Romanticism and Ideology

3 - 5 :   Blake - WW axis   -   cp. 57, 59, 63

43 :   Blake & sexuality ~ patriarchy

Romanticism and Ideology

Studies in English Writing 1765-1830

David Aers

Jonathan Cook

David Punter

ROUTLEDGE & KEGAN PAUL
London, Boston and Henley

First published in 1981
by Routledge & Kegan Paul Ltd
39 Store Street,
London WC1E 7DD,
9 Park Street,
Boston, Mass. 02108, USA, and
Broadway House,
Newtown Road,
Henley-on-Thames,
Oxon RG9 1BN
Printed in Great Britain by
Thomson Litho Ltd East Kilbride

British Library Cataloguing in Publication Data

Aers, David
  Romanticism and ideology.
  1. English literature - History and criticism
  I. Title   II. Cook, Jonathan
  III. Punter, David
  820.9   PR401

ISBN 0-7100-0781-7

Contents

INTRODUCTION
David Aers, Jonathan Cook, David Punter   1

1   BLAKE: 'ACTIVE EVIL' AND 'PASSIVE GOOD'
David Punter   7

2   BLAKE: SEX, SOCIETY AND IDEOLOGY
David Aers   27

3   ROMANTIC LITERATURE AND CHILDHOOD
Jonathan Cook   44

4   WORDSWORTH'S MODEL OF MAN IN 'THE PRELUDE'
David Aers   64

5   COLERIDGE: INDIVIDUAL, COMMUNITY AND SOCIAL AGENCY
David Aers, Jonathan Cook, David Punter   82

6   SOCIAL RELATIONS OF GOTHIC FICTION
David Punter   103

7   COMMUNITY AND MORALITY: TOWARDS READING JANE AUSTEN
David Aers   118

8   HAZLITT: CRITICISM AND IDEOLOGY
Jonathan Cook   137

9   SHELLEY: POETRY AND POLITICS
David Punter   155

NOTES   173

INDEX OF AUTHORS AND TITLES   191

Introduction

David Aers, Jonathan Cook, David Punter

The primary purpose of this book is to serve as an introduction to writing in the late eighteenth and early nineteenth centuries. It is thus not a work of research, but an educative and political contribution to literary study. We are very much aware that the key terms in the title, 'romanticism' and 'ideology', are problematic ones: that 'romanticism' is an ill-fitting label, whether we consider it in relation to genre or period, and that the relations between ideology and literature are the focus of more than one important and complex current debate.

If among literary historians and critics the period is classified as the 'romantic period', from other perspectives it is known quite differently: as 'the early industrial revolution', as a key stage in 'the making of the English working class'. We hope that this work will offer some connections with these other perspectives, in such a way as to show some of the relevant relations between literature and other forms of discourse, political, cultural and theoretical.

To be more specific, our aim is not to offer a survey of the decisive developments in English society and culture in the period, nor to offer a survey of those of its major authors who are canonized in our 'O' and 'A' level syllabuses and in the syllabuses for degrees in English literature. We have tried to adjust our critical task to the backdrop which already exists: the apparently unassailable hierarchization of writers which determines that 'romanticism' means, to most students, a unitary shadowy phenomenon which can be extrapolated as forming a middle ground bounded by six poets: Blake, Coleridge, Wordsworth, Byron, Keats and Shelley. Therefore we have indeed discussed four of these poets: but we have also deliberately introduced writers (Jane Austen, Hazlitt, Burke) who are usually studied in a different context; and genres (fiction, political writing) which are often cut off from the central body of poetry. But the body of accepted work is very large; and the attempt to redefine marginality and centrality in the period can only here - we think for reasons intimately connected with the nature of cultural hegemony - be glimpsed interstitially in the relations between the essays. This could be put another way. The nature of the history of literature, and of the history of institutions of literary education, is such that although students may - and even this

is rare - be able to take on for themselves sufficient authority to
defend the judgment, 'I do not like Wordsworth's poetry', it is not
possible for them to form the alternative judgment, 'Wordsworth is
a bad poet'. This, of course, is to make no comment about
Wordsworth's poetic power: but merely to point out that the balance
of this book is an attempt to steer a middle ground between the
recognizability which can only be achieved by location within the
canon and the renovation of critical tradition which depends on
interrogating that canon. Thus our relation to the canon is
tangential, but we acknowledge the necessity of working on the
basis of the cultural history we have.

We wish to concentrate on the understanding of texts as part of
a complex nexus of dynamic relations between literature, society
and available ideologies, taking ideology here in a simplified
general sense: 'a system of concepts and images which are a way of
seeing and grasping things, and of interpreting what is seen or
heard or read... [and of locating] the phenomena we perceive in a
network of causality, a given interpretative and evaluative
framework'. (1) We certainly do not intend to perpetuate the
increasingly common approach which goes under the general banner
of 'literature and its background'. This habitually erects a
static dualism in which a fixed general 'background' is sketched
in as a constant which is allegedly relevant for shaping our
perceptions of what writers in the period must have been saying
('the medieval mind', 'the seventeenth-century reader'). Often
the two terms 'literature' and 'background' are left as autonomous
units arbitrarily juxtaposed. Our perspective is rather that
writing is a social activity necessarily immersed in a diversity
of contemporary practices, ideological forms and problems: its
minute particulars articulate forms of life and outlook, imaging
and displaying the writers' attitudes towards received ideology
and existing circumstances, but also performing concrete work on
that ideology and those circumstances by virtue of the very
process of writing. The 'text' and 'background' approach seems
to us worth commenting on because, as a critical orthodoxy, it has
to a large extent replaced the notion of the transcendental
autonomy of the 'verbal icon' as a controlling academic myth.

Forms of language, ideology and socio-political relations are
the given basis on which the very possibility of any individual
growing up as a recognizable human being depends. As Aristotle
observed, 'man is naturally a political animal ... that a city then
precedes an individual is plain ... he that is incapable of society,
or so complete in himself as not to want it, makes no part of a
city, as a beast or a god'. (2) But within the given historical
circumstances, with the received forms of ideology and current
conflicts, individuals and collectives make their own history, and
an essential aspect of this making is the construction of meaning
according to their own aspirations, experience and practice. In
this process some writers may simply try to follow and apply the
received and dominant ideologies to contemporary circumstances
as they perceive them in the terms of such ideologies. But other
writers produce works which come out of a more critical relation
with dominant ideologies and given circumstances, and out of at
least some imaginative and intellectual engagement with current

ideological alternatives, be they overtly utopian or, at least on the surface, committed to empirical analysis and the historically 'possible'. This is clearly a particularly important issue in the period we are studying, both because it represents a significant stage in the development of historical thinking, and because we have a culturally significant problem to deal with in the way the very different types of engagement which we can see in the 'romantics' have been assimilated to a false unitary model. Even within their own works, writers in general and certainly the writers with whom we deal will not, of course, be consistent: it is possible to negate currently dominant ideology and the state of affairs which it legitimates while nevertheless preserving an affirmative and reconciliatory strand of meaning. (3)

The writers we have chosen represent different positions within a spectrum from revolt to counter-revolutionary affirmation of dominant ideologies and the 'status quo'. We have tried, further, to practise and thus advocate ways of reading which bring out the comprehensiveness or partiality of a work in relation to what existed and to what did not exist but was imaginable, its relation to the 'status quo' in a class-divided society and to the current conflicts between its defenders and its varied opponents. We have not adopted, or attempted to adopt, a single method in relation to our writers or texts, for we do not believe that the Marxist and sociological ways of thinking in which our work is grounded enjoin, or even permit, such satisfying homogeneity: instead, we have tried to perform a variety of kinds of critical work, and it is in keeping with the educative function of the book that it should be possible succinctly to describe these kinds of work.

Blake: 'Active Evil' and 'Passive Good' picks out the theme of labour in Blake's work, and traces it through various incarnations in order to demonstrate the kind of social concreteness the poet's work possesses. 'Blake: sex, society and ideology' is less simply thematic, in that here the cognitive and imaginative advances that Blake made in a specific sphere of thought, concerning the problems of sexuality, are brought into relation with the ways in which his work is none the less conditioned by the dominant ideology. In 'Romantic literature and childhood', contrasting attitudes towards childhood are used to initiate an investigation of conservative and radical formations within the 'romantic', focused on Wordsworth and again on Blake. 'Wordsworth's model of man in 'The Prelude'' is a close interrogation of Wordsworth's poetic language and an attempt to disclose some of the implicit arguments beneath the seriously encrusted surface of 'The Prelude'. It needs, perhaps, to be said at this point that the lengthy concentration on Blake and Wordsworth is intentional; that it is our belief that many of the most significant contradictions within the heavily striated reality of 'romanticism' can be extrapolated from a proper apprehension of the relation between Blake and Wordsworth, from, one might say, a discrimination between vision and 'vision'.

The essay on Coleridge is an exercise in de-fragmentation, an attempt to put the romantic Humpty Dumpty back together again, in however miniaturized a form, in order to demonstrate connections between poetic theory and historical understanding. 'Social relations of the Gothic' takes up an important set of fictions of the period, and demonstrates how their apparently escapist surface can be probed to reveal both social comment and also a set of narrative forms relevant to contemporary society. 'Community and morality: towards reading Jane Austen' argues that the significance of Austen's art and morality is far other than the 'universal' one still attributed to her work in literary history and criticism. 'Hazlitt: criticism and ideology' on the one hand seeks to reassert the value of a neglected figure of the period and on the other reconstructs an important political dialogue. 'Shelley: poetry and politics' questions traditional judgments on Shelley's involvement with practice and tries to offer a more specific version.

This diversity of approaches and concerns, however, can, like any other group of phenomena, be classed for convenience under a single heading. Our methods of reading try to grasp the complex ways in which ideology is at work within literary texts, without reducing the specific linguistic and aesthetic forms in question to some other realm of discourse: it is in the specific forms that we trace the role of ideology and the pressures of contemporary social life. Thus we follow a movement between detailed analysis of the language of texts and the relevant social, ideological and personal contexts mediated in them.

'Romantic language' is in itself a topic which could bear considerable elaboration. Much of the language which we criticize in this book has a heavily mystificatory function, often connected directly with the discharge of real or imaginary political duty. Thus, as we have written the book, we have sensed a number of tasks beginning to meet. The understanding of an ideologically charged language like that of Burke or Wordsworth is not a task remote from everyday concerns. The myths of the state and of personal creativity for which Burke and Wordsworth were largely responsible are still with us: in, for instance, the inflated, archaic and profoundly reactionary forms of parliamentary language, in the inflated, archaic and profoundly reactionary emphasis in literary education on falsely developed categories of personal taste, subjective response, isolated work. It would be difficult to deny that our acquiescence in the latter plays a part, however small, in sustaining the hegemony of the former. In the period which we discuss, specific changes occur in the relations between the realms of the public and the private, and they have substantially contributed to changes in the structure of real political power. Demystifying romantic language is thus a political task which goes hand in hand with more general educational tasks. The attempt to restore or achieve a proper intimacy with the literary text is not an exercise in naturalization, but a move towards the renewal of suppressed conflicts.

This brings us to a further point, which concerns our relation to Marxist criticism and interpretation of late eighteenth- and early nineteenth-century literature. There have been various signs of a 'rapprochement' between Marxism and romanticism, partly stimulated by the still increasing influence of the '1844 Manuscripts' on our version of Marx, partly by the Marxist critique of Stalinism which encouraged Marxists to recover the 'romantic' and humanistic components of Marxism, and partly by more general social and cultural developments which we have no room to discuss here. One of the most distinguished representatives of this 'rapprochement' in England is E. P. Thompson who has sought out the continuing relevance of romantic writing to radical politics in his revised study of William Morris, in his essays on Blake, Wordsworth and Coleridge and in passing uses of these writers throughout his work. (4)

Our own work casts some doubt on the attempt of Marxists to celebrate the romantic art of Wordsworth and Coleridge, as well as that of Blake, as an important critique of the contemporary capitalist social formation and ideology, as an anti-bourgeois alternative to existing forms of social domination. We have already noted the presence of highly contradictory moments of rebellion and reconciliation with dominant powers as a theoretical possibility within structures of writing, and we shall illustrate such tendencies; but we also want to say that our work on the most traditionally celebrated romantics, Wordsworth and Coleridge, shows a pervasive tendency on their part, even in their most overtly radical periods, to dissolve the social and political dimension of individual life and to lead the reader towards affirmative and reconciliatory attitudes to current modes of social control.

The mention of E.P. Thompson raises another set of arguments, summarized in the contemporary debate about the 'poverty of theory'. We have no explicit comment to make on this debate, but that very fact implies, as does this book as a whole, a minimal implicit comment. This is that, whatever the complexities of the relation between the development of theory and the concrete study of social, political and literary formations, there is none the less a role for a kind of work which, while focusing on specific intellectual problems, does not accept as a necessity a task of simultaneous theorization. It was Shelley, in his 'Defence of Poetry', who claimed that 'we have more moral, political, and historical wisdom, than we know how to reduce into practice; we have more scientific and economical knowledge than can be accommodated to the just distribution of the produce which it multiplies'. (5) As far as Shelley was concerned, it was poetry to which one had to turn in order to achieve those crucial elements of 'just distribution' and 'practice', but then, for Shelley, of course, poetry was a primary means of education. Now it is not, but the imagery of indigestion which succeeds Shelley's remarks may be none the less relevant. We do not believe for a moment that a useful literary criticism can proceed without benefit of theory, but we are also aware of the danger presented by the form in which some recent theoretical work has appeared - the danger, that is, of a discourse so arcane that to the uninitiated reader critical knowledge can be made to seem at best remote and at worst simply irrelevant. One point of our work is that questions of function are of primary importance and we believe that Marxism has an educative function to perform. If theoretical work is not to be divorced from this educative function, then it needs to be complemented by the kind of detailed attention to particular authors and works which we attempt.

We have written this book collaboratively: that is, we have engaged in continuing discussions of the work, and we have applied this discussion both to questions of organization and to the substantive content of our individual essays. This is not the highest conceivable level of collaboration, and it may be that what has emerged is less an indivisible harmony than a discordant polyphony; but, in view of the constraints of academic production, this would not distress us too much, provided the voices themselves are audible and clear.

Chapter 1

Blake: 'Active Evil' and 'Passive Good'

David Punter

In his 'Public Address' (c.1810), Blake comments: 'I am really
sorry to see my Countrymen trouble themselves about Politics'
(p.18), (1) and by doing so he sets a critical problem which has
absorbed students of Blake for many years. (2) It can be variously
formulated, but centrally it has to do with Blake's concept of the
relations between the individual and society. In so far as his
texts are polemical – which they certainly were in the earlier
years and which, I would contend, they substantially remained to
the end of his life – what is the essential site of that polemic?
Do the texts advocate a process of individual liberation, or one
of revolutionary social action? If both are advocated simultaneously,
what are the mechanisms by means of which the dialectical thrust of
the argument is maintained?
  This is a vast subject, and this essay can obviously provide
only a small contribution to it. A useful gloss on Blake's use of
the word 'Politics' is provided in Rousseau's 'Emile' (1757–60),
where we find the statement that 'society must be studied in the
individual and the individual in society; those who desire to treat
politics and morals apart from one another will never understand
either'. (3) The widely accepted separation between the concepts
of individual and society was an object of profound suspicion to
many writers of the romantic period, and this suspicion in turn
rests upon another emphasis within romanticism, which we can find
expressed by Coleridge: (4)

> It is at once the distinctive and constitutive basis of my
> philosophy that I place the ground and genesis of my system,
> not, as others, in a fact impressed, much less in a generalisa-
> tion from facts collectively, least of all in an abstraction
> embodied in a hypothesis, in which the pretended solution is
> most often but a repetition of the problem in disguise. In
> contradiction to this, I place my principle in an *act* – in the
> language of grammarians I begin with the verb – but the act
> involves its reality.

There is a certain amount of characteristically Coleridgean
verbiage here, but the central distinction is clear: 'fact' and

'act', noun and verb, stasis and process. Elsewhere Coleridge
writes that 'thinking can go but *half* way. To know the whole
truth, we must likewise *Act*: and he alone acts, who *makes* - and this
can no man do, estranged from Nature'. (5) This reminds us of
Marx's analysis of alienation in his 'Economic and Philosophical
Manuscripts of 1844', (6) but more significant for our purposes is
Coleridge's identification of activity and 'making': the kinds of
act which he is thinking of, and which he is claiming to be the
major constitutive factor in 'human-ness', in man's species-being,
are forms of making, forms of work, even though any sense of agency
is obliterated in the abstractness of his formulation. The link
between Blake and this general emphasis within romanticism is
provided by Hegel: 'What man is, is his deed, is the series of his
deeds, is that into which he has made himself. Thus the spirit is
essentially energy and one cannot, in regard to it, abstract from
appearance'. (7) What is particularly interesting here is Hegel's
use in this context of the Blakean term 'energy': the human spirit,
to Hegel, is not static but active, exuberant, continually in
movement and flux.

     If we see activity or energy - rather than reason, or any other
abstract faculty of mind - as the basis of the human, then the
question about relations between individual and society becomes
transformed. There are no 'mere' individuals, existing in
isolation, and there is, on the other hand, no 'society' in an
abstract sense: what we have instead is a continuous process of
activity and transformation, within which people work in relation
to each other and in relation to the natural world. The study of
these processes of work is too broad a matter to be confined
within a concept like 'politics'; thus in Blake we find, alongside
the apparent rejection of the political category as such, an
intense and continuing attention to areas of human life which are
heavily politically charged: questions of social relations, of
sexual behaviour, of the organization and role of the state and
commerce. Although there may seem to be a contradiction here,
it is by no means a confusion in Blake's mind: rather, Blake is
choosing precisely to point to the inadequacy of conventionally
accepted categories in order to advance an argument about the
eventual imaginative unity of human life and, in doing so, to draw
attention to the malevolent social purposes which are served by
separating the realm of politics from other areas of social
activity.

     What I want to examine, then, in this essay is a number of
aspects of Blake's attention to work. (8) Both as a London
tradesman, and as a hater of rigid rationalist philosophy, Blake
had every reason to be concerned with the everyday processes by
which men transform nature, rather than with the ways in which they
seek to explain the world abstractly to themselves; or perhaps
more accurately, he was concerned with the distinctions and
connections between those levels. I shall start by considering
some of the early work, leading up to some comments on the well-
known 'Tyger' poem from the 'Songs of Experience' (1789-94); I
shall then look at one of the short early prophecies, 'The Song
of Los' (1795), in which Blake's analysis of the relations between
work and social organization deepens; then at 'The Mental
Traveller', a lengthy ballad known to us from the Pickering

Manuscript, probably written around 1803, in which is inserted a
full-scale description and diagnosis of the history of
industrialization and its social effects; and finally at several
passages from 'Jerusalem' (1804-20), in which we can see in miniature
the more complex vision which informs the late works.

The whole philosophical effort of Blake's early work, not only
the poetry but also the various annotations and the tracts, is
directed towards a central opposition between passivity and activity.
'Active Evil is better than Passive Good' (409), he writes in the
margin of his copy of Lavater's rather saccharine 'Aphorisms' (1788);
and again, in more detail: (9)

> Accident is the omission of act in self & the hindering of act
> in another, This is Vice but all Act is Virtue. To hinder
> another is not an act it is the contrary it is a restraint on
> action both in ourselves & in the person hinderd. for he who
> hinders another omits his own duty. at the time (pp.226-7)

The problem Blake found with the thinkers of the eighteenth century
was that they assumed, first, that the nature of man was static,
and thus, as a consequence, that all actions carried the same
existential weight. What men did was merely to be considered as
an accompaniment to what they centrally were. This, to Blake,
was nonsense; one could paraphrase his opinion by saying that there
is no way to know whether a person is good unless he or she, at
least occasionally, does something which could substantiate that
view. In Plate 4 of 'The Marriage of Heaven and Hell' (c.1790-3),
he discusses the role which religion has played in perverting what
should be an obvious sense of connection between being and act,
and claims that:

> All Bibles or sacred codes. have been the causes of the
> following Errors.
>   1. That Man has two real existing principles
> Viz: a Body & a Soul.
>   2. That Energy. calld Evil. is alone from the Body.
> & that Reason. calld Good. is alone from the Soul.
>   3. That God will torment Man in Eternity for following
> his Energies.

In other words, religion has outlawed the body, and in doing so
has in fact cut off the mind from the real source of its energies:
'Energy', writes Blake, in the statements which the Devil's Voice
immediately puts forward as 'Contraries' to these religious
'Errors', 'is the only life and is from the Body and Reason is
the bound or outward circumference of Energy.'

What follows from this is a revaluation of the physical, and
of those forces which affect physical well-being. (10) The problems
of philosophy become inseparable from social justice, for
philosophy is conceived, not as dealing with an abstract,
disembodied model of man, but as related to man himself, in all
his complexity, body and soul, energy and reason, delusion and
potential. It is therefore not surprising that, even in his
early period when, on the whole, the issues at the centre of
Blake's mind were largely to do with religion, philosophy and

literary tradition, we none the less find him paying attention to
those social phenomena which ideology most centrally sanctions,
the processes of work. We find, for instance, the disturbing
ironies of the first 'Chimney Sweeper' lyric, from the 'Songs of
Innocence' (1789); here the child sweep, Tom Dacre, dreams about
his own freedom from drudgery and ascent to heaven:

> And so Tom awoke and we rose in the dark
> And got with our bags & our brushes to work.
> Tho' the morning was cold, Tom was happy & warm,
> So if all do their duty, they need not fear harm.

This final stanza opens up an enormous range of doubts in the
reader: what exactly are we supposed to think of the apparent
happiness which Tom has achieved? Is it merely an internalization
of repression? Or is there something in religious promises which
is genuinely satisfying? Or is Blake regarding religion cynically
as at least a momentary panacea for social evil? Or, in fact, are
we supposed to be laughing, very non-innocently, at Tom Dacre all
the way through? Ironically, the interpretative problems raised
by a so-called Song of Innocence are considerably resolved by the
companion poem in the 'Songs of Experience', with its uncompromising
final stanza which appears to lay the blame for misery squarely at
the feet of the controllers of ideological repression:

> And because I am happy, & dance & sing,
> They think they have done me no injury:
> And are gone to praise God & his Priest & King
> Who make up a heaven of our misery.

But even this leaves us with a distinct problem, about whether we
can justify our trust in the experienced voice. It might be, after
all, that the sweeping attribution of causation in this stanza is
the sign of paranoia, an indicator of a loss of trust so extreme
that every manifestation of the social world appears as part of a
perverted and threatening order.
    Blake's attitude towards state involvement in institutional
cruelty is bitter, and it is sometimes accompanied by an equally
sarcastic emphasis on the superiority of practical philanthropy
to intellectual speculation, as, for instance, in one of the songs
included in the satirical 'Island in the Moon' (c.1784-5) (pp.12-13).
The song is sung by the character called Obtuse Angle:

> To be or not to be
> Of great capacity
> Like Sir Isaac Newton
> Or Locke or Doctor South
> Or Sherlock upon death
> Id rather be Sutton
>
> For he did build a house
> For aged men & youth
> With walls of brick & stone
> He furnishd it within

With whatever he could win
And all his own

The poem goes on to describe in more detail Sutton's house, and
concludes with the question:

Was not this a good man
Whose life was but a span
Whose name was Sutton
As Locke or Doctor South
Or Sherlock upon Death
Or Sir Isaac Newton

Here different kinds of work are being very squarely contrasted:
the abstract, intellectualized labour represented by the baleful
geometrical rationalism of Newton, Locke and their deadly acolytes,
and the work represented by Richard Sutton, philanthropist and
builder of charity schools. Obtuse Angle is a character with only
partial perception, and we are not meant to take Sutton's rather
grim buildings as perfect; but we are meant to see that there is a
case to be made for the practical man, and, more importantly than
this, that work is of different kinds, and that according to the
work which he undertakes, so can man be judged. Sutton is
represented as possessive, narrow-minded and mercenary; nevertheless,
he is a man able to work on what comes to hand, rather than one who
seeks salvation through purely mental activity.
     But the most important locus for our purposes in Blake's early
poetry is a poem which has been all too widely considered in other
contexts, (11) 'The Tyger' from 'Songs of Experience', which is,
among many other things, a poem about work, about 'artifice' in
the widest sense. Blake's major concern is with the tiger as
product:

And what shoulder, & what art,
Could twist the sinews of thy heart?
And when thy heart began to beat,
What dread hand? & what dread feet?

The tiger is clearly in one sense a natural phenomenon, but the
whole poem brings this fact into question, brings it face to face
with the problems of work. For there are no answers given to the
many questions asked in the poem: one might begin by assuming that
the obvious solution is God, but the whole drift of the poem is
towards undermining that possibility, towards asserting that God
could not have had the strength, the courage to make the tiger:

In what distant deeps or skies
Burnt the fire of thine eyes!
On what wings dare he aspire?
What the hand, dare sieze the fire?

The answer to these questions seems to be less God than man: not
that man has made the literal 'tiger', but that it is a feature of
human work that it enables, for better or worse, men to produce

artefacts that are stronger or more dangerous than themselves. And
this interpretation is backed up by the industrial imagery of the
fourth stanza:

> What the hammer? what the chain,
> In what furnace was thy brain?
> What the anvil? what dread grasp,
> Dare its deadly terrors clasp?

The point here relates to Blake's well-known and irritating comment
that 'Natural Objects always did & now do Weaken deaden &
obliterate Imagination in Me' (Annotations to Wordsworth's 'Poems',
p.44), which has often been read as an extravagant aberration. Yet
surely what is implicit in this comment, especially when we note
that it occurs in the context of remarks on Wordsworth, is
principally a far more sophisticated concept of nature than was
common among the English romantics. It would be possible to claim
that while the tiger is a 'real', 'natural' beast, the images and
myths with which we, as people and as artists, surround it are
man-made, the fruits of imagination. It is this kind of dualism
which Blake will not stand: for him the tiger is simultaneously
the beast in the depths of the jungle and the beast in the depths
of our minds: to think of the tiger is to perform an activity,
to work on the given, to elaborate what may indeed be a 'natural'
basis - although very possibly a forever unknowable one - into a
fully-fledged act of human imaginative perception. The first
stanza runs, as everybody knows:

> Tyger Tyger, burning bright,
> In the forests of the night;
> What immortal hand or eye,
> Could frame thy fearful symmetry?

One interesting feature here is the word 'could': not 'did', which
would reduce the poem to a simple pondering on creation, but
'could', which immediately confuses the time-scale of the poem.
In the last stanza the word 'could' is replaced by 'dare'; here
the problems of production are projected decisively into the
future, and Blake simultaneously issues a challenge: the tiger
is not a fully achieved, given being, on which it is humanity's
duty merely to reflect, but half-formed, the site of future
'industry'. And to take up the implicit industrial metaphor again,
what, the poem asks, are we going to do about our capacity for
manufacture? 'When the stars threw down their spears/And water'd
heaven with their tears', are we going to adopt a similarly hopeless
attitude towards the dangers of industrial development, or are we
going to take up the challenge of 'framing' this 'fearful symmetry' -
providing it with a purposive context, such that the tiger can
continue to 'burn' without scorching us irreparably with its
terrible fires? 'The Tyger', of course, is a poem about art in
the narrow sense, about the adequacy of words and painting
confronted with the irruption of the violent: but as such, it
necessarily follows from Blake's philosophical premises that it is
simultaneously a poem about human perception and general human

practice, in which the concept of a given, static nature is
dissolved in the flux of activity and projected as a problem not
of apprehension but of transformation. (12)

And in case this view of Blake's way of connecting problems
seems rather far from 'The Tyger', we need only turn to the shorter
prophetic books, which were being written at substantially the same
time, and particularly to 'The Song of Los'. It is a brief work,
divided into two parts headed 'Africa' and 'Asia', which alerts us
to the fact that it continues Blake's treatment of the issues
raised in 'America' (1793) and 'Europe' (1794), which essentially
concern the conditions for the liberation of revolutionary energy
and its fate. It starts conventionally for this period in Blake's
development:

> Adam stood in the garden of Eden:
> And Noah on the mountains of Ararat;
> They saw Urizen give his Laws to the Nations
> By the hands of the children of Los.
>
> Adam shudderd! Noah faded! black grew the sunny
>   African
> When Rintrah gave Abstract Philosophy to Brama in
>   the East:

(SL, 3.6-11)

Essentially this describes the cessation of a golden age: Adam and
Noah are symbols of innocence, an innocence which is ruined when
Urizen, the god of reason, steps in and imposes moral codes and
rules of behaviour. It is puzzling that this should be at 'the
hands of the children of Los', since Los is the figure of prophecy
who stands against Urizenic domination, but, as has been pointed
out by other critics, (13) during the Urizenic stage of history no
force is powerful enough to resist, and even Los is tainted.
Blake may well also mean an irony, that men are gullible enough to
present themselves with the very rules which will do them harm and
cut them off from their destiny, as God could only impose the Ten
Commandments through the collaboration of Moses. This primal
event of repression spreads through the world, apparently through
the agency of Rintrah, who elsewhere represents anger, and here
perhaps imperial violence and domination, until:

> The human race began to wither, for the healthy built
> Secluded places, fearing the joys of Love
> And the disease'd only propagated:
> So Antamon call'd up Leutha from her valleys of delight:
> And to Mahomet a loose Bible gave.
> But in the North, to Odin, Sotha gave a Code of War,
> Because of Diralada thinking to reclaim his joy.
>
> These were the Churches: Hospitals: Castles: Palaces:
> Like nets & gins & traps to catch the joys of Eternity
>   And all the rest a desart;
> Till like a dream Eternity was obliterated & erased.

(SL, 3.25-4.4)

There are several possible meanings here. It might be the socially
privileged who are going into retirement: this is a double problem,
for they could be seen as the custodians of 'healthy stock' in relation to the poverty and disease they have visited on the poor, yet
they fear the 'joys of Love', which must entail both rejecting their
own sexuality and fearing any contact with 'the people'. More
probably, however, the image is principally one of mystical
withdrawal, and Blake is suspending his judgment on this response
to Urizen, and concentrating only on this enforced separation
between 'healthy' and 'disease'd', a false social division within
which all sorts of perversion become possible. The 'loose Bible'
which Antamon presents to Mahomet is the dialectical inverse of
the repressiveness of Christianity, a libertine gospel, whereas in
the north repression is sublimated into violence and discipline.
     All these societal principles, according to Blake, culminate in
institutions designed to 'catch the joys of Eternity', and imprison
imaginative potential; thus the possibility of human fulfilment
becomes further and further exiled. The second part of the poem,
'Asia', takes up this problem and depicts its impact precisely on
the world of work.

> The Kings of Asia heard
> The howl rise up from Europe!
> And each ran out of his Web;
> From his ancient woven Den;
> For the darkness of Asia was startled
> At the thick-flaming, thought-creating fires of Orc.
>
> And the Kings of Asia stood
> And cried in bitterness of soul.
> Shall not the King call for Famine from the heath?
> Nor the Priest, for Pestilence from the fen?
> To restrain! to dismay! to thin!
> The inhabitants of mountain and plain;
> In the day, of full-feeding prosperity;
> And the night of delicious songs.
>   (SL, 6.1-14)

The 'Kings of Asia' are symbols of unrepentant domination
archaically imaged in feudalism, (14) disturbed like spiders in
their webs by rumours of revolution in Europe. Yet the text seems
also to articulate a degree of pity: the kings are 'startled' by
the liberating power of Orc, and experience 'bitterness of soul',
as though the reasons why their rule should be overturned remain
mysterious to them: indeed, all their questions are of the form
of, 'We have always assumed this, or that, injustice to be part
of the natural order; how could we have known different, and how
could we possibly now adjust?' It has thus always seemed reasonable
to them that king and priest should be able to call on 'Famine'
and 'Pestilence' as means of social control: they are part of the
'natural' armoury of state domination, and Blake is astute in his
perception of the triple thrust of this domination: 'to restrain',
to discourage demands; 'to dismay', to inculcate fear; 'to thin',
to control population. The next two lines are ambiguous: it

might be that Blake is saying that while these devices are being practised, the means are in fact available to provide 'full-feeding prosperity', but more probably, in view of the connotations of 'delicious', he is alluding to the luxurious habits of despots and contrasting them with the fate of the people.

Shall not the Councellor throw his curb
Of Poverty on the laborious?
To fix the price of labour;
To invent allegoric riches:

And the privy admonishers of men
Call for fires in the City
For heaps of smoking ruins,
In the night of prosperity & wantonness
                    (SL, 6.15-22)

It is often said that the movement in Blake's language from the lyrics into the prophetic books is a movement towards obscurity, and of course this is partly true; but it is also worth noticing that a phrase like 'the price of labour' could not really have been accommodated within a lyrical and symbolic mode. In some ways, the looseness of form in these books permits clarity; at the very least, it permits a mixture of levels of discourse which is essential to Blake's purpose. What is at stake in these lines is the unreality of capitalist exchange values: the work which a man does stands revealed as having no relation to his prosperity, for the value of labour is being fixed from above. We should not, therefore, be deceived by the feudal connotations of the 'Kings of Asia', for this is not a feudal language, but a language of contemporary critique. The use of the word 'allegoric' is brilliantly ambivalent: on the one hand, Blake simply means that the riches which capitalism can give are not 'real', presumably partly because of the problems of paper money, partly because these riches pertain only to the cash nexus and prices remain manipulable by central government; on the other, he suggests the consolations of religion, the storing up of wealth in heaven which is advanced by the guardians of the state as a substitute for prosperity here below.

In the next four lines there is again a dialectical point: the 'privy admonishers of men', priests and moralists, wish for occasional destruction because it will remind the people of their moral lapses; yet Blake does not deny the 'wantonness' of the city, for he has already referred it back at root to the impositions of ideology. He continues:

To turn man from his path,
To restrain the child from the womb,
To cut off the bread from the city,
That the remnant may learn to obey,

That the pride of the heart may fail;
That the lust of the eyes, may be quench'd:
That the delicate ear in its infancy
May be dull'd; and the nostrils clos'd up;
To teach mortal worms the path
That leads from the gates of the Grave.
                    (SL, 6.23-7.8)

Is it not right, the kings of Asia are asking, that we, as guardians
of our people, should use economic means like the price of labour
and the availability of goods to induce subservience and moral
rectitude in our people? What is emphasized here is the diversion
of man from his real needs: he is turned from his path, his cycle
of reproduction is disturbed, his essential food is denied him, and
all so that 'the remnant may learn to obey' - we note particularly
the word 'remnant', a term for the Elect which, however, also
implies both the number of those who have been sacrificed and also
the bewilderment and disorganization of those few who survive the
ministrations of their own rulers. The kings of Asia see no
purpose in their subjects having senses: better by far to quench
them early, and they will then feel no discontent with their lot.

The poem then moves back into the symbolic mode, with Urizen
apparently drawing strength from Asia and setting forth to do
combat with the revolutionary forces of Orc; but Blake has already
made his point vividly. The repressive state can thrive only on
division of labour, on forcing man to renounce the possibility of
the satisfaction of real needs through working for his own purposes,
and to submit to a kind of labour which has its value only in the
context of the delusions of the cash-nexus. Yet how, one might
ask, can this happen? How has man through history managed to
fall into a condition of alienation so extreme that he is willing
to submit to such economic cruelty and injustice?

In 'The Mental Traveller', Blake makes a complex and sustained
attempt to answer these questions, which centrally involves
development of the connections between labour and sexual stereotyping. This is one of his most difficult poems, although not at
all for the usual reasons: it does not deal in abstruse mythological characters, and it is written in simple ballad metre. The
difficulty is of thought and narrative: in twenty-six bare stanzas
Blake, at one level, sweeps through the whole of human history,
economic, social and sexual, and discerns its patterns and forms.
But his account of six thousand years is simultaneously an account
of the progress of society in the late eighteenth century,
emphasizing problems of industry and sexuality, and in the latter
part there is also a systematic ambiguity about present and future.
The first five stanzas provide a stark beginning to the cycle:

I traveld thro' a Land of Men
A Land of Men & Women too
And heard & saw such dreadful things
As cold Earth wanderers never knew

> For there the Babe is born in joy
> That was begotten in dire woe
> Just as we Reap in joy the fruit
> Which we in bitter tears did sow
>
> And if the Babe is born a Boy
> He's given to a Woman Old
> Who nails him down upon a rock
> Catches his shrieks in cups of gold
>
> She binds iron thorns around his head
> She pierces both his hands & feet
> She cuts his heart out at his side
> To make it feel both cold & heat
>
> Her fingers number every Nerve
> Just as a Miser counts his gold
> She lives upon his shrieks & cries
> And she grows young as he grows old

The birth of the 'Babe' is a new beginning, but the babe was 'begotten in dire woe', born both of the decay of the older order and into a repressive and unnatural familial situation, a point to which Blake returns with considerable force at the end of the poem. Thus there is here in the babe a potential for development and change, but it is simultaneously negated by familial and social bondage; such minimal threat as is presented to the existing establishment is neutralized through the processes of socialization - familial, educational, sexual - represented by the 'Woman Old'. The woman is not a simple figure of violence: the fact that she 'Catches his shrieks in cups of gold' signifies that she values the child, but the problem lies in the nature of her values. Her behaviour towards the child is a caricature of possessiveness, and at the same time of scientific investigation; for the fulfilment of her wish to make the child wholly her own, it is necessary for her to investigate him in the finest detail, even if this process of analysis leads to repression and murder.

However, in this case, the process of analysis does not end, as it did for so many other romantics, in death: (15)

> Till he becomes a bleeding youth
> And she becomes a Virgin bright
> Then he rends up his Manacles
> And binds her down for his delight

What the old woman has been doing is forming her charge into a perfect male stereotype, and here she succeeds: she has managed to make him internalize the characteristics of domination which he needs in order to survive in society. At the same time she has deluded him into accepting her as a sexual partner, and thus compounding the ideological stereotyping which she practises. But the next stanza reveals that the woman is not only a symbol of socially acceptable sexual perversion:

> He plants himself in all her Nerves
> Just as a Husbandman his mould
> And she becomes his dwelling place
> And Garden fruitful seventy fold

As a woman, she has been inviting the male figure to rape her, and
has been actively forming him into the kind of person who will do
so: but she is not only a woman, but also nature, and she has been
encouraging the male to have a similar view of his relation to the
natural world, in other words to accept a similarly perverted
attitude towards the relations between transformation and appropriation, between labour and greed. Obedient to socialization, he sets
out to develop his 'talents', in the biblical sense, but something
curious happens:

> An aged Shadow soon he fades
> Wandring round an Earthly Cot
> Full filled all with gems & gold
> Which he by industry had got

> And these are the gems of the Human Soul
> The rubies & pearls of a lovesick eye
> The countless gold of the akeing heart
> The martyrs groan & the lovers sigh

He succeeds in piling up possessions, but these possessions are
powerless to endow him with reality; he is steadily reduced by
his unthinking acceptance of social values to a 'Shadow', stripped
of independent life, exiled even from his home because that home
is so filled with expensive but useless objects. The second of
these stanzas is puzzling, and appears to convey several different
arguments. First, to the person who considers everything under
the heading of exchange value no specific object has any special
worth, all is interchangeable. Thus the 'lovesick eye' is
translated on the market into 'rubies & pearls', which may, for
instance, be exchanged in a certain ratio for gold, which is the
market version of the 'akeing heart'. Second, and following from
this, Blake is suggesting the way in which, to the accumulative
habit of mind which repression and deflection have produced,
emotions and feelings harden: for the attributes of the soul to
be imaged as 'gems' by no means implies a positive value, for
Blake is surely thinking as much about the hardness, the resistance
of jewels as about their value - which, as we have seen, is in any
case suspect. And third, the very fact that the specific phenomena
which he mentions are all to do with yearning, with non-fulfilment,
points very clearly to the way in which accumulation of goods has
not satisfied real needs, but has instead encased them in false
ones, ones encouraged by a market system which works according to
dehumanized laws.

Now an old man, the central figure tries to make amends by
charity, and entertains 'the Beggar & the Poor', 'Till from the
fire on the hearth/A little Female Babe does spring'. This appears
as a moment of hope; we have been told at the very beginning that
the fate of the first babe was due to his sex, and here we might

suppose that all could now be different. But this second, female
babe is already at birth the product of a dehumanized society:

> And she is all of solid fire
> And gems & gold that none his hand
> Dares stretch to touch her Baby form
> Or wrap her in his swaddling-band

She is the victim of a ludicrous and dehumanizing protectiveness,
and it is hardly surprising that as she develops she shows only
callousness:

> But She comes to the Man she loves
> If young or old or rich or poor
> They soon drive out the aged Host
> A Beggar at anothers door

The 'aged Host' - still, we must remember, the original babe -
'wanders weeping far away', searching for sympathy, for human
feeling, since his own dubious offspring appears to have none.
The figure who has represented capitalistic accumulation and male
domination, albeit both induced by previous pressures, finally
abandons hope of salvation within the social order and sets out to
find an alternative mode of living and activity. He finds a
'Maiden',

> And to allay his freezing Age
> The Poor Man takes her in his arms
> The Cottage fades before his sight
> The Garden & its lovely Charms

> The Guests are scattered thro' the land
> For the Eye altering alters all
> The Senses roll themselves in fear
> And the flat Earth becomes a Ball

> The Stars Sun Moon all shrink away
> A desart vast without a bound
> And nothing left to eat or drink
> And a dark desart all around

Yet it is she who reveals to him the blanched reality behind social
illusion: with the ideology of success and the profit motive
stripped away, the 'Cottage' fades and is replaced by a 'desart',
the convivial 'Guests' who have been dining at his table vanish,
the universe itself is revealed as an invention of Urizen,
presiding deity of economic injustice, and the man returns to the
still point. Nothing, Blake is claiming, is eternal: all depends
on perception, and perception itself on social factors. But the
man has to find a vision to replace the one he has lost, and here
the poem becomes more complex.

From this point to the end, there are two possible readings, one
optimistic and one pessimistic, and both certainly present in the
self-censoring text: I will detail the pessimistic one, because

it seems to me more redolent of Blake's mood at this time.   In the
next stanza,

> The honey of her Infant lips
> The bread & wine of her sweet smile
> The wild game of her roving Eye
> Does him to Infancy beguile
>
> For as he eats & drinks he grows
> Younger & younger every day
> And on the desert wild they both
> Wander in terror & dismay

Since he has found that industry is incapable of supplying his
real needs, he finds alternative sustenance in the 'honey', 'bread'
and 'wine' of the maiden, but this only beguiles him back to
'Infancy'. Instead of providing a genuine social alternative, the
maiden allures him into a total rejection of responsibility. The
contemporary social and sexual order, by virtue of being a total
system, conditions its own opposite, portrayed here as a kind of
mindless hedonism. The man does not come through to a new
understanding, but merely wanders 'in terror & dismay', an outcast
from his own society but unable to conceive of a new one. He and
the maiden play various games,

> Till be becomes a wayward Babe
> And she a weeping Woman Old
> Then many a Lover wanders here
> The Sun & Stars are nearer rolld
>
> The trees bring forth sweet Extacy
> To all who in the desert roam
> Till many a City there is Built
> And many a pleasant Shepherds home
>
> But when they find the frowning Babe
> Terror strikes thro the region wide
> They cry the Babe the Babe is Born
> And flee away on Every side

As he becomes increasingly impotent, the world begins to reassemble
itself, and to forget the psychological and social development
through which he has gone, but this is only a superficial solution;
he continues to exist as a babe, a potential for change, and is in
due course discovered.

Many of the questions about 'The Mental Traveller' have centred
on the 'Terror' depicted in this stanza, and why it is felt; the
most likely interpretation, surely, is that Blake is giving an
oblique and double-edged warning about the next revolution. Urizen
has created Orc: mindless domination has created mindless
rebellion. The revolution of the bourgeoisie was fairly frightening,
but it was nothing, Blake is saying, compared with what the next
revolution will be like, the revolution which capitalism has itself
engendered. And yet the poem ends on an ambiguous note:

For who dare touch the frowning form
His arm is witherd to its root
Lions Boars Wolves all howling flee
And every Tree does shed its fruit

And none can touch that frowning form
Except it be a Woman Old
She nails him down upon the Rock
And all is done as I have told

Thus despite the terror the cycle of socialization is potentially
endless: the previous order has the power to neutralize its
potential successor unless an improbable qualitative change comes
about in socio-sexual life. The more optimistic account would
have to be based on a re-reading of several of these features.
First, one would have to construe the encounter between the man
and the maiden as a necessary 'rite de passage', in which a shedding
of previous accretions of belief occurs, and one would have to
accept that even terms like 'beguile' have a positive valuation.
Second, one would have to see the rebirth of the babe as the coming
of a genuine revolution: the 'frowning Babe' must, from all the
evidence, be Orc, but Blake did vacillate as to the advisability
of Orc's liberation, and it might be that he is here regarding it
as a necessary prelude to a wider change. And third, one would
have to see the last two stanzas, not as a statement of fact, but
as a challenge: is there in fact any force strong enough within
present society to thwart the revolution which is coming? Or,
failing that, as a gesture towards censorship, a kind of half-
retraction of the threat which is implicit in the previous
stanzas. In its closing ambiguities, the poem mirrors in its own
structure the contradiction which is also its principal content:
the contradiction in the nature of change and stasis whereby
generational progress stands continually revealed as a further
movement into the icy caves of Urizen. And there is one further
contradiction articulated in the very fabric of the text: between
the closed, repetitive, 'past' form of the ballad and the open,
uncertain, temporally indeterminate mode in which history is
represented. Here what is signified slides away from our
apprehension; as readers we are not led into a solution or closure,
but propelled outward and back to the revealed contradictions at
the core of social reality. We are ourselves involved more or less
forcibly in the process of imaginative work.
   Further depth here is provided in the way the first and second
parts of the central figure's life are related as work to play,
and both are found wanting: neither total competitivity nor total
leisure are adequate to man's real needs. One turns the human
being into a machine, the other into a child. And it is between
those poles that Blake saw man as oscillating under capitalism:
as a producer, he has little choice but to approximate as closely
as possible to the mechanical, but as a consumer he is expected to
display a child's gullibility and to be treated with a more than
parental contempt.
   'The Mental Traveller' is a schematic poem; its terseness and
tight narrative are geared to other purposes than expansion on

Blake's major themes of work and suffering. We can see the tone of his actual depiction of industrial scenes by looking at a few passages from 'Jerusalem', for instance at the portrayal of the armaments industry at the beginning of Plate 73:

> Lo! the Labourers at the Furnaces
> Rintrah & Palamabron, Theotormon & Bromion, loud labring
> With the innumerable multitudes of Golgonooza, round
>   the Anvils
> Of Death. But how they came forth from the Furnaces &
>   how long
> Vast & severe the anguish eer they knew their Father;
>   were
> Long to tell & of the iron rollers, golden axle-trees &
>   yokes
> Of brass, iron chains & braces & the gold, silver & brass
> Mingled or separate: for swords; arrows; cannons; mortars
> The terrible ball: the wedge: the loud sounding hammer
>   of destruction
> The sounding flail to thresh: the winnow: to winnow
>   kingdoms
> The water wheel & mill of many innumerable wheels
>   resistless

> (J, 73.4-14)

It has been said that Blake did not have any first-hand knowledge of industrial process, and this is true but slightly beside the point; (16) what is expressed here is the process of the bewildered consciousness encountering a profusion of industrial objects. And many of these objects fall for Blake into a curious category: on the one hand they are appurtenances of industrialization and carry an accompanying stigma, yet on the other hand they are in themselves 'wondrous', the astonishing achievements of human work, and thus possibly bear some partly hidden sign of the divine. The 'sounding flail to thresh' is not too far from the tiger: a source of power which has been let out like Frankenstein's monster, but under doubtful control. But the tiger is single, and what also astonishes Blake about industry is the sheer proliferation of objects, well represented in the tumbling line 'Of brass, iron chains & braces & the gold, silver & brass'.

And to criticize his knowledge of industrial process is not, of course, to say that he was unconcerned with the work involved: on the contrary, this is time and time again the centre of his analysis:

> Then left the Sons of Urizen the plow & harrow, the loom
> The hammer & the chisel, & the rule & compasses; from London
>   fleeing
> They forg'd the sword on Cheviot, the chariot of war & the
>   battle-ax,
> The trumpet fitted to mortal battle, & the flute of summer in
>   Annandale
> And all the Arts of Life. they changd into the Arts of Death
>   in Albion.
> The hour-glass contemnd because its simple workmanship.

Was like the workmanship of the plowman, & the water wheel,
That raises water into cisterns: broken & burnd with fire:
Because its workmanship. was like the workmanship of the
    shepherd.
And in their stead, intricate wheels invented, wheel without
    wheel:
To perplex youth in their outgoings, & to bind to labours in
    Albion
Of day & night the myriads of eternity that they may grind
And polish brass & iron hour after hour laborious task!
Kept ignorant of its use, that they might spend the days of
    wisdom
In sorrowful drudgery, to obtain a scanty pittance of bread:
In ignorance to view a small portion & think that All
                                        (J, 65.12-27)

There are many things that could be said about this passage. One
of the most important is that it repeats the critique of the
division of labour from 'The Song of Los', but in far more detail,
and with a more deeply felt sympathy for those who work for
purposes which they do not know and resign their stake in the
totality of life in exchange for 'a scanty pittance of bread'.
Blake does not here appear to believe that technological
sophistication is economically necessary; in his society, he sees
complexity being worshipped for its own sake, or perhaps rather
because complexity enshrines elites. But this passage is not only
a scathing portrait of industrialization: it is also a commentary
on the poet's task. The 'flute of summer' may well have been an
appropriate instrument in times of peace and stability, but now
England exists under a blackening cloud – a cloud of war and a
cloud of industrial smoke – it is no longer helpful. If the
warmongers and industrialists are forging themselves more
powerful implements, it behoves the poet to change his tactics
and to fight fire with fire, to abandon the simplicity of lyric
and to seek a poetic form adequate to new social content.
    In Plate 59 of 'Jerusalem' there is a good example of Blake's
attempt to weld together mythic references with the realities of
industrial life and work, when he describes the Daughters of Los
in terms strongly reminiscent of the Fates:

And one Daughter of Los sat at the fiery Reel & another
Sat at the shining Loom with her Sisters attending round
Terrible their distress & their sorrow cannot be utterd
And another Daughter of Los sat at the Spinning Wheel
Endless their labour, with bitter food. void of sleep,
Tho hungry they labour: they rouze themselves anxious
Hour after hour labouring at the whirling Wheel
Many Wheels & as many lovely Daughters sit weeping
Yet the intoxicating delight that they take in their work
Obliterates every other evil; none pities their tears
Yet they regard not pity & they expect no one to pity
For they labour for life & love, regardless of any one
But the poor Spectres that they work for, always incessantly

> They are mockd, by every one that passes by. they regard not
> They labour; & when their Wheels are broken by scorn & malice
> They mend them sorrowing with many tears & afflictions.
> (J, 59.26-41)

The passage goes on to depict the work of the other Daughters of
Los; between them, they are the figures responsible for maintaining
the basic continuity of 'material' life, for they weave the material
from which the world is made. In the myths from which this idea is
derived, there was no thought of enquiring into the state of mind of
such figures, but here it is the heart of Blake's concern. And the
consciousness of the Daughters of Los is riddled with contradictions:
on the one hand they are condemned to drudgery, 'Hour after hour
labouring at the whirling Wheel', on the other they feel an
'intoxicating delight' in their work, for they are aware of its
importance. It is unclear whether the mockery to which they are
exposed is justified, or whether they themselves have the last
laugh because of their hidden power; but what is clear is that this
kind of cottage industry, even if in the end the workers should be
capable of exercising their labour power, is moment by moment soul-
destroying, and the only way of performing it is by a series of acts
of self-abnegation. The Daughters of Los have given up expecting
any sympathy: they have come to assume that their tears and
suffering are necessary parts of the work process. Instead of
expecting any justice for themselves, they have externalized their
hopes into the 'Spectres' whom they are helping: they have thus
deferred any gratification into the future, and appear content to
take comfort from the eventual product of their labour even while
its current effects are evil and exhausting.
  Los is the figure in the prophetic books who most nearly
represents Blake himself, and his task in 'Jerusalem' is summarized
as follows:

> He views the City of Golgonooza, & its smaller Cities:
> The Looms & Mills & Prisons & Work-houses of Og & Anak:
> The Amalekite: the Canaanite: the Moabite: the Egyptian:
> And all that has existed in the space of six thousand years:
> Permanent, & not lost not lost nor vanishd, & every little act,
> Word, work, & wish, that has existed, all remaining still
> In those Churches ever consuming & ever building by the Spectres
> Of all the inhabitants of Earth wailing to be Created:
> Shadowy to those who dwell not in them, meer possibilities:
> (J, 13.56-64)

The world to Los - that is, to the poet - is not a world of
objects, no matter how fascinated by objects the poet may be; it
is a world of 'act/Word, work, & wish', and Los's principal task
is to give permanence to these phenomena, to assert their
importance as against the deadly, static world of Urizen. It is
only by means of deeds that human beings exist: permanence is not
a matter of stasis, but of 'ever consuming & ever building', of
continual transformations effected through work.
  As we saw at the beginning, there is a general emphasis within
romanticism on replacing an ideology of passivity, appropriate to

an age of social and political conservatism, with one of activity.
Schelling, in 'On University Studies' (1802), asserts typically that
the main task of philosophy is to manifest the unity of knowledge
and action, which for him are 'just as necessarily separate at the
temporal level as they are inseparable - because both are equally
absolute - in the Idea'. (17) But the very abstractness of this
pronouncement marks a falling away from a philosophy truly based on
a recognition of the importance of social activity: to find a more
concrete realization of the role of work we have to turn to another
writer who, like Blake, believed in the dialectical relation between
abstract thinking and concrete social life, and who, like Blake,
has therefore generally been regarded as an ideological
obscurantist. (18) Nothing could be less obscure than Hegel's
comments on labour, which are in substance identical to Blake's: (19)

> the value of labour decreases in the same proportion as the
> productivity of labour increases. Work thus becomes absolutely
> more and more dead, it becomes machine-labour, the individual's
> own skill becomes infinitely limited, and the consciousness of
> the factory worker is degraded to the utmost level of dullness.

It is this process of human reduction which Blake dramatizes so
often in the prophetic books, just as he has given us isolated
fragments from the drama in the early lyrics. What is also
important to Blake's analysis is the way in which labour becomes
deeply inscribed on our senses and perceptions, and thus carries
with it the forms of organization of human need. He was not alone
among the romantics in realizing that change in perception must be
accompanied by - perhaps could only be allowed by - change in
patterns of work: Hölderlin makes substantially the same point in
his 'Hyperion' (1799): 'let no one think to know our people, as
they are to be, from their flag alone; everything must be rejuvena-
ted, everything must be changed from the ground up; pleasure must
be full of seriousness, and all work gleeful!' (20) We could
paraphrase this comment by saying that it is impossible to know
people from their consciousness alone, as Marx was later to point
out: change of consciousness can happen only 'from the ground
up', by massive change in the material base, in the course of
which conventional distinctions between work and pleasure will be
obliterated.
    But Blake, unlike Hölderlin and many other romantic writers,
does not merely end up by describing an anthropomorphic universe,
a world in human shape which is mysteriously better than the
mechanical world of capitalism. He is fully aware that the world
is not in human shape, not, indeed, in fit shape for humans to
live in, but the centre of his concern is with the means by which
man can effect transformation in this situation. So often the
imaginative change in society which romanticism required was seen
as something final, a sudden stroke of humanization which was to
leave mankind exempted from work, basking in newly realized
divinity. To conclude the comparison with Hegel, we can cite the
'Phenomenology of Spirit' (1807), where he says that 'the life of
God and divine intelligence ... can, if we like, be spoken of as
love disporting with itself', but 'this idea falls into ...

insipidity, if it lacks the suffering, the patience, and the labour
of the negative'. (21)   The life for which we strive is not one in
which we will be immersed in play and pleasure, but one in which
these will take their proper place alongside productive work.   We
can fittingly conclude by quoting the lines, at the end of
'Jerusalem', in which Blake portrays the parallel situation: the
apocalypse is not the end, but the new beginning, in which real
tasks may be achieved, as opposed to the unreal ones which absorb
our time in a social formation governed by the cash nexus and by
the division of labour:

>And they conversed together in Visionary forms dramatic
>   which bright
>Redounded from their Tongues in thunderous majesty, in
>   Visions
>In new Expanses, creating exemplars of Memory and of Intellect
>Creating Space, Creating Time according to the wonders Divine
>Of Human Imagination, throughout all the Three Regions immense
>Of Childhood, Manhood & Old Age & all the tremendous
>   unfathomable Non Ens
>Of Death was seen in regenerations terrific or complacent
>   varying
>According to the subject of discourse & every Word & Every
>   Character
>Was Human ...

(J, 98.28-36)

Chapter 2

Blake: Sex, Society and Ideology

David Aers

> 'O Albion why wilt thou Create a Female Will?'
> (Blake, 'Jerusalem', 30.31)

> 'In Eternity Woman is the Emanation of Man she
> has no Will of her own'
> (Blake, 'Vision of the Last Judgement')

In his great study of Blake, D.V. Erdman observed that 'Blake's hostility to "female will" ... is not easy to evaluate', and he noted how Blake's views on women have received rather contrasting interpretations. (1) It could seem that the root of the problem here lies in some simple and avoidable incoherence in Blake's work, that he advocates positions which are just incompatible, either in the same poem or in different writings during the course of a long and highly productive life. One could point out that in the 'Visions of the Daughters of Albion' the central woman is a libertarian challenging male violence and repressiveness, whereas in 'Europe', published in the following year, it is woman who preaches that 'Woman's love is sin' (6.5) (2) and offers a classic programme of cunning sexual repressions. And it is, of course, striking that in the later works Blake's women tend to have a frightening commitment to sexual domination and the codes of conventional sexual morality. But the case is far more complicated than a matter of authorial incoherence or change of mind, as I wish to show. For in Blake's work we can follow the evolution of an original and profound understanding of the dialectics of sexual conflict and the internalization of repressive ideologies by their victims. Yet we can also see, as Blake himself did, how even the most radical penetration of dominant ideology or practice is likely to include some perpetuation of the forms being strenuously negated.

I will start with Blake's 'Visions of the Daughters of Albion', printed in 1793 (hereafter VDA). Harold Bloom called this poem a 'hymn to free love', (3) and most critics have handled it in this way, as 'a lament over the possessiveness of love and the hypocrisy of moral legislators'. (4) Erdman accepted this reading but brought out the direct relevance of the poem to the contemporary debate over the slave trade and to Steadman's powerful descriptions of slavery which Blake was working on at the time he wrote VDA. (5) The poem itself demands an approach which responds to the way in which Blake unveils the interactions between the most intimate areas of life and the total socio-political structures, within which life has to be led. In revealing this as a dynamic, two-way process, Blake shows that he already had the basis for a dialectical critique of the psychological and social phenomena which absorbed his attention.

Most readers of the poem will assent to the line of criticism
presented by Bloom's description of a 'hymn to free love' and to
Erdman's 'historical criticism'. But a dual assent is insufficient,
for it tends to dissolve the dialectic, to obscure the way in which
he grasps the minute particulars of life both as specific human
experiences and as concrete mediations of a social totality within
which they exist and have meaning. (6)

How Blake does this can be illustrated from Plate 5 of VDA.
Oothoon has been trying to make the sexual and social ruler, Bromion,
realize the potential multiplicity of unique energies and forms of
life (Plates 3 and 5), a multiplicity of which the conservative mind
is always terrified. Having gone on to point out the socio-economic
basis to perception (5.7-16) she asks,

> With what sense does the parson claim the labour of the farmer?
> What are his nets & gins & traps. & how does he surround him
> With cold floods of abstraction, and with forests of solitude,
> To build him castles and high spires. where kings & priests
>   may dwell.
>   (VDA, 5.17-20)

This is a striking illustration of the fact that our senses, our
sense-experiences and perceptions, are socially made, bound up
with our practical activity, and indeed, our class position.
Oothoon's statement naturally flows into the related consideration
that rationalizing discourse also relates closely to practical
activity and seems to serve the ideology and interests of a
particular class - the 'cold floods of abstraction' are tied to an
individualistic doctrine which isolates man from man, so enabling
ruling groups in Blake's society to build 'castles and high spires.
where kings & priests may dwell'. Abstractionism serves domination
and manipulation, the logical tool of Urizen, and it is characteristic of Blake to present the social basis and uses of such discourse:
he was never subject to the illusion, still harboured by many
intellectuals, that 'floods of abstraction' transcend the conflicts
of the specific, divided society in which the reasoner reasons. (7)

In this context, which has already shown the connections between
social exploitation (tithes, castles, spires, kings, priests),
perception, 'abstraction' and ideology, Blake shifts the subject to
sexual experience.

> Till she who burns with youth. and knows no fixed lot; is bound
> In spells of law to one she loaths: and must she drag the chain
> Of life, in weary lust! must chilling murderous thoughts. obscure
> The clear heaven of her eternal spring? to bear the wintry rage
> Of a harsh terror driv'n to madness, bound to hold a rod
> Over her shrinking shoulders all the day; & all the night
> To turn the wheel of false desire: and longings that wake her womb
> To the abhorred birth of cherubs in the human form
> That live a pestilence & die a meteor & are no more.
> Till the child dwell with one he hates. and do the deed he loaths
> And the impure scourge force his seed into its unripe birth
> E'er yet his eyelids can behold the arrows of the day.
>   (VDA, 5.21-32)

The link word 'Till' yokes this passage with the preceding lines
on exploitation and ideology, thus presenting the sexual situation
as an integral aspect and product of a society structured on
principles of division and domination. Blake registers the fact
that in such a society sexual energy is a threat to all 'fixed'
boundaries and conventional order. It must therefore be contained
within marriage, an economic and ideological institution determined
by the social structure he has just been depicting. (8)   By
describing the bands of marriage as 'spells of law' Blake suggests
how the law, far from being a central manifestation of human
community is more like the product of an enchanter, whose 'spells',
like Comus', 'cheat the eye with blear illusion' ('Comus', 155), but
are nevertheless real enough in the effects they have on those
subjected to the magician. The poet gives us, in fact, a witty
and dialectical image as part of his aim to free readers from any
reverence they may feel for the basis of current law (part of those
'cold floods of abstraction'). He reminds us obliquely that
magicians are often defeated and their spells destroyed, yet does
not deny the crippling reality of the spells while the magician
is allowed to impose them.
    With another brilliant shift Blake makes a further specific
connection between the wider structures of domination and the more
intimate sphere of sexuality. He evokes an image of women workers
in eighteenth-century mines and those emerging centres of manufacture,
early factories: the chains and rods are those of 'the great work
master' Urizen ('Four Zoas', II.25.5). As he wrote soon afterwards:

> The King of Light [Urizen] beheld her mourning among the Brick
>   kilns compelld
> To labour night & day among the fires, her lamenting voice
> Is heard when silent night returns & the labourers take their
>   rest
> O Lord wilt thou not look upon our sore afflictions
> Among these flames incessant labouring, our hard masters laugh
> At all our sorrow. We are made to turn the wheel for water
> To carry the heavy basket on our scorched shoulders, to sift
> The sand & ashes, & to mix the clay with tears & repentance.
>   (FZ, II.31.1-8)

Blake is disclosing in both these passages, from VDA and 'Four
Zoas', how industrial work discipline has demanded a total subjection
of the human personality to those who control and dominate production.
The richly diverse potential of human energies and joys are coercively
reduced to one-sided labour in the service of the 'performance
principle'. (9) For Blake, the industrial worker and the slave
have much in common, and as people reduced to being mere instruments
of labour, they can be presented in the same imagery. They live
in a world totally antagonistic to Oothoon's wished-for liberation
of energy and sexual drives, where she is,

> Open to joy and to delight where ever beauty appears
> If in the morning sun I find it: there my eyes are fix'd
> In happy copulation; if in evening mild. wearied with work;
> Sit on a bank and draw the pleasures of this free born joy.
> ...

I cry, Love! Love! Love! happy happy Love! free as the mountain
                                                                wind!
                                          (VDA, 6.22-7.2; 7.16)

In her imagined society such a liberation of Eros, would, in
Marcuse's words, 'necessarily operate as a destructive, fatal
force - as the total negation of the principle which governs the
repressive reality'. (10) It would, among other things, involve a
resexualization of the body, a spread of the libido which 'would
manifest itself in a reactivation of all erotogenic zones and
consequently, in a resurgence of pre-genital polymorphous sexuality',
changes which would make the body and the whole person strongly
resist reduction to an instrument of labour. (11)

But in the world that Blake examines, sexual activity is itself
absorbed into the nexus of social controls and containment. The
phallus becomes a mere instrument of punitive control reflecting
the workmaster's 'rod' and 'scourge', while 'lovely copulation' is
remade in the image of alienated labour, compulsively and joylessly
turning 'the wheel of false desire' (VDA, 5, quoted above; cf. FZ,
VII.92.17-33). The activity of begetting children is also engulfed
in this closed world and the infant's sexual life is doomed as the
ghastly circle of 'The Mental Traveller' is foreshadowed in VDA,
5.27-32. As I stated previously, this brief passage from VDA can
serve as an example of the dialectical forms Blake was developing.
He encourages the reader to explore minute particulars of experience
in terms of the social totality within which they are most compre-
hensible, but because he usually places such sharp imaginative
emphasis on the particulars of experience he is rarely in danger
of dissolving these in the face of some totalizing category.

Nevertheless, it seems to me that Blake had left himself with a
crucial problem which he could not face in the terms of VDA. The
question centres on the revolutionary consciousness of Oothoon,
but we can best come at it indirectly, and start by recalling the
passage I have just commented on, VDA, Plate 5. Here the alienated
woman was so immersed in the circle of exploitation that there were
no signs of her being able to generate any critique, let alone a
revolutionary ideology and practice. In a related way, Plate 1
contains Bromion's report on the situation where he states that the
daughters of the dominated 'worship terrors and obey the violent'.
Although he is a 'mistaken Demon' (5.3) we have no reason to dismiss
his claim here, however wrong he is in his analysis of the
phenomenon. What he appears to report is the possibility that the
repressed internalize the ideology and values of the oppressor,
they 'worship' their rulers in the way people have worshipped gods.
Once more Marcuse provides an appropriate comment when he adapts
Freud's account of the origin and perpetuation of guilt feeling to
explain the 'identification' of those who revolt with the power
against which they revolt: 'The economic and political incorpora-
tion of the individuals into the hierarchical system of labor is
accompanied by an instinctual process in which the human objects of
domination reproduce their own repression'. (12) Bromion may be
over-confident about his ability to control those he rules, but he
does have at least a practical knowledge of the mental process on
which his rule depends.

In Plate 6 Oothoon herself notices yet another counter-revolutionary form of female response to subjection as she asks: (13)

Who taught thee modesty, subtil modesty! child of night & sleep
When thou awakest. wilt thou dissemble all thy secret joys
Or wert thou not, awake when all this mystery was disclos'd!
Then com'st thou forth a modest virgin knowing to dissemble
With nets found under thy night pillow, to catch virgin joy,
And brand it with the name of whore; & sell it in the night
                          (VDA, 6.7-12)

This reaction is neither the absolutely exhausted subjection of
the kind we saw in Plate 5, nor the worship of the oppressor
reported by Bromion. It is a cunning strategy for using the
containing and perverting structures to salvage at least something
from a miserable reality which has been accepted: the woman
accepts her reduction to the status of commodity and sets out to
make herself as valuable a commodity as possible. This is a vital
insight, a crucial moment in the dialectics of sex, and one Blake
was to explore fully in later work. I shall return to it in
discussing 'Europe', but here Blake leaves it undeveloped.
Furthermore, and this is the problem I raised above, Blake presents
Oothoon as able to transcend the consciousness of her fellow women
absolutely: but how this can be so, how she has attained so clear
a revolutionary critique of sexual and social exploitation, and of
their interaction, how she has reached so full an understanding of
the psychological effects and perverted indulgences of repressed
sexuality (for example, VDA, 7.3-11), this remains a mystery.
For no one, not the most 'revolutionary' figure, stands clearly
outside alienated society, beyond alienation. Supersession of
alienated consciousness and oppressive reality can only come, if
at all, by a complex process of social practices, of human interaction gradually producing structural changes in all spheres of
human living. Certainly Blake had gained a marvellously dramatic
grasp of this by the time he wrote the 'Four Zoas', and in many
respects the grasp is evident in 'Europe', but it does seem that
in VDA he may have slipped towards an optimistic, idealist
illusion in his handling of Oothoon's consciousness. The illusion
lies in assuming that revolutionary consciousness can ever be as
uncontaminated by dominant structures and ideologies as Oothoon's
appears to be. The illusion is dangerous, and it encourages a
millenarian elitism which legitimates an attitude to the majority
of people as deluded objects to be liberated by the mysteriously
enlightened minority. Besides being a recipe for domination and
the consolidation of Urizen's rule, it is founded in a basic
misconception of the human subject. As Marx noted in his third
thesis on Feuerbach, attacking deterministic, mechanical
naturalism: 'The materialist doctrine concerning the changing
of circumstances and education forgets that circumstances are
changed by men and that the educator must himself be educated.
This doctrine has therefore to divide society into two parts, one
of which is superior to society.' No one is simply 'superior to
society', and yet Oothoon's consciousness does indeed seem to be
so. Here both the 'materialistic doctrine' criticized by Marx and

idealist assumptions found frequently enough among romantic writers
lead towards similar forgetfulness, a similar dissolution of the
complex dialectic towards which Marx points. (14)

The exuberant celebrations of sexual liberation towards the end
of 'America' (1793-5) presents similar problems.

> The doors of marriage are open, and the Priests in rustling
>   scales
> Rush into reptile coverts, hiding from the fires of Orc,
> That play around the golden roofs in wreaths of fierce
>   desire,
> Leaving the females naked and glowing with the lusts of youth
> For the female spirits of the dead pining in bonds of religion;
> Run from their fetters reddening ...
>
>   (15.19-24)

This actually involves a transition from a male-initiated
nationalist and political rebellion to a liberation of male and
female sexual energies from all fetters, internal as well as the
external ones imposed by traditional institutions. But Blake's
transition here is far too simple, for it ignores many fundamental
questions. How does a male-dominated political revolution (which
it clearly is in 'America' and the history Blake was mediating (15))
lead to the overthrow of traditional male domination over women in
the spheres of work, family, sexuality and relations in general?
How is the female consciousness and self-image, profoundly
accommodated to existing conventional society through training,
habit and years of practice, suddenly and totally transformed?
How are the males' deeply formed habits of domination and
exploitation so suddenly shed? 'Fetters', as Blake really knew,
are also 'mind forg'd manacles', 'knotted/The meshes: twisted like
to the human brain' ('London', 'Book of Urizen', 25).

It was in considering precisely this set of problems, I believe,
that Blake saw the need for deepening his sexual dialectic to
include the notion of 'female will', casting out the vestiges of
delusions about consciousness as free from all the effects of the
system against which it is struggling. Instead of Oothoon,
women's chief representatives in 'Europe' are the 'nameless shadowy
female' and Enitharmon. The poem's Preludium shows the former in
great confusion and despair (1.6-15) while the latter, with her
stamping signet, explicitly mirrors Bromion in VDA (2.8, 10; VDA,
1.20-1). In the centre of 'Europe' Blake includes a re-examination
of woman's consciousness in the alienated and oppressive world
depicted in VDA. Instead of Oothoon's critique and complaint, we
now hear woman's voice in these words:

> Who shall I call? Who shall I send?
> That Woman, lovely Woman! may have dominion?
> Arise O Rintrah thee I call! & Palambron thee!
> Go! tell the Human race that Womans love is Sin!
> That an Eternal life awaits the worms of sixty winters
> In an allegorical abode where existence hath never come:
> Forbid all Joy, & from her childhood shall the little female
> Spread nets in every secret path.
>
>   (6.2-9)

The strategy proposed is kin to the one that Oothoon rejected in
VDA, 6.6-13: woman accepts the alienation of her own sexuality in
a society organized around principles of domination and subjection,
and she internalizes its norms. Having done so, she tries to
manipulate the existing system of relations and values to carve out
an area in which she seems to be 'on top'. Both the orthodox
suppression of Eros, with all the traditional contempt for sexuality,
and the deferment of human fulfilment to a fictitious religious
future life, 'an allegorical abode where existence hath never come',
are strengthened. They are turned against the male who can thus
be trapped in the shared ideology of frustration and mutual
exploitation to pay court to Enitharmon and her progeny. Blake
has decided that in the world of VDA it is misleadingly undialecti-
cal to imagine a female consciousness like Oothoon's.
   From this group of insights Blake moves to the wider social
interactions of revolution and counter-revolution in contemporary
Europe, (16) and in Plates 10-13 he outlines the effects of
repressive material and ideological structures on consciousness.
For example,

                          then turn'd the fluxile eyes
     Into two stationary orbs, concentrating all things.
     The ever-varying spiral ascents to the heavens of heavens
     Were bended downward; and the nostrils golden gates shut
     Turn'd outward, barr'd and petrify'd against the infinite.
                              (10.11-15)

Again Blake characteristically stresses the social basis of
perception in these plates, a recognition which lies at the heart
of his sexual dialectics. The movement here, from the study of
fragmented female consciousness, to the wider conflicts in the
society and back to the specific question of women's consciousness
in the light of the total situation, is typical of Blakes'
exploratory method:

     Enitharmon laugh'd in her sleep to see (O womans triumph)
     Every house a den, every man bound; the shadows are filld
     With spectres, and the windows wove over with curses of iron:
     Over the doors Thou shalt not; & over the chimneys Fear is
                                                written:
                              (12.25-8)

Woman has become so integrated in the repressing system that she
can rejoice with Urizen and all rulers to see men bound and
fearful. (17) In this 'triumph' Blake explores the way forms of
political and sexual domination are internalized to generate a
'female will', leaving us not the idealized libertarian revolutionary of VDA, but with victims who have become the vicious
propagators of the very ideology and organization which oppresses
them and their male counterparts. 'Europe' concludes with the
hope that the current challenge to existing political and economic
order in France may be the present key to a future, more total
liberation which may include the sexual sphere (14.32-15.11).
But while the final plate involves highly generalized apocalyptic

violence, the outcome is, wisely, not predicted, and the question of sexual emancipation is correspondingly left in suspension: the dialectic is unresolved.

I now wish to point briefly at Blake's continuing development of these aspects of sexual dialectic he had forged in 1793-4. (18) It certainly plays a central part in the 'Four Zoas' and can be represented by this passage from the Second Night:

> Enitharmon answerd Wherefore didst thou throw thine arms
> around
> Ahanias Image I deceivd thee & will still deceive
> Urizen saw thy sin & hid his beams in darkning Clouds
> I still keep watch altho I tremble & wither across the heavens
> In strong vibrations of fierce jealousy for thou art mine
> Created for my will my slave tho strong tho I am weak
> Farewell the God calls me away I depart in my sweet bliss
> She fled vanishing on the wind ...
>
> ...
> The joy of woman is the Death of her most best beloved
> Who dies for love of her
> In torments of fierce jealousy & pangs of adoration.
>   (II.34.41-8, 63-5)

Enitharmon, repressed and fragmented in her own sexuality, desperately tries to impose the repressors' ideology and order on Los. It is she who invokes Urizen. The subordinate position of women, which Blake had just returned to on pages 30 and 31 of Night Two, breeds a fear which manifests itself in the desire to own, to possess, to control the male as women themselves are controlled. Herself an industrial slave (FZ, II.30, 31), she is convinced that her very survival depends on binding down the male as 'slave' to her own female will, using her only weapon - sex. The ghastly intellectual and psychological confusions involved in her strategy, as well as the male violence to which she responds ('Los smote her upon the Earth twas long eer she revivd', I.11.3), lead her to aggressive assertions of domination simultaneously combined with flight which is both the product of fear and the exercise of sexual enticement. Blake now presents all forward movement towards collaborative sexual relations in terms of these very fallen, realistic states of consciousness (see Nights, VIIa - VIII).

In his next major work, 'Milton', Blake shows the shadowy Female who opened 'Europe' responding to her lover, the revolutionary Orc. Now it was one of the marks of VDA that despite its frozen conclusion it encouraged readers to respond with thoughts such as this: 'desire cannot free itself from the restraints of law and convention until Orc arises again and destroys the whole mold that encases life and which has so far only begun to crack.' (19) But we have seen how Blake came to place the problems of freeing desire in a dialectic which grasped the consequences of internalization of 'restraints of law and convention' as a central human reality. Taking seriously the contradictions of consciousness which mediate the various drives for greater freedom within

particular social situations and ideological traditions, Blake
depicted Orc's energies and perceptions as extremely equivocal,
deeply effected by Urizen and the system against which he rebels.
Even those he loves and who love his energy see him as a terror,
mostly a dehumanized terror too. (20)   In 'America' Orc is already
depicted as tormented and dehumanized, although when he seized 'the
panting struggling womb' of the shadowy female, Blake claims she
'joy'd: she put aside her clouds & smiled her first-born smile',
welcoming him lyrically ('America', 2).   In 'Milton', however,
Blake more plausibly presents her as sharing the kind of female
will he described in Enitharmon:

> My Garments shall be woven of sighs & heart broken lamentations
> The misery of unhappy Families shall be drawn out into its
> border
> ...
> For I will put on the Human Form & take the Image of God
> Even Pity & Humanity but my Clothing shall be Cruelty
> And I will put on Holiness as a breastplate & as a helmet
> And all my ornaments shall be of the gold of broken hearts
> And the precious stones of anxiety & care & desperation & death
> And repentance for sin & sorrow & punishment & fear
> To defend me from thy terrors O Orc! My only beloved!
> ('Milton', 18.6-7, 19-25)

This is a typically fine passage depicting the contradictions of
ideology and feeling in female consciousness that Blake's
dialectic has enabled him to lay hold of and present so poignantly.
Like other women, she has to survive in an oppressive order run by
repressing and repressed males, and she employs the strategies of
the 'female will'.   The tragedy of the situation is deepened by
the fact that, as so often with Urizen, she takes up destructive
strategies with intentions that contain many admirable elements,
only these elements have been distorted by fear, by the received
ideologies, and by the genuine contradictions and complexities of
the social relations within which she lives.   She loves and wants
Orc ('my only beloved'), yet she fears him as a terror, and he is
indeed an extremely equivocal terror immersed in the same society
as herself.   She wishes to put on 'the Human Form', rather than
'The Human Abstract' (see 'Songs of Experience').   But in her fear
and confusion, doubtless thickened by such contemporary educators
as Hannah More, she self-protectingly reaches for a mixture of
vestigial Christianity (St Paul's breastplate, sin, repentance) and
traditional love ploys ('broken hearts', female 'cruelty') and the
use of sexual abstention to induce sexual 'anxiety' in the male
she both wants and fears.   Blake's sexual dialectic is indeed
grounded in a profound realism, alert to the dynamic movement and
complex contradictions of human consciousness. (21)
     His continued preoccupation with this approach to sexual
relations is evident in 'Jerusalem', where he gives readers an
immensely rich account of the psychology of repression, of the need
to understand how all who labour to build Jerusalem do so in a
multi-faceted situation where nobody is above confusion and
torment, where all are radically effected by fragmentation and

repression at the deepest levels of consciousness, in the most
intimate spheres of activity as in the most public. I have attempted
to show in an earlier article how this poem illustrates Blake's
dialectical vision of the 'collaboration' between man and woman so
essential in the struggle towards human emancipation which transcends
the sexual antagonisms he studied so profoundly. Here there is only
space to refer the reader to that discussion of 'Jerusalem'. (22)

So far I have concentrated on Blake's dialectical presentation
of sexual conflicts in his culture and his critical penetration of
conventional ideologies and their psychic effects. Yet his thinking
about consciousness, social and sexual organization encourages
readers to consider the poet's own vision in a similar way. If we
do so, one major question emerges. Granted that Blake's overall
exploration of contemporary sexual being comprises an extra-
ordinarily intelligent and radical critique of his culture, are
there really no affirmations of the dominant male culture and
received ideologies in his work? As we saw, his explorations of
consciousness in the later works hardly teach us to expect such
absolute transcendence of existing socio-cultural norms or their
psychic consequences. Far from it, he taught us to expect the
simultaneous presence of rebellion and affirmation in response to
the dominant culture. When we look at his work in the light which
he himself helped to generate, traditional features of male
ideology can be brought into focus. These are the features I shall
try to illuminate in the remainder of this chapter.

The survival of a traditional sexist hierarchy of values in
Blake's psychological symbolism and his vision of female roles
turns out to be quite visible. Obviously enough, his male and
female figures often (but rarely exclusively, and certainly not
always) represent aspects of the individual psyche. So in the
middle of a violent conflict with Enitharmon, Los says, 'in the Brain
of Man we live, & in his circling Nerves' (FZ, I.11.15). But even
when the poet's figures represent a concentration on the internal
organization of the individual, his use of male and female affords
insight to basic assumptions and their implications - just as they
do in Freud's use of 'masculine' and 'feminine' as psychic signs.
On the whole, after Oothoon, Blake's 'females' tend to represent
the receptive, the derivative, the soft, the passive qualities
whose fulfilment is in supporting the active, creative, male
qualities - unless they are, significantly, perversions of Blake's
ideal feminine, and in this case (the normal one, Blake laments)
they are presented as denying male gratification and as aggressive
agents of repression. Here the symbolism reveals a plain continuity
with traditional male perceptions of the good female, her ideal
qualities and orientation. It is typical that when Blake has
Ahania (Urizen's female counterpart or emanation) recall, in 'The
Book of Ahania', the good old days of unified life, she presents
herself in a thoroughly traditional female role as happily passive
recipient and servicer of Urizen's (male) creative energies
(5.25-37). As an image of female fulfilment the passage referred
to clearly affirms a highly conservative division of sexual roles
and images. The female's gratification is 'at thy feet', passively
and contentedly awaiting the evening return home of the idealized
male, energy-force and great intellectual, 'lap full of seed',

all of this begs reference to quotes?

'hand full of generous fire' and possessor of 'eternal science' to
boot. Although these divisions of role and image may have been
internalized by umpteen 'well brought up' females in Blake's culture
(as well as our own), they are manifestly a product of the male ego,
its vanity and its will to perpetuate inherited structures of
domination over women. Even when such imagery is meant to function
primarily as a figured reflection of internal movements within one
bi-sexual consciousness, it both discloses and affirms dominant male
ideology which inevitably feeds back into the realm of human inter-
relations from which it has been derived.

Such loaded usage is common in Blake's work. The 'Four Zoas',
for instance, opens with a passage which includes the statement
that 'In Eden Females sleep the winter in soft silken veils',
while the poet, in his own voice, immediately supports this view,
expressed by Enion. He tells the reader that Beulah is a 'Soft
Moony Universe feminine lovely/Pure mild & Gentle given in Mercy'
(FZ, I.5.1, 29-32). Much has been written about the state of
Beulah and its positive, though limited, role in Blake's economy
of salvation. One of its fullest portrayals is in the well-known
opening of the second book of 'Milton' (30.8-31). Necessary as
Beulah may be in Blake's framework, it is important to note just
how uncritically it perpetuates a stereotyping of sexual roles,
images and qualities. Beulah is unequivocally categorized in this
important passage in 'Milton' as female and a place inferior to
the one occupied by the 'Sons of Eden', whom 'the lovely' females
of Beulah address as 'our Fathers & Brothers' (not, of course,
mothers and sisters). 'Female' is perceived as a state whose sole
justification is in ministering to the infinitely more dynamic and
inspired male. Females are 'a mild & pleasant Rest' for the male
'Sons of Eden' engaged in the 'fury of Poetic Inspiration,/To build
the Universe stupendous'; they are 'mothers' and the providers
of 'love & pity & sweet compassion'. The male's justification for
existence is, in contrast, creative agency and not service or
gratification of the female. Here there is no equal and true
reciprocity but an ancient sexist hierarchy of being. The great
creative acts are allotted to males, 'man to man', for the females,
Blake assures us, simply could not live in Eden 'because the life of
Man was too exceeding unbounded'; so the females seek a shadowy
place, gratefully promising their 'Fathers & Brothers' that they
will dutifully 'obey your words'. (23)

Besides this, as we have seen throughout the chapter, Blake's
figures, quite as much as Spenser's or Langland's, (24) habitually
encompass both internal and a wide range of explicitly social
dimensions of existence. The passages we have just looked at are
no exception, but it is worth illustrating further how unself-
reflexively 'male' Blake could actually be, confirming how
traditional attitudes of male supremicism are very deeply rooted
in our cultural heritage. (25) In the First Night of the 'Four
Zoas' Los tells Enitharmon that woman was 'Once born for the sport &
amusement of Man', though now in her fallen condition she is, alas,
'born to drink up all his Powers' (I.10.25). It is tempting to
take this statement as Blake's critical reflection of the perverted
male mentality manifest in the fallen prophetic imagination. But
I doubt that this is correct. For Blake himself elsewhere gives

sympathetic expression to such views, assuming that Women's being
only has real meaning as support and entertainment for Man.   Here
we may recall how in VDA Blake had the libertarian Oothoon assure
Theotormon, paralysed with jealousy, that

> silken nets and trap of adamant will Oothoon spread,
> And catch for thee girls of mild silver, or of furious gold;
> I'll like beside thee on a bank & view their wanton play
> In lovely copulation bliss on bliss with Theotormon:
> Red as the rosy morning, lustful as the first born beam,
> Oothoon shall view his dear delight, nor e'er with jealous cloud
> Come in the heaven of generous love; nor selfish blightings
> bring.
>
> (VDA, 7.23-9)

One way of reading this passage is that Blake, far from presenting
it as a mark of understandable ideological confusion on the
generous Oothoon's part, actually means us to take it as an
expression of how he wants females to image their own role and
fulfilment, how he wants them to act towards males.   The woman here
may very well be Blake's paragon of non-possessive 'generous love'
because she accepts that female fulfilment is totally identified
with that of the male, however possessive and sullen he may be.
She serves the male with the most selfless devotion: however much
she may want the male she loves, with whoever he happens to be
enjoying 'lovely copulation bliss on bliss', all is well so long
as he is gratified.   As for the male, no reciprocal demands are
made on him (perhaps they would be a sign of depraved 'female
will').   It is also remarkable that no concern is expressed about
the use of 'nets and traps', instruments of violent coercion, with
which the necessary 'girls' for Theotormon will be caught.   Oothoon
(and, it seems, Blake) doubtless assumes they will be gratified by
the sexual favours of Theotormon - a common enough male fantasy and
one that serves to justify many forms of sexual exploitation and
even violence.   The libertarianism celebrated here actually
reinforces the traditional culture of male discourse which Blake's
poem sets out to undermine. (26)

'Jerusalem' involves some of the most moving and profound of
Blake's explorations of sexual relations.   Furthermore, one of its
major characteristics is a brilliant critique of patriarchalism as
it has evolved in our civilization, 'cruel Patriarchal pride/Planting
thy Family alone,/Destroying all the World beside,' 'the Patriarchal
pomp and cruelty' (J, 27.79-81, 83-4). (27)   Yet here too Blake
manifested the marks of the patriarchal culture against which he
was in such radical opposition.   Beulah, for instance, is still
envisaged in much the same way as in the passage from the opening
of the second book of 'Milton', but Blake adds to its activities
in a passage which should stir our memories.   It is a place,

> Where every Female delights to give her maiden to her husband
> The Female searches sea & land for gratifications to the
> Male Genius: who in return clothes her in gems & gold
> And feeds her with the food of Eden. hence all her beauty beams
>
> (J, 69.15-18)

He has thus cherished Oothoon's offer to Theotormon in VDA, 7, now
placing it in Beulah. Very traditional, unequal sexual roles and
divisions are thus retained. The vision is centred on the sexual
gratification of the male 'husband' and it is assumed, as male
libertines have customarily assumed, that this will necessarily
entail the fulfilment of the females whose real existence, after
all, is only in relation to the male's. The 'Male' does not
apparently delight to give his friend or servant (!) to the Females.
An indication of the extent to which such passages relapse into
startlingly conservative discourse is the way Blake uses, quite
uncritically, the social category 'maiden', one which is
necessarily part of a society divided into rulers and ruled on
lines he consistently opposed throughout his poetry. Another
indication of the breakdown of critical thought may perhaps be the
use of the category 'husband', for he had earlier laid emphasis on
the destructive effects of the institution of marriage and
associated human emancipation with its destruction (for example,
see the earlier quotation from 'America', 15).

More difficult to assess are the overall implications of the
roles of women in the processes of regeneration in 'Jerusalem'. We
saw how vital female collaboration is to these processes, but one
aspect of the collaboration demands a little further scrutiny -
namely, the consummation of female being in chapter four. The
problem I have in mind here can be illustrated from Plates 87-8 and
92, where Blake concentrates on the continuing conflict and
collaboration between Los and Enitharmon, already mentioned. Los
'began to utter his love' and frustrated sexual desire (much as he
had done in the first night of the 'Four Zoas') only to be repelled
by Enitharmon:

Enitharmon answered. No! I will sieze thy Fibres & weave
Them: not as thou wilt but as I will, for I will Create
A round Womb beneath my bosom lest I also be overwoven
With Love; be thou assured I never will be thy slave.
(J, 87.12-15)

According to Blake's own disclosure of 'sexual organization'
Enitharmon's fears concerning the male ego and the habitual male
domination over women are all too well-founded. Both 'love' and
the procreation of children had become instruments and means of male
domination and control. This is precisely what Enitharmon knows.
Of course, her reaction does not rest with the defiant 'I never
will be thy slave', but involves a counter-offensive to control the
threatening male. Expressing her jealousy she then tells Los that
he wishes to 'shut me in a Grave' (87.20-4). Her suspicions can
hardly be allayed when Los answers. For he (and, as we will see,
his creator) envisages the state of full humanity as one in which
'Man converses with Man'. True enough, men need 'their Emanations'
to achieve this unifying converse and these Emanations are, at any
rate theoretically, 'both Male & Female at the Gates of each
Humanity' (88.1-11). I will return to the decisive significance of
the choice of this 'emanation' imagery, but here one must note that
the 'Female' only survives as a function through which 'Man converses
with man'. (28)

In Plate 92 Enitharmon, 'in great terror', reiterates her justifiable anxiety about the females' fate in Los's (Blake's) universe:

My Looms will be no more & I annihilate vanish for ever
Then thou wilt Create another Female according to thy Will.

She fears that Los (and Blake - his is 'The Poets Song' mentioned in line 8) have a version of regeneration which involves the annihilation of her identity as a mere product of fallen divisions. The talk about the role of the Female Emanation in Eden has offered her no assurance about the continuity of her being. So she interprets these rather gaseous utterances as implying Los will obtain another female more fully in accord with male fantasies of 'Fibres of dominion'. More appropriately, she echoes Eve's fear in 'Paradise Lost' (IX.826-30), one whose content Adam also conceives independently even as he makes the sublime resolution to die rather than live without Eve (IX.908-13). However, although Blake calls Enitharmon Los's 'Wife till the sleep of Death is past' (14.14) she meets no such responses as Adam offered Eve. Whatever Los's expressions of 'love' and 'intoxication' at her 'beauty & perfection' (87.1-5),

Los answerd swift as the shuttle of gold. Sexes must vanish
                                                  & cease
To be, when Albion arises from his dread repose O lovely
                                               Enitharmon
                                            (92.13-14)

Enitharmon remains unimpressed as she again accuses males of 'the pride of dominion' while Los promises his Sons (!) that they will 'not Die' (93.17-19). In his assertions about the Sexes and Humanity, Los is his creator's mouthpiece. For example, Jerusalem tells the erring Vala that 'Humanity is far above/Sexual organiza-tion' (J, 79.73-4), and Los earlier emphasized that 'Humanity knows not of Sex' (44.33; see 63.20), while the narrator in 'Milton' proclaimed that 'The Sexual is Threefold: the Human is Fourfold' (M, 4.5). In the 'Four Zoas' Blake describes the regenerated state of Eden in terms such as the following: 'Then those in Great Eternity ... As one Man ... As One Man all the Universal Family ... consulting as One Man' (I.21.1-7). In the world of human fulfil-ment there are not, as now, 'Two wills' or 'two intellects' between individual males and females (II.30.48). Similarly, in 'Jerusalem' fulfilment is depicted as life 'as One Man ... As One Man all the Universal Family' (J, 33.15-26), while again the very existence of individuated male and female 'Intellects' and 'Wills' is merely a sign of the fallen and depraved condition of historical humanity (86.61). As usual the regenerate being is constantly referred to in the male gender even though gender has allegedly been transcended - 'every Man stood Fourfold' in the final resurrection at the close of 'Jerusalem', and all in eternity are 'as One Man' (J, 98.12, 39). In the light of such sexist currents we may not be too surprised that at the end of 'Jerusalem' Blake saw fit to incorporate an unironic line of advice in his own voice which has

clear signs of fairly traditional male arrogance - 'She who adores
not your frowns will only loathe your smiles' (85.24). The male
(Blake) images the adoring female prostrate before the irresistible
strong man, machismo rules. The self-image proved attractive enough
to Blake for him to use a variation of it in a lyric in his
Notebook: 'The Woman that does not love your Frowns/Will never
embrace your smiles'. (29)

The final topic I wish to mention is Blake's use of 'emanations'.
This is a category for examining the place of 'females' in humanity,
for although on a few isolated occasions Blake states that
emanations are male and female, the emanations given any extensive
life in the poetry are all explicitly females such as Enitharmon,
Vala, Jerusalem, Enion, Ahania, and so on - as anyone who even
consults the local contexts pointed to in the Blake Concordance
under 'Emanation/Emanations' can ascertain. Consistently Blake's
view is that 'In Eternity Woman is the Emanation of Man she has No
Will of her own' ('Vision of the Last Judgement', p.85), a candid
enough statement which accords with the elements in his work
affirming traditional male stances in his world.

Throughout the prophetic books Blake conflates Platonic myths
about the original androgynous humans with the patriarchal myth of
Genesis and Judaeo-Christian tradition, for he imagines female
existence as a tragic division in a being who is presented as male,
whatever the eternal Man's bi-sexual potentials. This we have
observed in some detail. The myth appears as early as 'The Book
of Urizen' where it is only after the male Los has been rent apart
from Urizen, and deeply affected by Urizen's fragmentation, that
'A female form' (Enitharmon) emerges. Even though Blake then
constructs a powerful version of the Oedipal romance with the
nuclear family of Los, Enitharmon and the man child Orc, he still
sees the pregnant Enitharmon merely as Los's 'own divided image'
(Plates 6-7, 13-20). The same is true of the 'Four Zoas', although
Los and Enitharmon are again depicted as 'husband' and 'wife',
called 'Parents' and developed as the participants in Blake's
profound psychoanalytic explorations of family and marriage, once
more using the Oedipus myth (FZ, V.58.1-25, 59.16-18, 60.6-63.22).
As for 'Jerusalem', there is little need to go over ground we have
just covered in discussing the relations between Los and his 'wife'
who is also seen as his 'emanation'. It might well be argued that
Blake's poetic realization of what he imagines as fulfilled humanity
is so lacking in that 'Definite & Determinate Identity' in which
'The Infinite alone resides' (J, 55.64), that there is little point
in analysing it at all. Yet one thing about this all too vaguely
presented image is clear and I have already drawn attention to it:
Blake's treatment downgrades the female and affirms many facets of
the dominant male supremicist traditions, despite his revolutionary
critique of the inherited culture.

It is worth recalling the antecedents of Blake's 'emanations',
for they shed some light on the structure of this idea. In his
prolific study of romanticisms, 'Natural Supernaturalism', M.H.
Abrams discusses the role of the specifically neo-platonic idea of
emanation and return in romantic writing. Although he does not
mention Blake's treatment of sex or emanations here, these pages
locate the premises forming Blake's choice of 'emanation' language.

There is no need to summarize Abrams's description of the relevant
metaphysical tradition for it is both lucid and accessible. But it
is interesting that the metaphysics of emanation and return to
perfect unity with the One had already been used to characterize
the nature of human sexuality. Abrams refers to the 'De divisione
naturae' of the Christian neo-Platonist John Scotus Erigena, where
man is envisaged as originally one and undivided (as in the myths
of the 'Symposium' and Genesis). All divisions, including sexual
differentiation, are the product of the primal fall. The redemption
through Jesus unites male and female, man and world, knower and
known, until all the divisions of nature are transcended in a
perfect reunion with the One. Abrams links the traditions
consolidated in John Scotus's eclectic work with the equally
eclectic works of hermeticism and Boehme, which Blake of course
knew well. (30) By selecting this model to represent the status
of woman, 'the Emanation of Man' (VLJ), Blake incorporated a
fundamentally sexist principle in the structure of his symbolism,
for the very existence of Women is inevitably presented as having
its sole telos in absorption into the 'One Man' (e.g. J, 98.39)
from whom they have fallen or emanated. Abrams does not point out
something we could well remember here. John Scotus is utterly
representative of the whole tradition of Christian allegorical
exegesis in treating the male as the spirit which contains all
good, and as a figure of Christ, while the woman is the inferior,
external region of corporality, nature and vain phantasies. (31)
To assert, as some prominent scholars do, that in Blake's model of
the human telos Woman 'is still an active part, though without
a separate will', seems quite mistaken. (32) For to dissolve
individuality of 'will' (and, as we saw earlier, 'intellect' too)
is the destruction of an absolutely essential aspect of human
identity. And Blake's symbolic eschatology manifestly consummates
the sexist moments of his own work.
   Indeed the whole vocabulary of human unification in 'One Man'
has dangerous implications. It encourages a vision which
substitutes a world of generalized symbols and abstractions for the
human world of concrete individuals and historical existence which
Blake explored so magnificently in the body of his work. At the
close of 'Jerusalem' we see the obliteration of not only Women and
Children but of the very possibility of all specific, irreducibly
particular relationships. We see the closure of the dramatic
interaction of human relationships and history and the substitution
of a cycle of emanation and return which has nothing to do with men
and women at any imaginable stage of existence (J, 99). Far from
the humanistic transcendence of individual and historical conflicts
promised earlier (J, 34.7-26, 38.12-30), this dissolves all human
identity into an undifferentiated unity. The fate of Women and
Children in this mythology could well be read as the perpetuation
of traditional forms of domination masquerading as the benevolent
transcendence of divisions. There is enough affirmation of
traditional male supremicism to make such a reading plausible, and
it would rightly highlight the dangers of the desire to terminate
the diversity, contingency and conflict of human interests in a
manner which has to dissolve individual, incarnate human identity.
The end of 'Jerusalem' includes a recurrent human nostalgia,

favoured in much romantic writing, for a totally unified state of being, 'All Human Forms identified' as 'One Man'. But this is a recipe for the destruction of the spontaneous forms of creative life to which Blake's work is dedicated to liberating and developing.

That Blake seems not to have focused on the repressive male traditions actually affirmed in his work shows the hold of received ideology and abstractions over even the most radical imagination. This finding would not have surprised him, for it confirms the soundness of his own dialectical way of exploring individual consciousness and social being. It is from this that we perhaps still have most to learn.

Chapter 3

Romantic Literature and Childhood

Jonathan Cook

A combination of social and ideological change gave peculiar
prominence to the subject of childhood in late eighteenth-century
England. Lawrence Stone in his book, 'The Family, Sex and Marriage
in England 1500-1800', has charted the unprecedented rise of a
culture of childhood amongst some sections of the aristocratic,
professional and gentry classes during the eighteenth century. (1)
This culture was characterized by an affectionate and tolerant
attitude on the part of parents towards their children, and a
respect for the individual integrity of the child as something more
than the inheritor of familial and social obligations. Signs of
this change in the relationship between parents and children
included more intimate modes of address, the production of a
literature designed to entertain children rather than instruct them,
the attentive reading of manuals on child-rearing, the education of
children at home rather than at school, and a refusal to use corporal
punishment. (2)
    The material basis for this new culture of childhood lay in the
accumulation of wealth from commerce and agriculture, wealth which
created opportunities for the kind of privacy and leisure which
allowed parents to pay close attention to the needs and potentials
of their children. The emergence of this new culture serves to
highlight the contrasting fate of the children of the poor. This
is not simply a matter of the persistence of forms of child labour
in the eighteenth century, but, as E.P. Thompson has powerfully
argued in his 'The Making of the English Working Class', a matter
of its intensification between 1780 and 1840 under the impact of
the new factory system. (3) However, economic development was a
necessary, but not a sufficient, cause for the creation of a culture
of childhood. Theoretical change played a central part, too,
particularly the various attempts that were made during the late
seventeenth and eighteenth centuries to expound a secular science
of human nature. One consequence of this was the common rejection
of the notion that the child was the depraved product of original
sin by theorists who were in other respects as divergent as Locke
and Rousseau. Another was a peculiarly heightened attention to
childhood as the place where theories of human nature could be
confirmed or disproved by observation or experiment. No doubt, the

experiences of children subjected to this kind of attention were
very different. Queeney Thrale in the eighteenth century and John
Stuart Mill in the nineteenth were both victims of an educational
regime based on an associationist theory of mind whereby the
child's identity was to be constructed by the assiduous interventions
of parents in regulating the kind and volume of ideas to be
implanted in the child's mind. (4) This is in marked contrast to
the reverential attention paid by Coleridge to his children at
play: (5)

> It is in very truth a sunny, misty, cloudy, dazzling, howling
> day, and I have been looking at as pretty a sight as a father's
> eyes could well see - Hartley and little Derwent running in the
> green where the gusts blow most madly, both with their hair
> floating and tossing, a miniature of the agitated trees, below
> which they were playing, inebriate both with pleasure - Hartley
> whirling round for joy, Derwent eddying, half-willingly, half
> by the force of the gust - driven backward, struggling forward,
> and shouting his little hymn of joy ...

This kind of writing is informed by Rousseauist assumptions
about the child's natural goodness or innocence. Education is as
much a matter of benign neglect as of supervision. Whatever
potentialities the child has should be allowed to develop
spontaneously. The natural world plays an important part in this
attitude towards childhood, not only as the best setting for this
kind of development, but also as a source which the writer can
draw upon to describe the behaviour of children. Coleridge reads
his children's activities in terms of events in the natural world,
and this forms the basis of his pleasure in the sight of them
realizing their identities through expression. In acting like
this they are most natural, and their action also brings them into
harmony with the natural world. Thus they provide the poet with
an ideal image of uninhibited, expressive self-hood which does not
carry with it the penalty of isolation or exile, so keenly felt
by the adult Coleridge. (6)
Evidently, Coleridge's delight in his children, and the
conception of self which underlies it, are at odds with the
educational ideas derived from an associationist theory of mind.
James Mill would have thought Coleridge mad for letting his
children frolic in the wind; he would have had them indoors
mastering the principles of political economy, on the assumption
that the child was an amorphous stuff waiting to be moulded by the
parent.
Thus the culture of childhood was by no means homogeneous in its
assumptions and ideas. Rather it was the site of competing
theories of self and the competing educational ideas that accompanied
them. The existence of these differences should not divert us,
however, from the identification of certain themes common to the
rival schools of thought. As I have already suggested, both the
associationist and the expressive notions of self shared a
rejection of the doctrine of original sin and therefore the innate
depravity of the child. They both shared, too, a basically asocial
conception of the self, although in different ways. For associa-

tionists the environment which creates and determines the self is figured in terms of sensations, ideas and their associations. There is little or no vocabulary to describe the making of the self in terms of the interaction of social and biological forces. The expressive idea centres on an opposition between the natural, pre-social self and a social world which threatens the natural self with inhibition and restraint. (7)

To identify these areas of common ground between rival theories is, in a sense, to identify the ideological limits of the culture of childhood, as it takes shape during the eighteenth century. A shared rejection of original sin, a shared belief in the asocial nature of the self, both set limits to the kinds of disagreement that occur over the identity of the child and the best means of her education, and, as I want to argue later in this essay, they set limits to the kind of social criticism that can emerge out of the culture of childhood when it encounters the fate of children of the labouring poor. Moreover, alongside the emerging secular culture of childhood, the older view of childhood as a vessel of original sin was given a renewed force through the impact of Methodism. Writing to her son John on the education of children, Susanna Wesley advised, 'Break their will betimes ... let a child from a year old be taught to fear the rod and cry softly'. (8) The most likely victims of this hysterical and sadistic insistence would be the children of the labouring poor, children whose fate would be either an early death or persistent physical labour, or both. In 'The Making of the English Working Class', E.P. Thompson has noted the connections between this kind of doctrine about childhood and the exploitation of child labour: 'the proverbial non-conformist mill owners, with their Methodist overlookers and their reputation as week-day child drivers, working their mills till five minutes before midnight on the Saturday and enforcing the attendance of their children at Sunday school on the sabbath'. (9)

The subject of childhood in late eighteenth-century England becomes a point of expression for long-term trends within intellectual culture: the emergence of different and competing secular models of the self, and the problematic relation of convergence and conflict between these secular models and the still persisting version of childhood derived from theology. These long-term trends are given a particularly intense focus by the social and economic contradictions of late eighteenth-century England - the increasing exploitation of child labour amongst the labouring poor set against the increasing opportunities for happiness amongst the socially privileged. In this respect childhood becomes a highly sensitive register for revealing the particular class interests which might underlie attitudes towards the child. But childhood is a subject in another sense too: not only something to write about, it is also an object of imaginative identification, a perspective charged with opportunities for social criticism and social withdrawal. In what follows I want to look in particular at the way two romantic writers, Blake and Wordsworth, respond to the challenges posed by the subject of childhood.

Childhood is central to Blake's concerns in the 'Songs of Innocence and Experience', (10) and one consequence of this concern is to give the 'Songs' a strong social and historical reference. The 'Chimney Sweeper' poems are a useful starting point for a more detailed analysis. As David Erdman has shown, Blake's proximity to the experience of the labouring poor in London gave him a sharp awareness of the economic exploitation of children, (11) and particularly the practice of selling young children into apprentice-ships, a practice which provides the context for the opening lines of the 'Chimney Sweeper' poem in 'Innocence':

When my mother died I was very young
And my father sold me while yet my tongue
Could scarcely cry weep weep weep weep
So your chimneys I sweep and in soot I sleep.
                    ('The Chimney Sweeper', 1-4)

The strangeness of these opening lines is in the child's calm in the face of the terrifying conditions of his own existence, and the poem goes on to explore the psychology of this passivity. The chimney sweeper derives support for his position from the dream of Tom Dacre which supplies a vision of liberation ('The Chimney Sweeper', 9-20). The real conditions of the sweep's existence are reversed in the imagery of the dream: open spaces instead of confinement, cleanliness instead of dirt, light instead of dark, a benign and present God in place of the absent father. But the chimney sweeper of 'Innocence' does not bring the dream into a critical relation to his own suffering. Instead, he makes his own suffering, and the suffering of other exploited children, into a condition for the prophetic truth of the dream and the comfort it supplies. The dream is a reward for acquiescence; its effect is to make intolerable conditions tolerable ('The Chimney Sweeper', 21-4).

One problem with the last stanza of the poem is whether we are to accept the chimney sweeper's interpretaion of the dream and the moral that goes with it. Or has Blake written a poem which provides us with an insight into the relations of dream to real existence, and into the part played by religion in providing an imagery and a set of fantasy identifications which not only compensate for the miseries of economic exploitation but help create a kind of person and a moral code which ensures the perpetuation of those miseries?

Viewed from the perspective of the 'Chimney Sweeper' poem in 'Experience', the problem seems solved. The chimney sweeper of 'Innocence' is revealed as a smug ideologue who inducts his fellows into an official morality which denies their real interests. Where the chimney sweeper of 'Innocence' sees duty, the chimney sweeper of 'Experience' sees exploitation, and where the chimney sweeper of 'Innocence' identifies himself with the images of religion, the chimney sweeper of 'Experience' sees institutional Christianity as a human construct which serves the purposes of domination. Thus, the sweep's parents

... are gone to praise God & his Priest & King
Who make up a heaven of our misery.

The poem of 'Experience' begins in sentimental vision. The
poet, presumably wandering through the streets of London discovers

A little black thing among the snow
Crying weep, weep, in notes of Woe!
                ('The Chimney Sweeper', 1-2)

But the expectation of pathos is rapidly dispelled as the child
answers the poet's questions. The poet may have discovered a
minute particular, but it is one which concentrates unexpectedly
powerful energies of expression and criticism. The sweep of
'Experience' displays a self-hood which remains independent of
attempts to exploit or deny him. He recognizes too, that his
independent powers of expression are the source both of attempts
to induct him into the religion of the Fall, and of the justification for his neglect ('The Chimney Sweeper', 5-10). The child's
critical powers reveal that what seem to be opposite attitudes,
indoctrination on the one hand, neglect on the other, are in fact
aspects of the same exploitation.
    'The Chimney Sweeper' of 'Experience' would seem to contradict
the poem of 'Innocence' as truth contradicts illusion. The sweep
of 'Experience' does not depend upon dreams inspired by religion
as his principal mode of relating to the world. Nor does he
depend upon the expressions of others as a means of self-definition.
His independent voice contrasts with the sweep of 'Innocence' who
seems to say what he knows his superiors want him to say. The
sweep of 'Experience' endures his hardship without fantasizing
it into the sign of future bliss.
    Taken together, the two poems reveal the relation between an
economic circumstance, the exploitation of child labour, and an
ideological circumstance, the role played by religion in adapting
people to exploitation. (12) The poem of 'Innocence' indicates
the conditions which make religion a consolation, a prospect of
'illusory happiness'. The poem of 'Experience' shows the part
religion plays in intervening between the sweep and his parents.
The effect of this intervention is to justify their denial and
neglect of his individual energy, to justify too their keeping
him in place as a chimney sweep.
    But the dialectic between the two poems cannot be wholly
resolved, I think, by taking the poem of 'Experience' as a truth
opposed to the illusion of the poem of 'Innocence'. There are
other implications and tones in the two poems which suggest
different orders of relation. The poem of 'Innocence' contains a
vision of the future, something that is lacking in the poem of
'Experience'; the poem of 'Experience' contains critical perception,
something that is lacking in the poem of 'Innocence'. It could be
that Blake is pointing to the difficulty of social change here.
The common condition of both poems, the relation of child labour
and institutional religion, is such as to bring about a dis-
sociation of those energies of vision and criticism which would
need to coalesce if substantial change was to be effected. (13)
Taken on its own, each poem seems to represent a complete state of
consciousness. Taken together, the poems reveal the limited and
incomplete nature of consciousness in a social world fissured by
contradiction.

Another problem posed by the two poems is how the common condition of child labour produces such different states of mind in the two children. Although their economic situation is identical, their family situation is not. The sweep of 'Experience' is not so vulnerable to the illusory comforts of religion because he has the behaviour of his parents to set against the ideals of parental love that exist in sublimated form in the 'Innocent' sweep's religious vision.

In the 'Holy Thursday' poems Blake begins from an apparently opposite starting point to the 'Chimney Sweeper' poems – the care that a society takes of its children through its charitable institutions. The poem of 'Innocence' celebrates the spectacle of charity children going to church to praise their benefactors ('Holy Thursday', 1-4). The poem of 'Experience' works as a virtual negation of the poem of 'Innocence'. Where 'Innocence' hears the children's songs 'like a mighty wind', 'like harmonious thundering', 'Experience' hears 'a trembling cry'; where 'Innocence' sees 'aged men wise guardians of the poor' and 'innocent faces clean', 'Experience' sees 'Babes reduced to misery,/Fed with cold and usurous hand'.

As with the 'Chimney Sweeper' poems, the 'Holy Thursday' poems raise the question of who sees truly and again the answer heavily favours the poem of 'Experience'. What is called into question by the poem of 'Experience' is accepted as a given by the poem of 'Innocence'. What the poem of 'Experience' reveals is the social condition which the spectacle of charity conceals, that without poverty there could be no charity and no pity either. (14)

In line with the structural principle of the 'Songs', the two 'Holy Thursday' poems give contrary perceptions of the same event. If the reader resolves the contradiction in favour of the validity of 'Experience', then the poem of 'Innocence' necessarily becomes a satire on the kind of person who could see the operations of charity in such terms. That 'kind of person', of course, could always turn out to be the reader. In the 'Songs', Blake evolved a mode which reveals the possibility that one kind of sentimental, aesthetic pleasure, whether derived from scenes of sweeps in heaven or charity children in church, necessarily has its basis in illusions about the social relations which produce charity children or child labour. The reader who takes pleasure in 'Holy Thursday' or 'The Chimney Sweeper' in the 'Songs of Innocence' is confronted in the equivalent poems of 'Experience' by the possibility that his pleasure would not have been possible without a deluded acquiescence in the exploitation and abuse without which the poems could not have been written.

Reading the 'Holy Thursday' poems in relation to the 'Chimney Sweeper' poems, we can begin to see something of the complexity and fullness of Blake's representation of childhood. From the perspective of experience, what seem to be antithetical episodes in a society's relation to its children turn out to be identical: charity and child labour are revealed as aspects of a common exploitation or neglect of children. In this sense, the poems work to reveal identities which the power of social appearances disguise. What is complex in the poems is Blake's understanding of social appearances as the interplay between a particular spectacle, whether it appears as actual event ('Holy Thursday') or as a dream ('Chimney Sweeper'), and the state of mind which at once sustains and feeds off that spectacle. This suggests that ideology operates not only at the public level of a ritual event, but even in the workings of the intensely subjective state of dreaming. The poems of 'Experience' penetrate through these ideological appearances to the social abuses which underlie them. In doing this, they seek to dissolve the pleasurable illusions by which the innocent mind perceives charity or child labour, and, if this is true, then what the world of 'Experience' gains in truth it loses in pleasure.

The issue raised by my reading of the 'Holy Thursday' and 'Chimney Sweeper' poems can be readily extended to other poems about childhood in the 'Songs'. The figure of the child as social critic, the form of childhood in the 'Chimney Sweeper' poem of 'Experience', recurs in 'The Little Vagabond', 'The School Boy' and 'A Little Boy Lost'. The critical force of the first two poems comes from stating the obvious, but suppressed truth ('The Little Vagabond', 1-4, 'The School Boy', 6-10). 'A Little Boy Lost' proceeds by a different method. The child states what he takes to be an uncontroversial truth about the centrality of self-love only to discover that this contravenes the order of a church which requires a masochistic submission of self to the worship of abstractions ('A Little Boy Lost', 9-16). The third and fourth stanzas of the poem capture the correspondence between sadistic impulses and the imposition of religion's institutional order. Within this kind of order, the exercise of authority is admired for its own sake - 'And all admir'd his Priestly care' - without consideration of its consequences.

The 'Nurses' Songs', like the 'Holy Thursday' poems are concerned with the care of children, but the focus here is not so much on the meaning of charity as on the mutually conditioning moods of nurse and children. The nurse of 'Experience' views her children in terms of envy and repression; she sees the children as enjoying what she can no longer have ('Nurse's Song', 1-4). They seem to be in a conspiratorial relation to her, 'whisprings are in the dale', hiding their pleasure from her. In this context 'care' is shown to be a form of possession. The nurse wants the children home so she can make sure they don't have anything she doesn't have and because she can then shape them in terms of her own repressed self-hood.

The 'Nurse's Song' of 'Experience' repeats lines from its equivalent poem in 'Innocence', but in contexts which give the lines contrasting implications. For the nurse in 'Innocence', the voices of children are linked to 'laughing', not whisperings, and the sound induces calm not resentment. The presence of a dialogue between nurse and children in the poem of 'Innocence' emphasizes its absence in the poem of 'Experience'. The interplay of voices suggests that the figures in the poem inhabit the same mental world and are conscious of doing so. Rhythmic echoes help establish this mental community: the children's request, 'No no let us play, for it is yet day', parallels the nurse's answer, 'Well, well go & play Till the light fades away ...'. One consequence of this underlying community is that the difference in the activities of nurse and children is not felt as threatening. (15)

The dialectical relation between 'Innocence' and 'Experience' is further reformulated through the 'Nurses' Songs'. I do not think it can be said that the nurse of 'Experience' sees more truly than the nurse of 'Innocence', any more than the poem of 'Experience' can be said to give a more truthful account of the relations between adults and children. Rather, the key term in the dialectic of the 'Nurses' Songs' is repression. The poem of 'Innocence' represents a vision of free relations in which the forces of desire and necessity and the natural and social worlds are harmonized. The poem images what it would feel like to be in such a harmonious world: each individual's contentment is implicated in the happiness of others; utterance is uninhibited; the passage of time is not punctuated by division and separation. The poem of 'Experience' provides an antithetical vision of repressed and concealed relations, characterized by a self-hood conditioned by envy, possessiveness, and an anxious relation to time. The poem of 'Innocence' is not true because it presents a vision of human relations which can, as yet, be realized only in an imaginary world. The poem of 'Experience' is not true in the sense that it is about a set of relations based on deception and concealment. Taken together, the two poems are like the terms of an equation as yet unsolved. (16)

Blake's concern with repression is central to another aspect of the representation of childhood in the 'Songs'. In a group of poems, principally 'The Little Girl Lost & Found' and 'A Little Girl Lost', Blake writes about the awakening of sexual desire and its consequences for identity. The subject is quite explicit in 'A Little Girl Lost', but I want to start with 'The Little Girl Lost' and 'The Little Girl Found', two poems which present an enigmatic and, I think, far-reaching account of the awakening of sexual desire.

'The Little Girl Lost' begins with an explicit statement of the poem's prophetic stance, in opening lines whose language recalls the first two poems in the 'Songs of Experience', the 'Introduction' and 'Earth's Answer', where the denial of sexual energies by 'Cruel jealous selfish Fear' is seen as the cause of earth's sleep. In its vision of earth's awakening 'The Little Girl Lost', then, is a poem about the surpassing of such inhibiting fears. Blake gives concrete form to his prophetic vision through the narrative of the young girl, Lyca, and her parents. The mode of the narrative is both distinctive and puzzling. Blake draws upon well-known sources in its construction: what Harold Bloom has referred to as 'the romance convention of the lost child cared for by beasts of prey' combines with the familiar Christian motif of salvation, a motif implicit in the poem's title. (17) But 'The Little Girl Lost' transforms its sources and produces meanings which, I think, challenge deeply rooted assumptions about the nature of sexuality.

As in many of the other songs, 'The Little Girl Lost' and 'The Little Girl Found' evolve out of radically opposed perceptions of a common situation. Lyca anticipates her imminent transformation, figured in the poem as a transition from waking to sleep, without anxiety:

Sweet sleep come to me
Underneath this tree

but is held back from sleep by an inhibition whose source is in her
parents' fears about her separation from them:

> Do father, mother weep
> 'Where can Lyca sleep'
>
> Lost in desert wild
> Is your little child
> How can Lyca sleep
> If her mother weep.
>   ('The Little Girl Lost', 17-24)

The child feels herself to be in harmony with those forces in
nature which her parents find threatening. What is meant by harmony
here is that instead of frightening Lyca, the natural world realizes
her conscious and unconscious wishes. Thus in the eighth stanza of
the poem Lyca calls upon the natural world to take on a less
threatening appearance; 'Frowning, frowning night' is to be soothed
by the light of the moon, presumably to alleviate her parents'
anxieties about nature's wildness, but also as the symbolic
expression of a wish that her parents should be less anxious: Blake
personifies the night as 'frowning' like a threatened or anxious
father whose darkness the moon will make light. Given that Lyca
can express her wishes to and through the natural world, she can
rid her mind of the image of her anxious parents, and attain the
'sweet sleep' she desires.

What follows is like a dream play, the enactment of Lyca's
unconscious wish to take on sexual being. She becomes the subject
of an erotic ritual superintended by 'beasts of prey/Come from
caverns deep'. Again Blake draws upon the resources of wild nature
to provide images for another wish fulfilment. The lion and
lioness become substitutes for Lyca's absent parents. They
initiate her into the world of physical desire instead of holding
her back from it ('The Little Girl Lost', 43-52). The poem's
language defines an unthreatening eroticism in relation to Lyca's
body. It seems merely prim to read this, as Keynes does in his
commentary, as an allegory of the soul's release from the body
after death. (18) The poem may subsume elements of Christian myth
but it does so in order to shift a Christian emphasis on the spirit
to a Blakean emphasis on the body, to make the salvation of the
soul a metaphor for the resurrection of the body, rather than vice
versa.

'The Little Girl Lost' is a poem which presents two interconnected processes with great subtlety. Lyca's sexuality depends
on her conception of her parents. The inhibition caused by the
image of her parents' anxiety is surpassed by the child imagining
them anew in a way that brings them into a less fearful relation
with the forces of desire. Lyca's parents are transformed in the
poem from 'Do father, mother weep' into lion and lioness by way
of the verse beginning 'Frowning, frowning night'. Only by
transforming her parents into creatures of desire can the child
achieve her own fulfilment, and to do that the human form of her
parents has to be displaced into the form of the lion and lioness.
One of the implications of Lyca's sleep is that this transformation

has to be effected at an unconscious level. Only by ceasing to be a
conscious object in the poem can Lyca preserve her relation to her
parents and attain sexual being.

   Events which have occurred in a symbolic form in 'The Little Girl
Lost' are re-narrated in a more literal form in 'The Little Girl
Found'. The second poem underlines what the reader already knows
from the first, that the parents' anxieties are premised upon an
illusion. They journey in darkness, 'Among shadows deep', following
'The fancied image' of their daughter who they imagine threatened
by the forces which have brought about her growth. In the poem the
wild nature that they fear becomes the instrument of their
education. 'A couching lion' by its gentleness removes the parents'
fears and so allows them to see a figure of desire not as
threatening but as noble ('The Little Girl Found', 33-40).

   As in the first poem, wild nature supplies the needs of the human
characters. In 'The Little Girl Lost' the lion and lioness become
the mother and father who could assist Lyca into the realm of
desire. In 'The Little Girl Found' the 'couching lion' becomes an
erotic partner for Lyca that does not fill the parents with
terror. The wild animals in the two poems are, of course, imaginary
figures. Their meaning inheres not in their realism but in the
crucial transitions they permit in the narrative. They overcome
what would otherwise be disabling contradictions between parental
love and the acknowledgment rather than the denial of sexuality.
(19) In this sense the two poems, although ultimately placed by
Blake in the 'Songs of Experience', by-pass a characteristic
formulation of 'Experience' which represents the terminus of desire
in repression and denial. 'The Little Girl Lost' and 'The Little
Girl Found' boldly imagine not the opposition between childhood
innocence and sexuality, but their compatibility.

   It is this attempt to create an imaginative order which
challenges deeply rooted assumptions about desire and innocence,
sexuality and familial relations that can make the two poems seem
difficult. The problems of writing against centuries of orthodox
morality make themselves felt in the overall structure of 'The
Little Girl Lost' and 'The Little Girl Found'. In order to
maintain Lyca as both an innocent and an erotic subject Blake has,
in effect, to remove her consciousness from the narrative. She
does not consciously perceive the new order of relations that
surround her. At the end of 'The Little Girl Found' she remains
what she was at the end of 'The Little Girl Lost', a 'sleeping
child/Among tygers wild', oblivious at a conscious level to both
her own change and the change in her parents. Blake's representation of Lyca in the closing verses of 'The Little Girl Found' is
one indication of an incongruity between the prophetic beginning
of 'The Little Girl Lost' and the unemphatic ending of 'The Little
Girl Found':

   To this day they dwell
   In a lonely dell
   Nor fear the wolvish howl
   Nor the lion's growl.

This seems a tentative conclusion to a sequence of poems which had

begun with a prophecy of the earth's awakening. Lyca's parents are
shown to accept their daughter's changed condition, but there is
little indication of the general renewal of relationship and the
liberation of sexual energies adumbrated by the beginning of 'The
Little Girl Lost'. The narrative of the two poems seems to end at
a stage prior to the fulfilment of Blake's prophecy and, indeed,
this might be an indication of the difficult task that Blake has
set himself: to invent a narrative mode which would take the reader
through to the fulfilment of the poet's prophecy and, by that token,
well beyond the historical experience of either poet or reader.

Like Blake, Wordworth found in childhood a medium for registering
and valuing social change, and, at an abstract level, the figure of
the child indicates parallel concerns in both writers. In Book
VIII of 'The Excursion' Wordsworth's criticism of the factory
system, and the economic theory which justifies it, builds up to a
description of the child produced by the cotton mill:

> He is a slave to whom release comes not,
> And cannot come. The boy, where'er he turns
> Is still a prisoner; when the wind is up
> Among the clouds, and roars through the ancient woods;
> Or when the sun is shining in the east
> Quiet and calm. Behold him - in the school
> Of his attainments? no; but with the air
> Fanning his temples under heaven's blue arch
> His raiment, whitened o'er with cotton flakes
> Or locks of wool, announces when he comes.
> Creeping his gait and cowering, his lip pale,
> His respiration quick and audible;
> And scarcely could you fancy that a gleam
> Could break from out these languid eyes, or a blush
> Mantle upon his cheek ...
>
>   ('Excursion', VIII.301-15)

This passage repeats a familiar Wordsworthian proposition about the
physical and mental damage that follows from depriving a child of
its right to experience of the natural world. But to understand
the critical force of this proposition we need to analyse the
structure of the eighth book of 'The Excursion', to analyse the
context in which Wordsworth's factory child appears and disappears.
(20)
  An elevated, and highly improbable conversation between three
figures, the Wanderer, the Solitary and the Pastor, gives shape to
'Excursion', Book VIII. The setting of this conversation is
pastoral: ideological, social and economic changes are surveyed
from a position of rural calm and this has a number of effects upon
the kind of social criticism advanced in the poem. The antithesis
between rural and industrial worlds underwrites the difference in
material condition and consciousness between the critic and what
is being criticized. Historical change is viewed from a position
outside history and this externality of view is reflected in the
description of the factory child whose mental state can be so
confidently inferred from a set of physical mannerisms. We can

note the contrast between this mode and the startling contradictions
between physical condition and consciousness represented in Blake's
'Chimney Sweeper' poem from 'Experience', and note, too, how
Wordsworth's writing creates the factory child as the victim of
his circumstances, an object of compassion, certainly, but
emphatically not the child as the critical and articulate subject
composed by Blake's writing in the 'Songs of Innocence and
Experience'.

The critical potential of the factory child is dissipated in
other ways by Wordsworth's writing in the eighth book of 'The
Excursion'. The Solitary takes up the Wanderer's account of the
effects of industrialization, but in a manner which oddly disperses
the subject:

> Yet be it asked, in justice to our age
> If there were not, before these arts appeared
> These structures rose, commingling old and young
> And unripe sex with sex, for mutual taint;
> If there were not, *then*, in our far-formed Isle,
> Multitudes who from infancy had breathed
> Air unimprisoned, and had lived at large;
> Yet walked beneath the sun, in human shape,
> As abject, as degraded?
>   ('Excursion', VIII.337-45)

The answer to this lengthy question is, predictably, yes. Rural
labour threatens 'liberty of mind' as much as factory labour; the
factory child finds his equivalent in the Solitary's description
of the plough-boy who combines physical strength with mental torpor
('Excursion', VIII.396-433). But the effect of this is not to
challenge the pastoral form of the poem by undermining the
distinction between 'healthy' rural conditions and a 'diseased'
industrial environment, because the Recluse's commentary upon the
effect of agricultural labour is subsumed in a concluding sequence
to Book VIII which reaffirms the difference between an unpressured
pastoral order and a problematic world of rural and industrial
labour in a way that comes embarrassingly close to revealing the
connections between a pastoral form and a particular class interest.
Their survey completed, the Pastor, the Wanderer and the Recluse
retire to the Pastor's mansion, a place represented by Wordsworth
as a haven of rustic order. Social criticism exhausts itself in
an act of gentlemanly withdrawal which suggests that the only
'solution' to social problems is to forget about them. As if to
secure this forgetfulness, a sequence of descriptions of childhood
which had begun with the factory child and continued with the
plough-boy, culminates in a description of the Pastor's son and
his friend, returned from a day's fishing ('Excursion', VIII.572-87).
Thus Book VIII ends with the discovery of a natural, uncorrupted
child whose absence had been felt in the earlier descriptions of
the factory child and the plough-boy. This discovery licenses a
different direction in Wordsworth's writing, one which can compare
human activity to natural processes in a poetic gesture which
seeks to release the figure it describes from the context of social
determination altogether. But, although Book VIII concludes with a

picture of childhood which attempts to erase the disquieting
implications of its earlier presentations of the children of the
labouring poor, the poem unwittingly reveals the social basis of
leisure and privilege in the Pastor's mansion, which sustains the
'naturalness' it celebrates. A contradictory social world is not
so easily to be wished away, although it is clear from the poem's
structure that it is not Wordsworth's purpose to dwell upon different
forms of childhood as the focus of contradiction. The Wanderer is
moved by the appearance of the Pastor's son not to a reflection of
what it is that makes childhood in a country house so different from
childhood in a factory. Instead, he enters into a lengthy discourse,
taking up part of the Ninth Book of 'The Excursion', whose starting
point is a celebration of that 'active Principle' which is so
visible in the Pastor's son ('Excursion', IX.1-44). The Wanderer
gives us a statement of Wordsworthian doctrine that will be familiar
to readers of 'The Prelude' (cf. 'Prelude', II.238-75). One point
to notice here is that the general statement of a principle which
is held to apply to 'every Form of being' is then validated by
examples drawn exclusively from the natural world. This seems
further evidence of a tendency, inherent in the structure of
Wordsworth's writing, to move away from any continuous imaginative
engagement with a social world which the poet, none the less, feels
obliged to notice. Thus, after some hundred lines that celebrate
the workings of the active Principle in young and old alike, the
Wanderer returns to the problems of industrialization and poverty.
Wordsworth's belief in the universal workings of the 'active
Principle' encounters embarrassing evidence to the contrary in the
lives of the poor and their children. The poem becomes somewhat
confused at this point, advancing incompatible explanations for
the conditions of the poor, but as we shall see this confusion has
a strategic purpose. The Wanderer advances something very close to
a materialist explanation of the separation of the poor from natural
being, the source of which lies in the alienating conditions of
work, and which is in line with the earlier criticism of political
economy as the legitimating ideology of a factory system ('Excursion',
IX.113-22; VIII.283-302). But this materialist 'moment' in the
poem remains an undeveloped fragment within the Wanderer's discourse.

He recalls the descriptions in Book VIII of the factory child and
plough-boy and then moves to a series of assertions which make the
unnatural lives of the poor simply inexplicable. Nature, the
'active Principle' is now conceived as a form of revelation
available to all without the need of any intermediary ('Excursion',
IX.206-49); and the poem bends away again from an engagement with
the social origins of ignorance and suffering, shifting to a
language which construes man's relationship with nature in
religious terms. What could have developed from the brief
materialist moment of the poem is thus forestalled, but in the
process the poor become momentarily unthinkable. It is not difficult
to see why: if what is aesthetically and morally natural is so
generously revealed why do the poor remain without benefit of
revelation? To answer that question would demand a return to that
engagement with the relations between work and consciousness so
briefly entertained in the poem.   Rather than do that, the
question and the problem it poses *and* the emotion which evidences

the problem, are simply cut out. The 'sadder grief' caused by 'so
wide a difference between man and man' to the mind enraptured by the
equality of all before nature's revelation is displaced as the poem
returns, significantly, to its previous point of security - those
'blooming Boys (whom we beheld even now)/Blest in their several and
their common lot!' The hiatus in the poem's logic is glossed over
by the Wanderer's reversion to those emblems of naturalness, the
Pastor's son and his friend. The optimistic tenor of the poem,
initiated by the Wanderer's celebration of Nature's continuous
revelation, can then be sustained and this mood conditions the next
appearance of the poor in the poem when the Wanderer prophesies
the coming of universal education:

> O for the coming of that glorious time
> When, prizing knowledge as her noblest wealth
> And best protection, this imperial Realm,
> While she exacts allegiance shall admit
> An obligation, on her part, to *teach*
> Them who are born to serve her and obey;
> Binding herself by statute to secure
> For all the children whom her soil maintains
> The rudiments of letters and inform
> The mind with moral and religious truth ...
> ('Excursion', IX.293-302)

The state, personified as a powerful but benign matriarch,
guarantees its stability by increasing educational provision. It
is important to note how knowledge is defined in this passage - at
least, that knowledge which is deemed appropriate to the poor:
'the rudiments of letters' but not full literacy; the inculcation
of 'moral and religious truth' as a means of innoculating the poor
against the kind of subversion that is referred to later on in the
same passage in the figure of the rude boy who 'lifts his wilful
hand on mischief bent/Or turns the Godlike faculty of speech to
impious use'. The purposes of education are, then, to keep the
poor in their place and naturalize hierarchical relations. (21)
   This reading of Books VIII and IX of 'The Excursion' reaffirms
what has been written elsewhere in this and other books; that the
social character of Wordsworth's poetry is overwhelmingly
conservative. It also shows how that conservative character is
inscribed in the text of Wordsworth's poetry. The sequence of
poetic utterances which make up Books VIII and IX are so ordered
as to secure the massive complacency of the poem even when this
seems most threatened by the difficulty which Wordsworth has in
reconciling his own abstract doctrine of the 'active Principle',
informing all things, with his own perception of the contemporary
state of the labouring poor. As we have seen, an attempt to
reconcile the two creates a logical incoherence in the poem which
is then overridden by shifting its subject in such a way as to
secure an appearance of unity. Childhood is central in effecting
this shift, just as it is central in approaching the historical
conditions of poverty and alienated labour which haunt the poem.
But if childhood is a means of approaching this historical condition
it is also the means of escaping it. Childhood allows the poet to

imagine the impossibility which is at the heart of the poem's
ideological effect: namely to recognize the conditions of poverty
and alienated labour as historical and, therefore, alterable, to
advocate their alteration, and, within the same discourse, to affirm
that this alteration can be effected without in the least threatening
the prevailing social formation.   Childhood marks the moment when a
historical perception of labour and poverty intensifies in the poem;
equally childhood marks the moment when the same historical perception
is expelled for the sake of an ahistorical doctrine, Wordsworth's
religion of nature.   In this sense we might say that childhood is
crucial to the grammar of Wordsworth's conservatism, as it is
realized in Books VIII and IX of 'The Excursion'.

It could be argued against this analysis that it is based on
poetry written in the period of Wordsworth's poetic decline and is,
therefore, untypical of his representation of childhood.   Evidence
drawn from the earlier poetry suggests that this is not so.   In
'Alice Fell', a poem written in 1802, childhood becomes a means of
mediating poverty so that it becomes the occasion of tender
sentiment rather than indignation.   The poem begins by creating an
expectation of the supernatural: the gentleman poet, being driven
in his chaise on a stormy night, is troubled by a strange sound:

> As if the wind blew many ways
> I heard the sound - and more and more
> It seemed to follow with the chaise
> And still I heard it as before.
> ('Alice Fell', 5-8)

But this haunting turns out to have a natural source in the
weeping of an orphaned girl, 'sitting behind the chaise alone'.
The child's emotional state, her misery at the destruction of her
cloak, becomes a mystery quite as compelling to the narrator as any
supernatural event.   What the narrator's questions reveal is that
Alice Fell's distress over her cloak seems more powerful than other
more explicable sources of misery:

> My child, in Durham do you dwell?
> She checked herself in her distress
> And said, 'My name is Alice Fell;
> I'm fatherless and motherless
>
> And I to Durham, Sir, belong'.
> Again, as if the thought would choke
> Her very heart, her grief grew strong;
> And all was for her tattered cloak.
> ('Alice Fell', 41-8)

In common with a number of Wordsworth's other poems about
childhood, 'Alice Fell' shows a child teaching the poet about the
mysteries of the 'human heart'; in this case the lesson concerns
the capacity of strong emotion to attach itself to apparently
trivial objects.   As if in gratitude for his teaching the gentleman
poet gives a charitable gift to the child:

Up to the tavern door we post;
Of Alice and her grief I told
And I gave money to the host
To buy a new cloak for the old

And let it be of duffil grey
As warm a cloak as man can sell!
Proud creature was she the next day
The little orphan Alice Fell.
                    ('Alice Fell', 53-60)

'Pity would be no more,/If we did not make somebody poor', wrote
Blake. Yet the closing verses of 'Alice Fell' suggest that pity
and the charitable act it promotes are constitutive of our humanity.
The poem affirms charity as the right relation between rich and
poor and can thereby resolve the misery of the poor child in the
reassurance of the last two lines: the grief-stricken Alice Fell
becomes a 'Proud creature' as a result of the charitable act.
Moreover, the poem defines what is moving about poverty and it is
not that it exists at all, but that, in what I take to be an
unintended paradox, the material poverty of the child does not
inhibit the emotionally abundant occasion which her meeting with
the socially privileged narrator affords. The poem's ideological
effect is both powerful and insidious because it rests upon the
unstated assumption that the social division between rich and poor
is itself the condition of the emotionally elevating experience
that the poem records.
     The brevity of 'Alice Fell' may make it a more readable poem
than the ponderous philosophizing of 'The Excursion', but this
analysis suggests that the two poems are part of some conservative
constellation of attitude and belief. The contrast with Blake is
particularly instructive: Wordsworth's poetry does not work by
those sudden dislocations of perspective which are one important
effect of the structure of Blake's 'Songs'. The concluding lines
of 'Alice Fell' invite the reader to complacent reflections on the
emotionally educative experience it describes: a warm cloak in
exchange for emotional uplift and all's well with the world. There
is no room here for the sharp, antagonistic voice that informs the
'Holy Thursday' poem of 'Experience'. Unlike Blake, Wordsworth is
not concerned with the creation of a poetic form which can
imaginatively convey the reader into the reality of contradictory
perceptions of the social world.
     There is one further aspect of Wordsworth's writing about the
child that I want to discuss, and it has to do with the part played
by childhood in the poet's account of the formation of the self.
Two poems in particular, 'The Prelude' and 'Ode: Intimations of
Immortality', constitute Wordsworth's major statement on the
relation between childhood and maturity and both poems provide
further evidence of the centrality of childhood in the construction
of Wordsworth's conservatism.
     In Book I of 'The Prelude', the subject of the poet's own
childhood is approached through a series of interconnected with-
drawals. The opening lines of the poem record the poet's escape,
'... coming from a house/Of bondage, from yon City's walls set

free', and this withdrawal from the city into the country is the
condition of an unpressured attempt by Wordsworth to discover a new
self-definition ('Prelude', I.10-19). As we soon discover, the
direction taken by Wordsworth's free self is backwards. His
wanderings take him back to his place of origin both geographically
and temporally. As if led by a force beyond his own will, the poet
returns to the Lake District ('Prelude', I.81-4), and then, later
on in Book I, he recollects his childhood self as the poem commences
its principal subject, the 'Growth of a Poet's Mind'.

But the subject of childhood is not in an unproblematic sense
the free choice of the poet's imagination. If 'Prelude', Book I
records a twofold withdrawal, from the city into the country and
from the present into the past, this is connected to an important
theme in Book I, Wordsworth's failure as a poet. Imaginative
stirrings fail to find their issue in poetry ('Prelude', I.101-9,
134-56, 238-76) and, as a corollary of this, Wordsworth enters into
a lengthy discussion of his difficulty in finding the subject
appropriate to the epic poem which he feels it is his vocation to
write ('Prelude', I.177-238). Wordsworth's discovery of his own
childhood and subsequent development as the subject of his poem
occurs as if by accident, in a moment of reproach for his failure
to produce poetry ('Prelude', I.272 ff). The poet's recollection
of childhood brings with it a landscape imbued with pleasure. The
guilt or self-doubt which shadow Wordsworth's positive construction
of his withdrawal as the realization of 'liberty' and vocation, can
be momentarily forgotten, even resolved, in the poet's immersion
in his past.

It is difficult to know what the exact sources of Wordsworth's
guilt are; whatever else it may contain, 'The Prelude' does not
give us any clear sense of its genesis. His self-confessed failure
as a poet may provide part of the answer, but what then are the
sources of that failure, particularly in the context of a poem which
begins with an affirmation of the poet's own capacity for joy and
with promises of renewed poetic activity? We may surmise that
Wordsworth's relation to France is one source of his guilt. Book I
of 'The Prelude' was composed during a period when Wordsworth was
in the process of abandoning both Annette Vallon, the mother of his
first child, and his support for the French Revolution. But what
is important for the purpose of this essay is that childhood is
approached in 'The Prelude' in a context haunted by guilt and self-
doubt. Wordsworth recalls his childhood in order to postpone an
encounter with the problems of vocation and purpose which divide
him as an adult.

Given the determining pressure of this context, it is not
surprising then that one important aspect of Wordsworth's
reconstruction of childhood is a celebration of the idyllic unity
that obtains between the child and the natural world:

> Oh, many a time have I, a five years child
> A naked Boy, in one delightful Rill,
> A little Mill-race sever'd from his stream,
> Made one long bathing of a summer's day,
>   ('Prelude', I.291-4)

These lines present an unproblematic selfhood, whose reality is simply confirmed in a pleasurable, sensuous contact with nature. But they indicate something else central to Wordsworth's account of his childhood and that is the overwhelming importance of natural, rather than social, determinations in the creation of the poet's self. Whatever else may be true of the much-discussed 'spots of time' in 'The Prelude', they are composed out of the encounter between the solitary poet, whether as child or young man, and the natural world and a necessary condition of these moments, so crucial to the 'growth of a poet's mind', is the displacement of the social world. This displacement can be encoded in very obvious ways as in, for instance, the passage from Book I which builds from the recollection of the young Wordsworth's delight in skating ('Prelude', I.452-89). (22)

For Wordsworth, the essentially asocial character of formative movements of experience is established in childhood. The repetition of such moments into adult life and their retrieval in poetry is the guarantee both of continuity and growth in the poet's mind. It is worth stressing how deeply this tendency goes in Wordsworth's writing. In a celebrated passage from Book II of 'The Prelude' Wordsworth describes the earliest experiences of the child with its mother:

                              ... Bless'd the infant Babe,
(For with my best conjectures I would trace
The progress of our being) blest the Babe,
Nurs'd in his Mother's arms, the Babe who sleeps
Upon his Mother's breast, who, when his soul
Claims manifest kindred with an earthly soul,
Doth gather passion from his Mother's eye!
...

In one beloved presence, nay and more,
In that most apprehensive habitude
And those sensations which have been deriv'd
From this beloved Presence, there exists
A virtue which irradiates and exalts
All objects through all intercourse of sense.
                    ('Prelude', II.238-43, 255-60)

Here we find a characteristic mode of writing which effectively makes the mother indistinguishable from an array of natural presences which have a similarly formative effect upon the child - the river Derwent, for example, which 'compos'd my Thought/To more than infant softness'. One consequence of this kind of writing is that it cannot focus upon the family as the arena in which identities are both formed and repressed. It cannot do, that is, what Blake does in poems like 'The Little Girl Lost' or 'The Little Girl Found', or 'Infant Joy' and 'Infant Sorrow'. Wordsworth's refusal or inability to write about the family as a specific determinant of identity can be understood as one more aspect of that general exclusion of the social world which, as we have seen, is a central device in formulating the version of the self propounded by 'The Prelude'. (23)

One consequence of this version of the self in 'The Prelude' is
that when society intervenes it does so as a secondary process working
upon the subject already constituted by nature, and its effect is
inevitably to confuse or dissipate the natural self. An extreme
account of this process is found in 'Ode: Intimations of Immortality'
where, it seems, any human contact has a corrupting effect upon the
self disclosed in childhood ('Intimations Ode', 86-99). Wordsworth
describes the child as indifferent to its parents' attentions. The
mother's affection is little more than an unwanted distraction:
'Fretted by sallies of his mother's kisses'. The parents initiate
a process which brings the child to abandon its own identity in
favour of socially prescribed roles:

> The little Actor cons another part;
> Filling from time to time his 'humorous stage'
> With all the Persons, down to palsied Age,
> That Life brings with her in her equipage;
> As if his whole vocation
> Were endless imitation.
>   ('Intimations Ode', 103-8)

These lines form part of a general movement in the poem which
stresses the transition from childhood to maturity as an experience
of declining power. This is not the only construction of this
transition that the poem offers - adulthood brings with it a
knowledge of 'man's mortality' that is unknown to the child - but
it is the one that subtends all others. Childhood is presented
in the poem as a time of uninhibited expression and activity:
'Thou Child of Joy/Shout round me' or 'And the Children are culling/
On every side/In a thousand valleys far and wide,/Fresh flowers',
or 'And the Babe leaps upon his Mother's arm'. Opposed to this,
and yet earnestly trying to reach back to it, is the adult poet,
a melancholic figure whose primary relation to the world is passive
and contemplative ('Intimations Ode', 172-9).

Throughout the poem adulthood is encoded in terms of contemplation and reflection and not in terms of action and expression.
Custom, inhibition, a knowledge of mortality weigh down upon the
adult poet. All that he can hope for by way of consolation is a
continuity in that relation with nature that was founded in his
childhood.

But this is the only source of continuity in a poem that otherwise
stresses the radical division between child and adult. The poem
works to invert common sense assumptions about the relations between
infancy and maturity: children do not grow but decline into
adulthood; children are powerful, adults are weak; children possess
autonomy, adults are dependent. Coleridge was amongst the first
to notice the perversity in the poem. (24) But the treatment of
childhood in the 'Ode' is simultaneously the point of emergence
for a distinctive persona for the adult Wordsworth, one that is
more firmly fixed than the diffuse narrative presence of the poet
in 'The Prelude'. Out of the antithesis between the exuberant
child and the elegaic consciousness of maturity, Wordsworth defines
the subjective ground which will later find its less introspective
equivalent in the Wanderer and the Solitary, those spokesmen for

the political and social conservatism of 'The Excursion'.

A number of conclusions can be drawn from this essay. One is to warn us against the notion that there is a single 'romantic' image of childhood. A subject that in Blake's writing is central to the articulation of a radical poetic form becomes for Wordsworth a crucial moment in the creation of an essentially conservative account of the relations between consciousness and society. Whereas in Blake a society fraught with division and contradiction is the medium in which consciousness takes on its shape and its limitations, in Wordsworth the same historical society is so transformed as to cease to be a significant agent in the formation of identity. This is one aspect of what the study of childhood can tell us about the work of the two poets. It is central in another and related sense too, because the different constructions of childhood in the work of Wordsworth and Blake take us close to a major difference in the argument implicit in their writings. In Wordsworth childhood is one part of a repertoire of poetic means which seek to persuade us that humanity can be preserved in the face of intensifying social contradictions; in Blake the same subject is used to an opposite effect, to persuade us that our humanity can only be realized in the surpassing of social contradiction.

Chapter 4

Wordsworth's Model of Man in 'The Prelude'

David Aers

> When we consider all that is necessary to human life,
> however, it becomes clear that man is naturally a
> social and political animal, destined more than all
> other animals to live in community ... one man alone
> would not be able to furnish himself with all that is
> necessary, for no one man's resources are adequate to
> the fullness of human life. For this reason the
> companionship of his fellows is naturally necessary
> to him.... This is further evident from the fact that
> men alone have power of speech.... The fellowship of
> society being thus natural to man, it follows with
> equal necessity that there must be some principle of
> government within the society.
>
> St Thomas Aquinas, 'De Regimine Principium',
I.1 (trans. J.G. Dawson, ed. A.P. D'Entrèves,
'Aquinas. Selected Political Writings',
(Blackwell, Oxford, 1965)

Like most of the writers now grouped as 'romantic', Wordsworth often
expressed rather exalted views about the knowledge he communicated
as a poet. 'Poetry is the most philosophic of all writing ... its
object is truth.... Poetry is the image of man and nature', indeed,
'Poetry is the first and last of all knowledge - it is as immortal
as the heart of man'. As for the poet himself, 'He is the rock of
defence of human nature; an upholder and preserver, carrying
everywhere with him relationship and love' - an attractive image,
for poets, as for those engaged in teaching, studying and enjoying
poetry. Wordsworth especially stresses the poet's grasp of 'the
mind of man' in interaction with 'the objects that surround him',
with 'nature'. He styles himself and Coleridge 'Prophets', come
to teach men about 'Nature' and 'the mind of man'. By writing
about himself, a poet, his theme, he assures us in 'The Prelude',
is 'Genius, Power, Creation and Divinity itself'. (1)

    The dominant stream of commentary on Wordsworth's work seems to
have been much impressed by many of the poet's views, especially,
in recent years, those embodied in 'The Prelude'. Probably the
most studied and celebrated achievements have been those concerning
the artistic exploration and re-creation of the active interchange
between 'the Mind of Man' and the 'external world', between what
he calls in 'Tintern Abbey' 'my purest thoughts', 'my moral being'
and his 'anchor' in 'nature and the language of the sense'. A
host of essays, and even books, have traced the details of the
'rhetoric of interaction' between 'mind' and 'external world',
while at the same time honouring the poet's grasp of the
development of individual consciousness. Perhaps more surprisingly,
many critics seem to have been impressed by Wordsworth's claims
about the poet 'carrying every where with him relationship and
love', treating the man's own work as an example of this, and
largely ignoring David Ferry's arguments that Wordsworth's poetry
manifests 'contempt and fear of the society of mankind' preferring
'abstractions' to 'men'. (2)

In this chapter I shall take Wordsworth's writing as seriously
as he himself, his admirers and his classic status as a major author
in the official study of English literature all demand. My focus
will be the 1805 text of 'The Prelude' and my aim is to analyse the
model of man informing this central work. In examining this we may
gain not only insight into a major poet in the established canon but
also learn something about the canon itself.

Man, as St Thomas Aquinas wrote in the passage quoted as epigraph to
this chapter, is necessarily a social and political animal, destined
to live in community, depending on interaction with other people
for his language, his sense of his needs, his human identity. 'He
that is incapable of society, or so complete in himself as not to
want it,' Aristotle comments, is 'a beast or a god.' (3) It may
be necessary today to remind ourselves of such truisms and to
consider their implications, for a version of human personality has
emerged in our culture over three to four hundred years for which
the myth of Robinson Crusoe provides the appropriate archetype.
In this the individual ego is presented as a supra-social entity,
freely electing whether to contract into or out of society, an
autonomous and free agent whose standpoint is independent of any
particular social order. Such a picture is not only inadequate for
the basic reason St Thomas offers; it entails an unexamined
attribution of particular cultural attitudes, language, assumptions
and desires to the figure said to be 'man' or 'natural man'. What
is allegedly extra-social or pre-social, as Alasdair MacIntyre
observes, 'turns out to presuppose the existence of some social
order'. (4) Even if the necessary social nature of man is
acknowledged the tendency in this tradition is to abstract the
consideration of 'Man', 'Nature', 'Human Life' and 'moral judgments',
Wordsworth's avowed subject, from virtually all connection with the
determinate productive activity through which people create the
possibilities of continued human existence. Man does not live by
bread alone, but he does not live at all without it, and the ways
in which it is produced and exchanged, the overall relations of
domination, conflict and collaboration will contribute decisively
to the forms of life available to human beings. Here one could
refer to pertinent and well-known texts of Marx, from the 1844
manuscripts and the 'German Ideology', but for the moment I would
rather recall the medieval poet who wrote 'Piers Plowman'. While
no one could suggest he undervalued the 'spiritual' and 'moral'
dimensions of human life, his poem constantly and painfully
acknowledges and explores the problems of production, commercial
exchange and earthly institutions in his own quest for a salvation
that was plainly Christian. I have written about this elsewhere,
and the point of mentioning Langland's work here is to recall how,
when a pre-romantic poet took the general notion of the incarnate
nature of man seriously, he was constantly obliged to return to
the social and collaborative existence without which there simply
would be no human spirituality. (5) Now Wordsworth himself
certainly believed that he did take the incarnate nature of 'the
Mind of Man' seriously and had transcended the 'Abstraction'
substituted for 'Man,/The common Creature' in later seventeenth-
century and Enlightenment moral philosophy (and in eighteenth-

century verse): his poetry dealt with 'solid life', and presented:

> A more judicious knowledge of what makes
> The dignity of individual Man,
> Of Man, no composition of the thought,
> Abstraction, shadow, image, but the Man
>   ... whom we behold
> With our own eyes;
>   ('Prelude', XIII.82-7)

Yet if we attend to his treatment of 'the Mind of Man,/my haunt,
and the main region of my Song', in its relations to the 'external
world' (Prospectus to 'The Recluse'), I think we will find a model
of man which has marked continuities with the Crusoesque
'abstraction' he claims to have transcended.

One relevant contrast with both Langland's and, more especially,
Blake's writing is that while Wordsworth has much to say about
'creative agency' (II.401) he virtually ignored the role of work
in shaping people's attitudes and lives. Even when he did
acknowledge the effects of labour on human personality it is in
passing and reveals an inability to attend to the issue:

> True it is, where oppression worse than death
> Salutes the Being at his birth, where grace
> Of culture hath been utterly unknown,
> And labour in excess and poverty
> From day to day pre-occupy the ground
> Of the affections, and to Nature's self
> Oppose a deeper nature, there indeed,
> Love cannot be; nor does it easily thrive
> In cities, where the human heart is sick,
> And the eye feeds it not, and cannot feed:
>   ('Prelude', XII.194-203)

The passage is offered as a concession to his basic belief that
virtually all differences in forms and conditions of work and in
social circumstances are merely 'outside marks' (XII.217):
Wordsworth invites his readers to believe that only in the most
exceptional cases will one have to pay attention to such factors
when exploring 'human life'. Furthermore, he presents these
avowedly extreme and exceptional circumstances in such an excessively
vague manner that his readers are quite unable to say exactly what,
if anything, he had in mind. After all, the most right-wing
employers and politicians of Wordsworth's world and our own could
assent to the tautology that 'oppression worse than death' and
'labour in excess' could have destructive effects on human beings.
Since Wordsworth's imagination is not engaged enough with the subject
to display what he might mean in concrete terms, it is not surprising
that, here again unlike Blake, he does not explore the complex
connections between 'labour', 'culture', 'nature' and 'love', key
terms in the passage. Instead, he moves easily to generalized
assertions that 'love' does not 'easily thrive/In cities, where
the human heart is sick,/And the eye feeds it not, and cannot
feed'. Again the world of work is conveniently brushed aside, the

all-important differentiations between various kinds of work in
cities, between various kinds of collaboration, domination and forms
of life collapsed into a 'sick' corporate urban 'heart' deprived of
'food' from the 'eye'. We come across this passage having read
Book VII, devoted to London, so we will have already met this process
enacted at some length, seen Wordsworth's 'moral judgments' on an
undifferentiated 'rabblement', 'many-headed mass', anti-creators of
'hell' and 'slaves of low pursuits' (see VII.295, 466-7, 648-704).

His ideal may sound charming enough as it is briefly mentioned
in Book VIII: 'Man free, man working for himself, with choice/Of
time, and place, and object' (152-3). In so far as one can make out
the assumptions here, this seems to be a world of nothing but
totally self-subsistent agrarian owner-occupiers, a world which
never had existed and if it did would certainly exclude poets of
leisure, like Wordsworth and Coleridge, living off the surplus
extracted from other men's labour-power. But the force of such
myths was bound up with their convenience in diverting attention
from the forms of life presently available in rural England where
bigger landowners, developments of markets and agrarian capitalism
had long since destroyed even the remotest possibility of such a
life for most people five hundred years before Wordsworth set pen
to paper. (6) They allowed a gesture towards the fundamental area
of social subsistence while avoiding imaginative and intellectual
engagement with man in the present world.

But here a reader might suggest that we briefly turn away from
'The Prelude' and look at the eighth book of 'The Excursion',
Wordsworth's 'account of changes in the country from the manufac-
turing spirit', and what is more, 'chiefly as it has affected the
humbler classes'. (7) One might indeed expect this to qualify the
picture of desocialized man that Wordsworth constructed in 'The
Prelude' and which I am currently following.

Wordsworth exults in 'the force of those gigantic powers' which
human technology can now control, and his 'dominion over nature
gained' ('Excursion', VIII.199-216). He does not pause to wonder
how the technological forces he admires could ever be compatible
with the mythologizing ideal we met in 'The Prelude' and discussed
earlier. Instead, he expresses his dislike for the 'outrage done
to nature' through shift work during the night, a system clearly
aimed at maximizing the exploitation of capital invested in the
machinery (VIII.151-85). Wordsworth is offended at the ending of
'pensive quiet' in rural England, that 'domain of calm simplicity'
before the Industrial Revolution, and he continues his Wanderer's
comments by expressing his own 'keen regret' at the disappearance
of 'The old domestic morals of the land ... and the stable worth/
That dignified and cheered a low estate':

Oh! where is now the character of peace,
Sobriety, and order, and chaste love,
And honest dealing ...
That made the very thought of country-life
A thought of refuge, for a mind detained
Reluctantly amid the bustling crowd?

There is more in this vein (see VIII.232-65). The first point to note
in the present context is the tell-tale disappearance of work and all
attention to the actual life-processes of those agricultural
labourers, servants, small tenants, and small-scale freeholders
towards whom Wordsworth seems to be gesturing. The poet's model of
man made this all seem mere 'outside marks', to use the terms in
'The Prelude' (XII.217). The next point is Wordsworth's disinclina-
tion to explore the abstractions that compose the statement. One can
have no idea from his poetry as to just what 'morals' and practices
he has in mind. (8) Nor can one have much sense of what he has in
mind by 'the stable worth/That dignified and cheered a low estate' -
certainly there is not much here other than a combination of stereo-
typed class mythology about English agrarian history and a total
failure to subject the imagination to the range of struggles and
aspirations of generations of men and women in rural England. The
unreflexive class-bound nature of Wordsworth's standpoint is marked.
It is overt in the untroubled assertion about the 'order' of the
past and in the view of 'country-life' as a 'refuge, for a mind
detained/Reluctantly amid the bustling crowd'. Such 'a mind' was
certainly not given to meditating on the plainly conflicting versions
of 'order' in agrarian England from the thirteenth century to
Wordsworth's own day, and as plainly it belonged to someone whose
social and economic assumptions and experiences had little in common
with those in genuinely 'low estate' to whom he refers so knowingly.
 The Wanderer does go on after this to attack the use of child
labour in industrial production and the destruction of children's
health in contemporary cotton mills, along with the destruction of
their 'liberty of mind' (VIII.262-334). Wordsworth then allows the
atheistic Solitary to remind the poet and Wanderer of the kinds of
mental 'torpor' he had found in rural life and ask 'what liberty of
mind' there was in the uneducated rural idiocy he depicts (VIII.391-
433). Yet in all this Wordsworth does not give any poetic attention
to disclosing what he might mean by 'liberty of mind', let alone
what this might entail in social and political practice. With this
blankness comes a feature we have already mentioned in connection
with the treatment of city and country, and which seems fairly
typical of his work and outlook. Namely, the processes of domination
in contemporary work (whether industrial or agricultural), and the
overwhelming apparatus of judicial, political and military support
for employers, are dissolved into thin air. Throughout his account
Wordsworth obscures the human agents and groups who direct and most
benefit from the processes to which he is looking. The approach is
very much in keeping with the model of man developed in 'The Prelude'
and the perspectives it suggests to the poet. The following passage
near the opening of the eighth book of 'The Excursion' shows some of
the linguistic marks of the approach:

> I have lived to mark
> A new and unforeseen creation rise
> From out the labours of a peaceful Land
> Wielding her potent enginery to frame
> And to produce, with appetite as keen
> As that of war, which rests not night or day,
> Industrious to destroy!
>   (VIII.89-95)

By using the nominalization 'creation' (rather than the linguistic
form from which it is derived - X created Y) Wordsworth can place
an abstract noun as agent in a phrase describing physical and social
processes. (9) That is, creation rises, wields her (is there a
reason why the abstraction is made female?) potent enginery to frame,
produce and destroy. She walks about England erecting cotton mills
and organizing industrial production, while the human agents who
actually own the 'enginery' and who control, hire and fire labourers,
and who take the profits ('Gain' VIII.184), who deploy the apparatus
of state power, these agents and groups of agents are deleted.
Wordsworth continues with the systematic deletion of the dominating
agents in the following passages (e.g., VIII.117-27, 167-96), but
once the reader has noticed the characteristic and its main syntactic
forms (nominalization, abstract nouns as initiating agents, passive
voice used in ways that allow the writer to ignore agents in a
process), its recurrence should be plain enough in these passages and
later ones (as VIII.288-336). The approach makes it especially easy
to pose as defender of 'liberty of minds' without having to oppose
any of the powerful groups and individuals currently transforming
and dominating the lives and habitat of most human beings in England.
The poet's model of 'mind' is not without social, political and
ethical consequences, nor without literary consequences in the
favoured modes for writing 'On Man, on Nature and on Human Life'.
   The ideological and linguistic features I have just been
discussing are part of a sustained desocialization in the model of
man found in Wordsworth's mature work - including 'The Prelude'.
He manifests a consistent tendency to delete the social activities
and relationships which are essential to human identity, to strip
man of all specific determinants as a historical being, erecting a
cult of abstract individualism quite as thoroughgoing as any he
attacked (cf. 'Prelude', XII.69-87 and such typical claims as that
at IV.222-5). Here it is appropriate to turn to Book VIII of 'The
Prelude' headed 'Love of Nature leading to Love of Mankind', a
subject that should encourage the poet to focus on his models of
human personality, of the 'Mankind' he loves.
   The book opens rather unpromisingly, for Wordsworth tells his
readers that the preceding book on the city showed his 'love of Man,/
Triumphant over all those loathsome sights/Of wretchedness and vice',
that he has shown his 'Love human to the Creature in himself'
(VIII.64-7, 77). We discussed both the generalized contempt
informing the poet's superficial writing on the city and the one-
dimensional model of man it assumed, and the opening of Book VIII
warns us that Wordsworth still has no qualms on either issue. He
will continue to assert that *he* is the poet who engages with 'the
frame of life/Social and individual', with living 'individual Man',
the Man who is 'no composition of thought,/Abstraction, shadow,
image' (XII.39-40, 84-5), and he has found readers to believe him.
But even his explicit exemplification of his 'Love of Mankind' in
Book VIII actually reveals the basic model he assumes as one that
does not encourage serious engagement with the complex life-processes
of human beings, let alone 'Love of Mankind'. Wordsworth chooses
to represent 'Mankind', as David Ferry observed many years ago,
through a series of mountain shepherds who are themselves 'abstractions', although the poet insists that these passages demonstrate

both his 'first human love' and its development when he was 'mature/
In manhood' (VIII.178, 324-5), denying any debts to literary
pastoral traditions (183-91). He gives us four exempla and a fable
to illuminate his 'human love' (178) and his model of 'mankind'
(VIII.77-101, 101-19, 324-90, 390-428; and the story is recounted
in 222-311). Even if there were space here to discuss all the
exempla, which there is not, it would be rather unnecessary since
the mode and implications of the exempla are fairly uniform. The
final one is representative, very impressive and often-quoted:

> ... Mine eyes have glanced upon him [the Shepherd],
>   a few steps off,
> In size a giant, stalking through the fog,
> His sheep like Greenland Bears; at other times
> When round some shady promontory turning,
> His Form hath flash'd upon me, glorified
> By the deep radiance of the setting sun:
> Or him have I descried in distant sky,
> A solitary object and sublime,
> Above all height! like an aerial Cross,
> As it is stationed on some spiry Rock
> Of the Chartreuse, for worship. Thus was Man
> Ennobled outwardly before mine eyes,
> And thus my heart at first was introduc'd
> To an unconscious love and reverence
> Of human Nature;
>   (VIII.400-14)

As in the first two exempla the Shepherd is seen through a mist
or transformed by the setting sun or located on distant heights as
an enskied object, and as before it is explicitly intended to
disclose the 'human Nature' he loves. Yet one of the main features
of this image is the way it effects a complete desocialization of
man. The shepherd is extracted from any contexts which would give
him his particular occupation and in which his practice has purpose
and meaning. Social, economic and cultural dimensions of existence
are dissolved. But if we ignore or destroy these dimensions of
human existence we ignore or destroy the human. And the poetry
does register this. For the desocialized shepherd is completely
dehumanized. He becomes an alien form or a fixed object in the
self-gratifying contemplation of the beholder (poet and reader).
He is seen as 'a Power/Or Genius' ruling the region (VIII.393-5),
a 'giant' in the fog, a glorified 'Form', and in the culminating
lines as a sublime 'object' likened to 'an aerial Cross ... stationed
on some spiry Rock ... for worship'. Aristotle, we remember, thought
that desocialized being would only be for 'a beast or a god':
Wordsworth envisages misty giants, glorified form and object, while
still asserting that he *is* talking about 'human Nature ... the
human form', about 'Man/With the most common' (VIII.412-16, 423-4).
At the end of the passage in question it seems that despite the
self-congratulating tone in the lines he has now paused for
some self-critical assessment of his model of man. He now admits
that for the man who was 'Husband, Father; learn'd ... suffer'd with
the rest/From vice and folly, wretchedness and fear;/Of this I little

all these assumptions of subjective purpose an [U]. in part are oddly old-fashioned

saw, car'd less' (423-7). But neither self-criticism nor criticism
of his model is at all his purpose. First of all he puts the
acknowledgment in the past tense, distancing that state from the
poet who is writing 'The Prelude'; second, he asserts most brusquely
that, even then, concerning these aspects, 'I ... something must
have felt' (427-8); and third, he thanks 'the God/Of Nature and of
Man' for this way of perceiving human beings, 'thus purified/Remov'd,
and at a distance that was fit', far from 'the deformities of
crowded life' (436-40, 465). So it is through these very modes
of perception and the evolution of his desocialized model of man
that he claims to manifest 'the love of Human kind' and the grasp
of 'the frame of life/Social and individual' (586-8; XII.39-40)
essential to the self-proclaimed vocation of Poet-Prophet and
Moralist. The poetry, however, has negated such claims, ironically
revealing the dehumanization of 'mankind' in the desocialized
abstraction that Wordsworth projects.

Wordsworth's account of his sympathy with the French Revolution does
little to modify the tendencies traced above. By the time Wordsworth
wrote about France in 'The Prelude' he rejected all radical political
activism, even if its aspirations were ones he found laudable and
directed against the most repressive, demoralizing and impoverishing
of regimes. He believed it was inevitably contaminated by abstract
schemes of reform, abstract versions of human nature, an unworthy
contempt of traditions supporting the status quo. David Ferry was
quite right to stress that while Wordsworth did admire the ideals
he puts in Beaupuy's mouth in Book IX he treats these as part of
the follies of his youth. This is true even of the often cited
lines about the 'hunger-bitten Girl,/Who crept along, fitting her
languid self/Unto a Heifer's motion' (see IX.510-33). The passage
sweeps from indignation at an instance of poverty (albeit rather
a conventionally picturesque one) to a belief in the presence of
'a spirit' which will ensure the ending of such poverty, the ending
of 'legalized exclusion, empty pomp ... sensual state and cruel
power' and the establishment of political democracy, 'whence
better days/To all mankind'. The sweep is significantly
incoherent, hastily brushing aside all analytic, political and
social problems, a blind and ignorant faith appropriate to 'an old
Romance or tale/ Of Fairy, or some dream of actions' (IX.306 ff;
and X.697). And Wordsworth wanted us to realize this, for, as
Ferry notes, his overall purpose is to suggest that 'thinking
things could ever be set right by political action or indeed by
any sort of human endeavour' exhibits great 'naivety'. In Books
IX and X Wordsworth is trying to dramatize a series of well-
intentioned 'abstractions', placing them as the peculiar failing
of radical thinkers, certainly not of his present standpoint. (10)
Nevertheless, we do learn more about Wordsworth's present model
of man in his explicit attack on the French Revolution in Book X
and the attack on his own alleged abstractionism in those pre-
'Prelude' days of young radicalism and the Salisbury Plain poems.
The attack on the Revolution concerns France in late 1793 and
early 1794, the year following the Montagnards' victory over the
Girondins with whom Wordsworth's sympathies remained (X.308-46).
This is how the poet describes the period, and a rather lengthy

quotation is necessary to do justice to the mode:

                        Tyrants, strong before
In devilish pleas were ten times stronger now,
And thus beset with Foes on every side
The goaded Land wax'd mad; the crimes of few
Spread into madness of the many, blasts
From hell came sanctified like airs from heaven;
The sternness of the Just, the faith of those
Who doubted not that Providence had times
Of anger and of vengeance, - theirs who throned
The human understanding paramount
And made of that their God, the hopes of those
Who were content to barter short-lived pangs
For a paradise of ages, the blind rage
Of insolent tempers, the light vanity
Of intermeddlers, steady purposes
Of the suspicious, slips of the indiscreet,
And all the accidents of life were press'd
Into one service, busy with one work;
The Senate was heart-stricken, not a voice
Uplifted, none to oppose or mitigate;
Domestic carnage now filled all the year
With Feast-days; the old Man from the chimney-nook,
The Maiden from the bosom of her Love,
The Mother from the Cradle of her Babe,
The Warrior from the Field, all perish'd, all,
Friends, enemies of all parties, ages, ranks,
Head after head, and never heads enough
For those that bade them fall: they found their joy,
They made it, ever thirsty as a Child,
                        (X.310-38)

This passage has no self-critical irony and is emphatically a judgment
from the present self-proclaimed prophet and moralist who has
transcended the 'abstractions' of radicalism. There is a remarkable
blend of extreme generalization (e.g. 318-27) and uncontrolled
hysteria culminating in the final lines quoted. The poet has
settled for stereotype (the old man in the chimney-nook, the
'maiden' at the 'bosom' of her lover ...), the most absurd
imprecision (in 1793-4, 'all perish'd, all'), complete with 'blasts/
From hell' and 'childlike'(odd, this) but insane Frenchmen
delightedly killing 'all ... all ... of all parties, ages, ranks' -
yet still able to fight a victorious war against European counter-
revolutionary powers!

The grounds of this surprisingly crude writing are in Wordsworth's
desocializing model of man and the abstractionism that he so
repeatedly asserts he has transcended. In his own account we
follow how he had originally seen the political and social
Revolution in the terms of natural processes (IX.251-2). His model
of man meant that, as with the shepherd, it was easy to reify human
beings as objects in the natural world. (11) But when the practices
of human beings in real conflicts resisted this reification he did
not, as he alleges, abandon a commitment to a desocialized and

'abstract' version of 'human Nature'. He did not subject his
imagination and ideas to the diverse aspirations, motivations and
circumstances of very different social groups active in the period
about which he was writing. One could not even begin to gather
from his approach that the abhorred Jacobins and Robespierre were
actually trying to represent particular social, political and
economic interests of the French middle classes; that the militant
wing of the bourgeoisie wished to define 'Liberty', 'Democracy',
'Fraternity' in nationalistic terms which would secure the property
and wealth of the middle classes (from aristocracy and the lower
classes), reassure the richer bourgeoisie and subordinate the
popular forces, especially the 'sans-culottes' on whose mobilization
their own victory over king, nobles and foreign enemies depended.
Within Wordsworth's language one could not begin even to ask why
lower-class urban men and women were rioting in Paris in the summer
of 1793. One could certainly not begin to explore these peoples'
concern with immediate and very pressing problems of subsistence,
prices and wages in a situation of serious lack of provisions, nor
to examine the way that through these active concerns they were
pushing against the Jacobins and towards a form of popular democracy
which was deeply uncongenial to most Jacobins. (12) The point is
not Wordsworth's failure in social and political observation but
the way his model of man precluded a host of central considerations
concerning the human lives on which he was commenting.

Book X leads from Wordsworth's meditations on the French Revolution
to an account of a period of reflection on ethics and politics
which apparently led him, very temporarily it seems, to yield up
'moral questions in despair' - until his recovery from dejection
was inspired by Dorothy, Coleridge and 'Nature' (X.806 - XI.397).
His overt target in this part of 'The Prelude' is again a radical
Utopian philosophy 'That promised to abstract the hopes of man/Out
of his feelings', abstracted man from 'The accidents of nature,
time and place' in pursuit of 'social freedom' (X.806-30, 873-901).
The poet overlooks the irony, one we have noted before, that his
own model of the individual is as 'abstract' as any enlightenment
Robinson Crusoe, certainly as much as Godwin's. Rather surprisingly,
his depiction of his recovery illustrates this together with a
marked lack of self-reflection. He insists that his past analytic
errors (X.873-901: in those days when he was a naive democratic
republican) were really caused by his fundamentally sound 'heart'
being 'turn'd aside/From nature by external accidents', 'external
accidents' which apparently refer to his residence in France and in
counter-revolutionary England. (13) He maintains that through all
these merely 'external accidents' his own 'true self',

> was no farther chang'd
Than as a clouded, not a waning moon
> (X.916-18)

Nature and Dorothy,

> Gave me that strength and knowledge full of peace,
> Enlarged, and never more to be disturb'd,

> Which through the steps of our degeneracy,
> All degradation of this age, hath still
> Upheld me, and upholds me at this day
> (X.926-30)

So that he can confidently say, 'I stand now/A sensitive, and a
creative soul' (XI.256-7). In his own case, then, history, change
of circumstances, encounter with vital and quite new ranges of
human experience can be placed as 'external accidents' which cannot
effect the 'true self'. Thus, while he attacked 'abstract' moral
and political philosophy for 'shaking off/The accidents of nature,
time and place' in its version of man (X.806-30), he himself does
just this both in constructing his model of man and in describing
the development of his own being amidst the 'accidents' of the
human world and his biographical experiences. David Ferry's comment
here is pertinent: 'The true self is inviolable and unchangeable.
It proceeds according to its own laws, which are remarkably like
cosmic and other nonhuman natural laws.' (14) This reflects the
absence of any dialectic between developing individual identity and
a specific human, historical world.

One of the most discussed passages in 'The Prelude' is the poem's
culminating image and meditation in Book XIII, among the major
revelations about the 'Mind of Man' in the poem. Book XII ended
with the usual claims about the 'ennobling interchange/Of action
from within and from without ... Both of the object seen, and eye
that sees' (XII.278-379). It is characteristic both in reducing
the action 'from without' to desocialized 'Nature' and reducing
the perceiving agent to a 'within', or a disembodied 'eye', equally
desocialized. From this Wordsworth passes to the ascent of Snowdon
and the ensuing meditation. It is in the meditation that he
selects from the multiplicity of potential symbolic significances
of the 'scene' after it had 'pass'd away', and directs us to take it
for 'The perfect image of a mighty Mind' (XIII.69). (15) It
comprises a careful attempt to finish 'The Prelude' with a last
account of his model of the mind of man at its most powerful.
  Having written of the 'domination' that 'Nature' exercises over
the visible world, turning it into appropriately educative symbolic
scenes which even 'the grossest minds must see and hear/And cannot
chuse but feel', Wordsworth attributes similar powers to the human
minds at their best, according to his model of man. In this
passage, too long to quote here (XIII.91-105), man can transform
and create 'a world of life', but the mind is quite disembodied,
utterly independent of the social relations that alone make fully
human activity possible. At the same time, Wordsworth imagines
and writes in a manner which precludes all specificity concerning
'all the objects of the universe' with which the 'higher minds'
allegedly 'deal'. Nevertheless, it is important to note that he
still claims this dealing is in our world, in accordance with the
view that he is the poet of 'human nature' in this world - 'the
world/Of all of us, the place in which, in the end,/We find our
happiness, or not at all' (X.726-8).
  As so often, Wordsworth fails to see that if 'objects of the
universe' are encountered and transformed this is through collabora-

tive human activity, that individual engagement with Nature is mediated through specific and plainly changing cultural forms, including a particular language with its own effects on perception. However marked some of the changes in his vision between the bulk of the opening two books and the bulk of the rest of the poem, between 1798-1800 and 1804-5, this failure permeates 'The Prelude' in all its different stages of composition. It is rather a serious shortcoming in a poet who had so much to say about interaction between man and the 'external world', and it involved his fundamental ideas of creativity. The long passage from Book XIII, just discussed, makes the strongest claims for what he elsewhere calls 'creative agency', 'creative sensibility' and 'creative soul' (II.371-401; XI.257). This 'power', we noted, allegedly transforms, creates, and can 'build up greatest things' (XIII.84-107). But (as the eighth book of 'The Excursion' and the seventh book of 'The Prelude' acknowledged) the 'objects of the universe' include the objects and environment being transformed and created by men in an increasingly urban and industrial society, together with the related agrarian dislocations, conflicts and sufferings endured by so many agri-cultural workers. How then does the 'creative agency', which Wordsworth celebrates as a this-worldly one, deal with such prominent features of our universe? The answer is, of course, that it simply does not. It offers instead an effortless transcendence which allows the poet and his readers to enjoy the sense of an exhilaratingly powerful creative dialectic between 'mind' and 'active universe', an 'intercourse' as Wordsworth often says. This accords with his treatment of agency (illustrated in 'Excursion' VIII) and the presiding model of man in 'The Prelude', a fit basis for such gratifying but profoundly fallacious forms of transcendence. The claims about 'creative agency' in the historical world are all too vacuous and entail an evasion of this very world, where 'in the end,/We find our happiness or not at all'.

Indeed, it is worth observing that one of the effects of envisaging human creativity in this desocialized manner is to obscure even the possibilities of imaginative, intellectual and practical engagement with either the social world Wordsworth pointed towards in the eighth book of 'The Excursion' or the changing agrarian world to which he withdrew. It directs readers' imaginative energies (which, Wordsworth stresses, involve the fullest exercise of 'reason', XIII.167-70) away from the life-processes of human beings in a manner which could only legitimate and strengthen the development of industrial society under the domination of the present owners of capital and land in the interests of 'Gain' ('Excursion', VIII.184). In this respect Wordsworth's meditation suggests how far he was from acknowledging that the poet and his vision was a victim of the divisions of labour and power so eloquently described by writers as diverse as Adam Smith and Blake, how far he was from suspecting that the cult of desocialized but creative individualism might have social foundations. When Wordsworth *did* attempt to offer an image of a social community he admired, he wrote that most revealing poem, 'Home at Grasmere'. Here he celebrated his 'last retreat' (at the age of twenty-nine) to what is presented as a secluded 'paradise', surpassing 'the bowers/Of blissful Eden', in which he again easily transcends all social and historical pressures. (16)

In the culmination of 'The Prelude' Wordsworth maintains his
desocialized model of man in a mode which does not even allow
thoughts about the mystically unified 'true Community' of Grasmere
(see 612-19), even though he is, as we saw, allegedly talking about
activity in the human universe. It is typical of the mode that the
writer can use the notion of domination without any consciousness of
the host of problems this raises. For if the 'higher minds' dominate
and transform the world as 'Nature' is said to do, then will they not
necessarily be dominating the lives of other beings? Exercising
'power' is not easy to distinguish from the multiplicity of forms of
coercion Blake explored and dramatized so fully throughout his work.
Wordsworth almost goes out of his way to stimulate such questions
by categorically asserting that the creativity he purports to
describe is personal 'freedom', indeed, 'this alone is genuine
Liberty' (XIII.121-2). But the last thing Wordsworth really thought
of in using the vocabulary of 'domination' and 'Liberty' here
(XIII.77-122) was the implicit human and Urizenic problems. Such
thoughtlessness in such a major issue constitutes significant
intellectual and imaginative failure closely bound up with the
model of man that informs 'The Prelude'.

Although the subject is complicated and beyond the scope of
this chapter, I will hazard a brief comment on the kind of
religiosity that the Snowdonian 'scene' exhibits (especially
XIII.69-113). One does not have to be a theologian or Christian
dogmatist to find that the exaltation of 'whatsoe'er is dim/Or
vast' and the putative role of 'sensible impressions' in stimulating
'communion with the invisible world' are very confused. The passage
uses vaguely religious language and invokes a non-specific
'religion', 'faith' and 'invisible world'. Yet by talking about
'sense of God' and 'the Deity', the writer suggests that the
experience in question does provide knowledge of the realm to
which theology has claimed insight, and it is hardly surprising
that Wordsworth chooses to talk about himself as a prophet speaking
'lasting inspiration', one who hopes to teach us about our
'redemption' (XIII.439-44). Without a doubt, the imaginative and
theological imprecision of the writing contribute to delivering
the 'dim' and 'vast' experiences he exalts from the tests of
engagement with actual life-processes in the human world, while
never denying, unlike traditional religions, that the present world
is the place for 'the highest bliss/That can be known'. This
accords well with an increasingly secular and industrial society
where religious institutions, authority and doctrine do not play
a major role in shaping peoples' outlook, but where there may well
be many individuals desperately seeking ways of maintaining the
sense of a powerful, creative ego in a society where they find no
obvious forms of expression for their particular sense of creative
potential. For such people, the very imprecision of the text, and
its evasion of both the social world and traditional religious
discourse, and institutions, is essential to its attraction. It
may offer an exceptionally proud and self-gratifying way of total
accommodation with the world of Urizen and the powers that be. It
does not even demand retreat to Grasmere. (17)

In one chapter it is impossible to pursue the analysis of Wordsworth's

model of man much further, but I will conclude by pointing towards
two areas which are closely related. The first is the poet's version
of 'Nature'. This is a topic around which a large literature has
accumulated and here I only wish to offer very brief points which
come directly out of the preceding discussion, but were not made
explicit there. Nature acts as a substitute for imaginative and
intellectual engagement with the development of embodied human
beings in their diverse circumstances. It (or rather 'She') is a
screen against the actual worlds of adults and children, one which
enhances the reduction of the 'external world' to the abstraction
'Nature'. This is totally independent of human life-processes but
yet is credited with personal agency and concerns throughout 'The
Prelude'. By attributing a benevolent teleology and direct agency
to this 'Nature' Wordsworth allows himself and his readers the
gratification of an extremely comforting theodicy shorn of all the
more uncongenial Christian and neo-Platonic doctrines on which
western theodicies had been constructed. (18) It is true that by
the time his beloved brother was drowned (February 1805) he was
coming to want more traditional supernatural guarantees than those
afforded by his secularized theodicy, but it still informs the
conclusion of the 'Ruined Cottage', 'Tintern Abbey', 'The Prelude'
and a great deal of the poetry for which he is now celebrated. (19)
Furthermore, and doubtless this is a comment from one of 'the
grossest minds' that Wordsworth was sure 'Nature' would correct
(XIII.74-84), the poet fails to incorporate the fact that the
nature he met in late eighteenth-century England, even in the
Lake District, was very much a humanized nature. It was a landscape
transformed and made accessible by sustained, human activity. Not
by the 'higher minds' of the Wordsworthian model, but by generations
of human settlement, collaborative work and technology through
which uninhabitable forests had been turned into land cultivatable
by specific communities, by 'sordid men,/And transient occupations
and desires/Ignoble and deprav'd'. And nature was only inhabitable
in the present for the poet, one of the self-proclaimed 'Prophets
of Nature' we recall, through the continuing labour of men and
women in a rapidly changing social structure which would involve
further and drastic transformations of the human habitat. The
poet's 'intercourse' with Nature was mediated in ways that his
poetry simply evaporates. There is no way that one could write
with any honesty of Wordsworth what John Barrell writes of Clare:
for Clare, 'a place is a manifold of images, not of visible images
only, and not only of topography, but of the people and living
things that work and live in the place'. (20) For Wordsworth, the
'spirits' of clouds, lakes and places that fill MS JJ and still
appear at times in 'The Prelude', are, like 'Nature', a fantasizing
substitute for the social individuals and historical practices
which have created specific places, a fit mate for the desocialized
and abstract 'Mind of Man' of which Wordsworth was such a great
projector.

The final topic that I wish to mention, however briefly, is
Wordsworth's ethics, his sense of 'truth in moral judgments'
(XIII.118). The poet-moralist's normative model of man as
desocialized individual made it likely that his moral ideas and

judgments would be wholly inadequate to form any viable principles of human practice in nineteenth-century England. It was also rather likely that in evaporating the social foundations of morality, Wordsworth's own moralizing would be especially prone to confusion.

His tendency to revere sheer power may offer an example of the problem his approach encounters. In the boat-borrowing episode, for instance, the boy's feelings moved from 'troubled pleasure' and physical (even sexual, 401-3) exhilaration to extreme fear and unfocused anxieties ('huge and mighty Forms ... mov'd slowly through my mind/By day and were the trouble of my dreams'). The poet then claims that these intense feelings were 'purifying',

> And sanctifying, by such discipline,
> Both pain and fear, until we recognize
> A grandeur in the beatings of the heart.
>   (I.437-41; see I.373-441)

The neo-religious moralism of the claim is evident in the vocabulary - 'purifying', 'sanctifying', 'discipline of pain and fear' (one of the Christian God's favoured ways of educating his saints). But it is altogether lacking in any poetic foundations or clear conse- quences. For the experience so brilliantly realized in the poetry involves the sensations I mentioned above, 'a dim and undetermin'd sense/Of unknown modes of being', with the very indeterminacy part of its overwhelming hold on the child (and, it seems to me, over the adult writer). The moralizing of this experience can only 'sanctify' sheer intensity of feeling, indeterminate 'pain and fear', exalting the confessedly 'dim and undetermin'd sense/Of unknown modes of being' (this kind of religiosity we discussed above in connection with Book XIII). Yet these are all morally neutral and, very unpromisingly for Wordsworth's claims as a moralist, vacuous in terms of any ethical content and guidance. Because the poetry is informed by the model of man I have been describing, Wordsworth fails to submit these notions to an imaginative engagement with social practices and relations which might have subverted them and encouraged self-critical reappraisal within the poem. His famous meditation while writing about the crossing of the Alps calls for similar remarks (VI.525-48). 'Power' and 'might', 'vapour' and the sense of being 'lost as in a cloud' constitute his experience here too. Yet the disclosure is allegedly about 'our destiny, our nature, and our home' which apparently is 'with infinitude ... with hope it is ... Effort, and expectation, and desire/And something evermore about to be'. The claims characteris- tically combine neo-religious gestures and a generality which is as much part of Wordsworth's 'moral judgments' (XIII.118) as of his wildly eclectic metaphysics. His approach dissolves incarnate existence into a vague life force, an abstract nisus with a teleology whose blankness is remarkable ('something ever more about to be'). We cannot miss the poet's admiration for 'power', 'strength', 'infinitude', 'effort', in the pursuit of that 'something', but this is, once again, lacking in any particular ethical content. Indeed, if it holds any implications for human practice they are a rather sinister worship of any 'power' and commitment. It was Wordsworth's distinguished admirer, the Victorian

moralist and educationalist Matthew Arnold, who insisted that 'we
can never forsake' the view that the correct response to active
working-class dissidence in capitalist society is an exercise of
power: 'flog the rank and file, and fling the ring-leaders from
the Tarpeian Rock'. (21) This was, of course, not Wordsworth, yet
for all its overtly didactic aims the poet's combination of
admiration for 'power' and dissolution of all specific social
relations meant that his moralizing could legitimate virtually
any practice which is intensely felt, dedicated to 'something'
beyond the present state of affairs and touched by the conviction
that the practitioners are an elite of 'higher minds'.

A reader may well object that this ignores Wordsworth's own
advocation of 'intellectual love', 'the universal heart' and his
affiliations with the main current of eighteenth century ethical
argument which made sympathy a key notion. Unfortunately Wordsworth's
idea and presentation of sympathy is also quite devoid of moral
content, of any specifiable guiding principles for human practice
in Wordsworth's world, or any other. It also fosters attitudes
which allow poet and reader to accommodate uncritically with any
ruling powers, however unjust, immiserating and cruel their
government. The ending added to the 'Ruined Cottage' before
Wordsworth began 'The Prelude' may serve as an example. (22) In
this poem Margaret loses her husband, a victim of unemployment,
poverty and war, her elder child to the parish in her poverty, her
younger children in death, and her own desire to live. Nevertheless,
her psychic disintegration, her death and that of the child and,
one supposes, husband, do not lead Wordsworth to meditate on the
social dimensions of the most intimate areas of experience, although
his own text has painfully disclosed these. Instead, he avoids
any criticism of the distribution of power, resources, opportunity
and free choice in the social world he depicts, a refraction of
his own world examined in the Salisbury Plain poems. He celebrates
the misery and death of this rural family in terms such as the
following:

>   the calm obvious tendencies
> Of nature ...
>
> ...
> So still an image of tranquility
> So calm and still ...
> ... I turned away
> And walked along my road in happiness.

I think Edward Bostetter's comment on a like-minded addition to MS B
of the poem is penetrating:
> The danger in all this is that it relieves the individual ...
> of any responsibility to act within the present frame of things.
> He can salve his conscience, free himself from any sense of
> guilt by saying that all men could, should, and ultimately will
> feel [sympathy] as he feels. He need only wait. And in the
> meantime he can gain a quiet and pleasant glow of satisfaction,
> even an exhilaration, from his superior awareness and
> sensitivity ... he can be justified in drawing strength and
> happiness from their suffering.

This is fine and just critical interpretation, showing great
insight into the characteristic sympathy evolved in Wordsworth's
poetry and morality. (23) Wordsworth never grasped the Urizenic
nature of such compassion or sympathy - unlike Blake: (24)

> Pity would be no more,
> If we did not make somebody Poor:
> And Mercy no more could be,
> If all were as happy as we ...

As Blake dramatized so often, much of the attraction such sympathy
holds is the legitimation it offers for the aestheticizing of
avoidable human suffering. Its ethical vacuity in terms of any
guidance for forming principles relevant to action, positively
recommends it. The only guidance it does offer the reader is to
withdraw into his/her privacy and let those who direct and benefit
from tyranny, inequality, poverty, and war create more human
tragedies to provide 'tranquillity' and 'happiness' for meditative
teachers and moralists like the poet. (Wordsworth's admirers could
well reflect slightly more on the class basis of such an ideology
of suffering, however unsavoury such considerations may be to their
own enjoyment of the poet's sympathy and 'happiness'.)
  A reader who accepts the gist of these comments on the Wordsworthian 'heart' and sympathy, may suggest that I have overlooked an
important notion in his moral thought - the role of 'duty'
('Prelude', XIII.264-5). However, this too turns out to be the
victim of his model of man as desocialized and abstract individual.
The term is kept in such isolation from specific human contexts
and interactions, so removed from any imaginative engagement with
the social world, that we cannot know what it might or might not
entail in practice. Like his notions of 'power' and 'sympathy'
it could be filled with virtually any content. This is also true
of 'duty' and 'Reason' in the later 'Ode to Duty' (1807), and what
Alasdair MacIntyre wrote at the end of his illuminating critique
of Kant's notion of duty is most pertinent to the problems of
Wordsworth's ethical language and ideas: (25)

> the consequences of his doctrines, in German history at least
> [discussed by MacIntyre], suggest that the attempt to find a
> moral standpoint completely independent of the social order may
> be a quest for an illusion, a quest that renders one a mere
> conformist servant of the social order much more than does the
> morality of those who recognize the impossibility of a code
> which does not to some extent at least express the wants and
> needs of men in particular social circumstances.

Wordsworth's quest for such an 'illusion' was part and parcel of
his model of man. Perhaps it is also worth remembering how his
own history provides an example of MacIntyre's argument - the long
period of devoted service to Lord Lonsdale in which he attacked
social reformers and democrats, campaigned actively for the
continuation of the economic, political and social power of the
Lowther family in the north-west and for their class in the nation.
He came to uphold, overtly, 'habit and time-honoured forms of
subordination ... an humble reliance on the wisdom of our Forefathers, and a sedate yielding to the pressure of existing things,

NB

or ... to religious trust in a superintending Providence, by whose
permission laws are ordained and customs established'. Our forefathers apparently did not include Milton, let alone Winstanley
or John Ball, and he stated that the 'best' available test of
'discretion and knowledge' was 'property'. (26) This illustrates
the kind of links between the desocialization of man in Wordsworth's
chief model, the attempt to develop 'truth in moral judgments' from
this model and the collapse into conformist service of the dominant
powers in the existing social order.

Chapter 5

Coleridge: Individual, Community and Social Agency

David Aers, Jonathan Cook, David Punter

> Alas! dear Sir! what is mankind but
> *the Few* in all ages? Take them away,
> and how long, think you, would the
> rest differ from the Negroes or New
> Zealanders ...
> > (CL, vol.IV, p.714, 22 March 1817)

The publication of Coleridge's 1795 lectures on politics and
religion together with recent study of his views and activities in
the mid-1790s make it clear that Thelwall was perfectly justified
in remembering Coleridge as a radical who held a number of
unorthodox social and political opinions which went beyond those
common among English or French Jacobins. (1) This is particularly
striking in his various statements about the corrupting role of
private property, inequality and adverse material circumstances.
It was no ordinary Jacobin who saw original sin as private
property — 'The real source of inconstancy, depravity and
prostitution is *Property*, which mixes with & poisons everything
good — & is beyond doubt the Origin of all Evil.' Sin is no
longer an innate and mysterious corruption, but rather the
contingent effect of a determining environment, and in 1795 he
notes: 'That vice is the effect of error and the offspring of
surrounding circumstances, the object therefore of condolence not
of anger, is a proposition easily understood and as easily
demonstrated.' (2) Such opinions might lead one to believe that,
like Rousseau or Blake and some earlier radicals, Coleridge had
moved the old debates concerning original sin and the causes of
individual depravity from metaphysical speculation and theology to
the fields of social and economic criticism, and towards empirical
historical investigation: from concern with an abstract, desocialized
individual towards the development of an ethic indissolubly linked
with political inquiry into the distribution of power, resources
and opportunities in existing societies. But a close reading of
some of the most important poetry Coleridge produced in this period
(1793-8) will not corroborate such belief, although it will
illuminate his version of individual, community and social processes
at this stage of his life. From a reading of some earlier writing
we will move on to consider the form of idealism pervading his
later work. We hope this chapter, despite its necessary brevity,
will cast some light on the question E.P. Thompson put in the
misleading form 'disenchantment or default' and on some important
aspects of the developing ideology of a major figure in the history
of English 'Romanticism'. (3)
    One of Coleridge's earliest surviving poems is an ode on the

destruction of the Bastille. The poem displays some features which
are worth noticing because they are not merely the product of
youthful incompetence in the use of eighteenth-century modes of
personification. In the first stanza the poet claims that age-old
'Tyranny' has been defeated:

> Yet Freedom rous'd by fierce Disdain
> Has wildly broke thy triple chain,
> And like the storm which Earth's deep entrails hide,
> At length has burst its way and spread the ruins wide.
> ('Destruction of the Bastille', 7-10)

The social agent effecting the alleged liberation is an abstract
noun, 'Freedom', apparently stimulated by the personification
'Disdain'. Coleridge combines this use of abstractions with
conventional apocalyptic analogies in which violent political events
are seen in terms of violent natural phenomena. The effect is to
preclude any attention to concrete historical processes, to the
empirical questions about who was actually doing what to whom and
with what motivations. Given the similarly abstract vein in which
the forces of tyranny are described in stanza four, the mode in
which the fifth stanza treats revolutionary 'Liberty' is hardly
unexpected, though it is of interest:

> I see, I see! glad Liberty succeed
>   With every patriot virtue in her train!
>   And mark yon peasant's raptur'd eyes;
>   Secure he views his harvests rise;
>   No fetter vile the mind shall know,
>   And Eloquence shall fearless glow.
> Yes! Liberty the soul of Life shall reign,
> Shall throb in every pulse, shall flow thro' every vein!
> ('Destruction of the Bastille', 23-30)

A striking feature is the absence of transactive (even of transitive)
verbs, although the poet is overtly meditating on what he takes to
be revolutionary human action and the transformation of society.
The abstraction 'Liberty' simply 'succeed(s)' and 'shall reign'.
Grammatical form, as Halliday and others have demonstrated, is one
of the ways a writer manifests his perception of the world. (4)
Here, by selecting non-transitive verbs, the poet gives the
impression of an almost magical triumph of the abstraction 'Liberty',
one in which the human groups, institutions, traditions and material
factors which may resist the unspecified bearers of 'Liberty' just
disappear. Even the peasant is presented in a way which dissolves
the fundamental activity on which his existence as a peasant was
based - not to mention the existence of those overlords who
depended on extracting his labour and rent. Like some baroque
mystic, Coleridge's peasant strikes a purely contemplative pose
marked by 'raptur'd eyes'; all he has to do is behold 'his harvests
rise'; labour, markets and all material problems vanish. In this
transformation of agricultural work the peasant becomes an utterly
non-social seer fixed in an eternal present. Coleridge concludes
the stanza with a further reflection on the post-revolutionary era

(the last four lines of the quotation above). Here 'mind' is clearly a desocialized entity: no reader can have any idea about the implications of such a statement for domestic, social or political life. The poet asserts that 'Liberty the soul of Life shall reign' but fails to apply any version of the concept of 'society' to 'life', even though his subject is a particular revolution. This, we shall see, is a failure that foreshadows major elements in his later work. In the final stanza Coleridge extends his unexamined assumption that France now comprises a homogenous national unity to voice his aspiration for some such unit throughout the world, 'Till every land from pole to pole/ Shall boast one independent soul!' (lines 37-8). This is hardly distinguished by its imaginative clarity ('independent' of whom? What is the 'soul' of a 'land' and where would one look for it?), but it does express a longing for a unified and undifferentiated social totality. Yet this totality is no more than a remarkably vague and desocialized abstraction, a sign of intellectual and imaginative failure that turns out to be far more significant than the passing confusion of apprentice work.

In 1794 Coleridge expressed his desires for a revolutionized society in pantisocratic schemes, evolved in the face of an increasingly violent counter-revolutionary English ruling class. (5) While he continues to deploy a host of personified abstractions in the ways we have just outlined, he now acknowledges that a hidden oasis may well be more to his taste than the kind of conflict with the forces of triumphant counter-revolution carried on by Thelwall and the London Corresponding Society (see 'To the Reverend W.J. Hort', 15-22, and 'To a Young Ass', 19 ff: the locus of human 'freedom' is, unironically, said to be 'far from men', in some 'romantic glen' where the massive problems of the relations between individual and collective are effortlessly dismissed). It could be argued that the poem 'Reflections on having left a place of retirement' (1795, published 1796) squarely faced the social issues he was tempted to evade. Certainly 'Reflections' is a poem dealing with his guilt at the wish for withdrawal to a 'dell' or 'Cot' safely removed from the risks run by Thelwall or Hardy; its overt argument is of course that he must and will commit himself to struggle in society, as he was to do with the 'Watchman' of spring 1796. Nevertheless, the poem is actually a celebration of the retreat he is, on the surface, negating: the 'Valley of Seclusion' attracts far more imaginative and intellectual attention than the social activity to which he is allegedly committing himself. He allows himself to surmise that the effects of such a landscape are powerful enough, per se, to detach a 'wealthy son of Commerce' from his habitual passion for accumulating wealth and to stimulate 'wiser feelings'. The poet does not attempt to convey what these 'wiser feelings' are as the 'wealthy son of Commerce' enjoys his Sunday walk in the country. Perhaps one of the reasons for this reticence is that the poet is actually representing what was already a characteristic attitude among the 'wealthy' urban bourgeoisie to the country as an asocial and temporary retreat from the world of 'Commerce', an attitude which he also, to some degree, shared. The human beings who make rural England inhabitable as

they strive for their subsistence with both nature and, often, the
dominant possessing classes, are simply evaporated. (6)   There is
no sign that Coleridge was self-conscious here about these particular
continuities of attitude between himself and the wealthy son of
'commerce' from Bristol, and he has nothing to say about the urban
visitor's daily pursuit of what he quaintly calls 'idle gold'.   The
realities of eighteenth-century English commerce and imperialism,
indivisible as they were, are elegantly contained within his landscape and art, in sharp contrast to the contemporary work of Blake.

In fact Coleridge presents the landscape, 'a godly scene', in a
mode which makes even sheep-farming into something natural and
timeless, divorced from any specific social practices.   The human
world is deliberately absorbed into the natural in a meditative
form which dissolves history and event into a desocialized,
unhistorical present.   Coleridge emphasizes this by asserting that
the scene, one of sheep, clouds, fields, hamlets and so on, 'seem'd
like Omnipresence'.   That is, a symbol of 'God' rather than a
manifestation of embodied humanity living in the natural world.
All human differentiation is absorbed into this 'Omnipresence' and
the poet enjoys the 'Blest hour' freed from human relationship
and time (lines 38-42). (7)

The following lines overtly reject this celebration as a
pampered dream (43ff).   Yet the poet's self-accusations seem oddly
off the mark.   The charge of simple cowardice (46-8) has no grounding
in the poem so far and one wants to know what practice he feels he
should undertake.   He wishes to join 'my unnumber'd brethren [who]
toil'd and bled' but this formulation conveys nothing about the
kind of toil and blood-shedding he envisages.   At first he seems to
picture some generalized philanthropy (lines 48-56), but he completes
his pledge by proclaiming that he goes 'Active and firm, to fight
the bloodless fight/Of Science, Freedom and the Truth in Christ'
(60-2).   We honour the bravery of his public lectures and political
publications of 1795-6.   Yet we also note that these lines themselves
constitute a failure to realize the alleged commitment imaginatively
or intellectually and as an assertion of active commitment they
contain some curious features.   Having expressed guilt at retiring
from those who 'toil'd and bled', he now promises to 'join head,
heart, and hand/Active and firm' in what he confidently asserts is
a 'bloodless fight'.   Again the problem is to identify what the
poet imagines, and it is striking that he uses the verb 'join' to
refer to him joining his apparently fragmented self together rather
than to joining any particular group of his 'unnumber'd brethren
[who] toil'd and bled'.   It is also significant that the lines
obscure who he imagines his opponents to be: he goes 'to fight' not
human groups or concrete forces but 'the bloodless fight'.   This
resistance to specificity even when pledging himself to historical
action, a resistance embedded in the grammar, is also marked in
his characterization of the 'fight' as 'the bloodless fight/Of
Science, Freedom, and Truth in Christ'.   That is, a fight of
abstractions presented in such a generalized manner that any
bearings they might have on conflict among his 'unnumber'd brethren'
and their opponents are quite concealed.   The form of writing
positively discourages historicizing questions about 'Freedom' (for

whom to do what?) and 'Truth' (whose Christ - Bishop Watson's or
Blake's, Hannah More's or Gilbert Wakefield's?) as particular
social groups and historically specific conflict are dissolved. (8)
It is not surprising that the poem concludes by immediately
withdrawing from the 'honourable toil' of the supposedly 'bloodless
fight', to 'dream' once more of the secluded 'Cot' and the
millennium when all people will have such picturesque rural
dwellings and 'none greater', a millennium to be ushered in by no
human agency but by God (63-71). This confirms the abandonment of
history, society and politics in a poem whose overt theme is
'Reflections on entering into active life', as it was originally
entitled, a poem written well before the period for which E.P.
Thompson puts questions about Coleridge's 'disillusionment' or
'default'.

In April 1796 Coleridge wrote, 'I build all my poetic pretentions
on the Religious Musings', (9) and to this major attempt at the
poetic embodiment of his religious and social radicalism we now
turn. The opening vision of the crucified Christ is in terms of
the 'majesty of portraiture' in which the scene 'imaged the supreme
beauty uncreate' (lines 17ff). Instead of any attempt to focus on
the human suffering of the 'Man of Woes!/Despised Galilaean'
(lines 8-9) and the religio-political dimensions of the Crucifixion,
so stressed by Blake and Christian radicals through the ages,
Coleridge aestheticizes the historical event in ways which tend to
dissolve the humanity of Jesus and substitute a neo-Platonic idea
(lines 23-4). In fact the crucifixion was a punishment for
escaped slaves and for rebels against the Roman state, a terrible
death used by the Romans against Jewish freedom fighters.
Crucifixion was a political punishment for rebellion in very
specific historical circumstances. Jesus was the 'despised' man of
sorrows esteemed as one 'stricken, smitten of God, and afflicted'
(Isaiah 53), condemned by official religion and state powers, the
man who asked that the cup of suffering pass from him (Matt. 26)
and cried out 'My God! My God! Why hast thou forsaken me?' (Matt. 27).
Yet the 'radical' Coleridge turned this event into a 'lovely' death
when 'anguish winged the prayer/Harped by Archangels, when they
sing of mercy' and Heaven is filled with 'ecstasy'. Jesus on the
cross becomes a neo-Platonic, almost gnostic light of doctrine
and knowledge. The passage leads into a statement about union of
the illumined soul with God, 'absorbed' (passive voice) 'to perfect
Love' and 'exclusive consciousness of God' (lines 43-5). Jesus
on the cross, the political dimensions and implications of the act,
problems in the theology of evil and suffering, all are effortlessly transcended in this mystical union, brazenly glossed in
1797 by a footnote to Hartley and Pistorius who are respectively
alleged to have 'demonstrated' the poet's metaphysical claim and
'proved and freed [it] from the charge of Mysticism'. The theology
here entails a superficial dissolution of the historical and social
individual so absolutely illumined and so easily 'absorbed' into a
self-annihilating union with deity.

From here Coleridge moves to the 'Elect', the 'deeply principled
Minority, which gradually absorbing kindred minds shall at last
become the whole'. (10) This group of people, whom we meet again
and again in Coleridge's work, are as impassive, 'unmoved' (line 78)

and noumenal as the poem's Jesus. Coleridge claims that each of
these elect souls,

> Stands in the sun, and with no partial gaze
> Views all creation; and he loves it all,
> And blesses it, and calls it very good!
>   ('Religious Musings', 111-14)

The poet expresses his belief in the possibility of a completely
impersonal knowledge of 'all creation', achieved by an utterly
desocialized individual grasping an undifferentiated totality, his
own standpoint and perceptions free from all the multivarious
mediations through which specific individuals engage with their
world and interpret it. A truly angelic form of cognition.
Coleridge also asserts that the totality he perceives is a fraternity
in which we 'know ourselves/Parts and proportions of one wondrous
whole'. But this fraternity is also desocialized into a vaguely
pantheistic whole with 'God/Diffused through all' (lines 126-31).
He then attacks the egotistic 'anarchy' of people lacking a 'common
centre', a social atomization in which each individual is 'A sordid
solitary thing,/Mid countless brethren with a lonely heart/...
Feeling himself, his own low self the whole' (lines 149-52). Here
we meet the recurrent aspiration for some universal human
community in which contemporary individual and social fragmentation
is superseded. But in voicing this aspiration Coleridge un-
selfconsciously discloses problems that he failed to make topics
for sustained investigation, although they have grave implications
for his social and psychological explorations. As we noted,
earlier in the poem, Coleridge had developed a version of union
with God which discounted both empirical individual and any specific
historical community. He now rejects contemporary individualism,
yet fails to consider how much his own form of piety may be a
refraction of what he rejects. The coveted universal community he
now invokes is 'one wondrous whole' which 'fraternises man' and in
it he finds, 'self, that no alien knows' (lines 128-9, 154). But
this transcendence of individualism and 'alienation' ironically
involves an utterly desocialized community, a metaphysical
abstraction in which all conceivable human agencies, empirical
differentiations and historical particulars are obliterated. The
context the poet creates is one in which the language of fraternity
and community has no concrete meaning, in contrast to the role of
'brotherhood' in Blake's 'Four Zoas' or 'Jerusalem', or in the
practice of groups such as the London Corresponding Society.
    Despite the poem's dissolution of social processes and
historical humanity, Coleridge was concerned about 'The present
State of Society', in the words of the poem's 'Argument', and
desired its radical reformation. To these issues he addresses
himself explicitly (lines 198ff).
    Most orthodox Christian authorities had seen private property as
the product of the fall, but Coleridge adapts this idea to suit a
Panglossian, partially secularized theodicy. (11) Private
accumulation of wealth leads to a fusion of 'vice and virtues';
class divisions, domination and all social 'ills' are 'the immediate
source/Of mightier good' in the intellectual, material and aesthetic

progress of humanity (198-229). The events of history, whatever
human misery they entail, are comfortably absorbed into a provi-
dential pattern which legitimates everything. The poet-histori-
osophist, calmly confident that he knows the final goal of history,
can pass easily over the seeming 'ills' of human development seeing
them as 'the immediate source/Of mightier good'. As in all such
schemes the empirical individuals and the specificities of actual
human history are treated with grand disdain, dissolved into the
irresistible progress of providence or 'Weltgeist'.

We have already met the Coleridgean 'elect', but it is worth
again drawing attention to their reappearance here (224-59). These
calm spectators of social chaos are contrasted with the demagogues
who rouse 'the unnumbered tribes/That toil and groan and bleed'.
But Coleridge wants to believe their detachment is historically
effectual. The first transformation he undertakes to gratify his
wishes is one we saw in his earlier treatment of the Bastille.
His language, characteristic here of 'romantic' writers, transforms
political and social action into natural phenomena - popular
insurrection becomes 'the mad careering of the storm'. With this
transformation he can then present the detached elite of
Coleridgean seers exercising demiurgic powers 'over the wild and
wavy chaos' as they 'tame the outrageous mass, with plastic might'
(239-47). Not only do they 'tame the outrageous mass' (with poems
like 'Religious Musings'?) they apparently create new and 'perfect
forms' (246-8). The construction of new social forms is thus
imagined not as a collaborative set of social practices involving
'the outrageous mass', but as an aesthetic exercise of 'plastic
might' by an ill-defined elite. The language allows Coleridge to
enjoy solipsistic revery in a form which still seems to engage with
current social conflicts - thus avoiding the feelings of guilt
associated with what Milton castigated as 'cloister'd and fugitive
virtue'. The failure of such language to describe purposeful human
activity, whether collective or individual, is total.

As Coleridge turns again to the present, perhaps one of the most
striking features of his vision is its continuing lack of
differentiation. The majority of people are placed in one group:
'The wretched Many! Bent beneath their loads/They gape at pageant
Power, nor recognise/Their cots transmuted plunder' (260-4). One's
first response to this is justifiably that the 'wretched Many'
hardly had to wait for Coleridge to work out that the power and
ease of the possessing classes depended on the labour of others,
for this transparent fact had been generally acknowledged throughout
the Middle Ages and early modern period by people from diverse
social groups. Perhaps, however, by singling out 'pageant Power'
Coleridge invites his readers to think about the concentration of
power in the state apparatus with the supporting theatre of terror
and seemingly neutral justice which legitimized the 'plunder'. In
this way ruling class domination and 'plunder' occur in a 'pageant'
form which encourages ignorance concerning the source and function
of state power, an ignorance which is a vital component of its
perpetuation. But while these complexities may perhaps have been
in Coleridge's mind, the far from complex contempt he felt for the
'Many' is expressed in his choice of the word 'gape' to describe
their gullible presence in the ruling-class theatre. Furthermore,

his choice of the nominalization 'transmuted plunder' actually
simplifies the processes in which the people's labour is controlled,
appropriated, reified and turned against them. It directs the
readers' attention away from the concrete social and psychological
realities of these processes, showing how Coleridge, in even his
most radical democratic period, quite lacks Blake's kind of
imaginative engagement with the realities of domination and
conformism in his culture. (12)

Of course, Coleridge's poem does assure the 'Children of
Wretchedness' (a significantly non-specific grouping) that massive
social change is imminent, 'the day of Retribution nigh' (line 303).
Paraphrasing from the sixth chapter of the Book of Revelations he
finds 'the Great, the Rich, the Mighty Men,/The Kings and the Chief
Captains of the World,/... shall be cast to earth' (lines 308-15).
But there is evasion here over the power that will bring about this
downfall of political, religious and economic tyranny. Coleridge
selects passive verbs with the key agents deleted. So ruling
classes 'shall be cast to the earth' and 'down-trodden', but by
whom we are neither told nor even encouraged to ask. The grammatical
form Coleridge selects once again reveals much about his world view
and its version of historical processes and agency. The poem as a
whole probably invites the reader simply to accept that God is the
agent of desired historical change, thus evading the vital questions
concerning what and who are the contemporary mediations of this
supernatural power.

Coleridge, however, is uncomfortable with even this use of the
Christian Apocalypse. For he immediately presents the deleted
revolutionary forces as 'the Giant Frenzy' who 'Mocketh high
Heaven', a simple and unironic judgment worthy of Urizen and Burke.
Instead of exploring the possibility that God may work through
groups who mock conventional 'heaven', instead of trying to achieve
some specificity here, Coleridge moves on to pious hopes that
social change will actually come not through 'Giant Frenzy' but
through 'Faith' and 'meek Piety'. These abstractions will lead to
a form of communism in which the social product will be shared
equally and humanity will be one happy 'vast family of Love'
(lines 339-42). Once again Coleridge fails to attend intellectually
or imaginatively to central questions concerning historical agency
and social being.

Nevertheless, he does have advice for the 'Children of Wretchedness', the 'numberless,/Whom foul Oppression's ruffian gluttony'
torments. The oppressed people must 'Rest awhile', a phrase he
reiterates. 'More groans must rise,/More blood must stream, or ere
your wrongs be full', he assures them; but they must certainly not
become self-organizing agents of self-defence and social change
(300-8). They must accept their fate as passive victims, a
sentiment preached to them by Burke, Hannah More, Bishop Watson
and the massed bands of Urizen's followers. It is especially
important to note the message here, for it comes at the height of
the most overtly radical democratic phase of his life and writing.
It is intrinsic to his poem and manifests clear connections with
his later political stance towards any lower class political
organization. Certainly there was nothing here for Pitt or the
Association for the Protection of Liberty and Property against

Republicans and Levellers to worry about. Individual, communities
and contemporary social conflicts are evaporated in the assertion
of a generalized theodicy which demands passive obedience from the
'numberless' oppressed, the 'wretched Many' - 'Rest awhile', indeed.
The poet longs to grasp 'that blest future' when he will finally be
able to dismiss history, to cry out 'Time is no more' in the light
of 'unimaginable day' (357-401). Fittingly, he concludes 'Religious
Musings' with an exultant dissolution of social and individual
histories of humanity into 'a dream' and 'shadowy' vision. The later
ode on France (first published April 1798) (13) simply continues
the displacement of liberty we observed earlier. For example, in
lines 15-21 the idea of 'liberty' can be freely applied without any
recourse to even the concept of society. Its realm is Nature, and
in an utterly desocialized Nature the poet can proclaim his
congratulation of himself on his devotion to Liberty (lines 39-40).
The second and third stanzas recall a time when he claims to have
thought the French Revolution might be a manifestation of Liberty,
yet our own readings of the texts he produced in the earlier period
have hardly revealed a scrupulous attention to the relevant social
and political practices, and he seems to admit this cheerfully enough
when he confesses that he expected the abstraction 'Wisdom' to be
the decisive teacher of France, informing her practice in quite
unspecified ways (lines 59-63). After attacking French imperialism
(stanza four) he concludes the poem with a stanza which illustrates
the displacement of 'liberty' from human community on to the
utterly desocialized Nature we noted in the first stanza (98-105).
'Liberty' is now experienced and extolled where the poet can be
with winds, waves and trees, apparently in Crusoesque isolation.
He writes this passage without any self-reflexive irony or criticism,
without any sense of the impoverished and fantasizing version of
individual and now invisible community he is projecting. One could
do worse than recall the passage from St Thomas with which we
headed the earlier chapter on Wordsworth.

Before moving on to the most famous conversation and mystery
poems it is worth drawing attention, however briefly, to some
features of a much commented upon poem, 'The Eolian Harp'. The
first seventeen lines seem to have been written in the period of
Coleridge's self-alignment with radical politics (1795), and they
celebrate a moment of sensual gratification and promise between
Coleridge, 'pensive Sara' and Nature in a rural retreat. Most of
the poem that has elicited lengthy commentary, however, seems to
have been written rather later (1797), leaving aside the much later
additions and revisions of 1803 and 1817. (14) In the central
sections of 'The Eolian Harp' Coleridge draws out the possible
metaphysical and psychological meaning of the initial harmonious
scene, leading into speculations on the nature of a cosmic unifying
principle adumbrated by the poet's sensuous apprehension of nature
(lines 36-46, second draft). But instead of pursuing these speculations the poem cuts them off by reintroducing 'pensive Sara' now
characterized by a 'serious Look' rather than a 'soft cheek'
(47-62). She reminds the poet of what he seemed to have overlooked,
the need for unphilosophical, faithful and very humble piety
accompanied by sharp awareness of original sin. The final paragraph
of the poem downgrades the previous activity of sensuous and meta-

physical imagination, placing it as the product of 'the unregen'rate
soul' of the fallen sinner. The real compensation for this may well
be that the rejection of imagination and metaphysical speculation
seems to hold out the possibility of absorption in a community,
however abstractly formulated - 'the *family* of Christ' (54).   Be
this as it may, in 'The Eolian Harp' orthodoxy, imagination and
metaphysical speculation come into conflict and, in the process,
imagination again reveals an asocial drive. While the imagination
may conceive of various forms of relationship, their starting point
is with the solitary individual and their finishing point with God.
What permits imagination is the denial of the social world. Equally,
the denial of imagination is the price of the poet's re-entry into
the social world of the conventionally pious. The poem's structure
of transgression and denial has its specific effect on the poem's
changing conceptions of community. What is presented at the
beginning of 'The Eolian Harp' as a spontaneously given moment of
well-being has been redefined by its end as an undeserved gift of
God to a sinful man, a gift which includes 'Peace, and this Cot' as
well as Sara. The conclusion thus settles for a society premised
upon authority and its familiar, guilt. The ending of 'The Eolian
Harp' opens up a perspective on to Coleridge's writings in which
authority and guilt are increasingly seen as the necessary ground
of any social and political order.

In a letter written to his brother in early March 1798, Coleridge
affirmed his belief in the orthodox doctrine of original sin. (15)
The letter as a whole is a significant document in charting the
path to his later conservatism. The earlier optimism about
historical evolution is cancelled as Coleridge emphasizes 'that
from our mothers' womb our understandings are darkened', and
whereas once Coleridge had sought the origins of moral depravity
and self-division in alterable social conditions, his thinking here
ends with the theological conception of original sin as the base
line of explanation. His overt commitment to original sin coincides
with an increasing distrust of politics in general and an outright
rejection of radical politics in particular.   In the letter to his
brother, Coleridge refers contemptuously to the 'Philosophers and
Friends of Freedom' who presume to be able to break with the
pessimistic law that history now teaches Coleridge: 'History has
taught me, that RULERS are much the same in all ages and under all
forms of government: they are as bad as they dare to be. The
Vanity of Ruin and the Curse of Blindness have clung to them like
an hereditary Leprosy' (CL, vol.I, p.395). Government, in this
understanding, is simply an outgrowth of man's inherently depraved
nature. Radicals are presumptuous not only because they ignore
history's repetitious lesson but also because they deny the truth
of original sin in their conviction that human ignorance and self-
division can be overcome in the reordering of society.
    But this is not all that Coleridge has to say about government.
If belief in original sin now allows him to be contemptuous of
attempts at political and social reform, it also permits him to
state an essentially conservative view of the necessity of existing
governments. What from one point of view looks like an hostility
towards society's rulers (particularly if they happen to be the

rulers of revolutionary France) can consort oddly with a disclaimer about any subversive intentions:

> Do not therefore, my Brother consider me as an enemy to Government and Rulers; or as one who says that they are evil ... I regard Governments as I regard the abscesses produced by certain fevers - they are the necessary consequences of the disease, and by their pain they increase the disease but yet they are in the wisdom and goodness of Nature; and not only are they physically necessary as effects but also as causes they are *morally* necessary in order to prevent the utter dissolution of the patient (CL, vol.I, pp.395-6).

Metaphors of disease, frequently used by Coleridge to elaborate his conviction of the depravity of human nature, are here turned to a justification of government as a necessary regulative force against the anarchic and disintegrative tendencies of fallen humanity. Clearly, there is no room in this conception for a view of government as an instrument of beneficial social change.

The letter of March 1798 reveals Coleridge's embarrassment at his earlier radical affiliations, 'but I have snapped my squeaking baby-trumpet of sedition and the fragments lie scattered in the lumber-room of Penitence'. This has its consequences for his definition of the purposes of imagination and philosophical thought:

> I have for some time past withdrawn myself almost totally from the consideration of immediate causes which are infinitely complex and uncertain, to muse on fundamental and general causes - the 'causae causarum' - I devote myself to such works as encroach not on the antisocial passions - in poetry, to elevate the imagination and set the affections in right tune by the beauty of the inanimate impregnated as with a living soul, by the presence of Life - in prose, to the seeking with patience and a slow, very slow mind ... what our faculties are and what they are becoming (CL, vol.I, p.397).

If Coleridge's work from 1794-6 involved an uneasy amalgam of metaphysics and reverie with political and social concerns, these comments suggest, in the context of a generalized craving for respectability, the triumph of metaphysics and reverie over an attempt at direct engagement with politics and society. Coleridge's abandonment of 'the consideration of immediate causes' is an abandonment of that limited abstract materialism, expressed in his earlier doctrine of necessity, which at least broached the problem of the environmental sources of evil.

Coleridge's stated purpose for poetry, 'to elevate the imagination and set the affections in right tune by the beauty of the inanimate impregnated, as with a living soul, by the presence of Life', seems to correspond to one of the most celebrated aspects of his work, the conversation poems. Although the letter suggests that these were written in the context of a general withdrawal from political concerns, it is possible to see the conversation poems as a continuation of the optimism of Coleridge's earlier poetry.   'This Lime Tree Bower, my Prison' perpetuates the kind of theodicy we

noted in 'Religious Musings' but with an important difference. (16)
In 'This Lime Tree Bower' the demiurge's providence is exclusively
confined to Nature. No attempt is made by the poet to see its
operations in history or to comprehend contemporary politics as a
manifestation of divine providence. In the poem Coleridge can
confidently assert that he knows 'That Nature ne'er deserts the
wise and pure:/No plot so narrow but Nature there/No Waste so vacant,
but may well employ/Each faculty of sense' ('This Lime Tree Bower',
60-3). The price of continuing optimism is a withdrawal from any
imaginative exploration of the social and political world as the
possible site of an ordering principle which can realize new forms
of being for the impoverished and deprived rather than just for the
poet's friends. The conversation poems mark a point in the
evolution of a poetic mode which can now exclude the pressures of
political obligation, pressures which were felt, however abstractly,
in 'Reflections' and 'Religious Musings'. In 'France: an Ode', as
we noted (p. 90) the world of political action and struggle is
written out of the poem. Liberty can only be discovered in
communion with nature, as disillusion with a particular historical
event allows the poet a general withdrawal from political and social
concerns altogether. One cannot help feeling that by 1798 the
French Revolution had provided Coleridge with an excuse for what
he had wanted to be for a long time, a respectable rather than a
radical writer. Although the position arrived at by the end of
'France: an Ode' is recognisably different from, and, in an
important sense, more decisive than the awkward social engagement
of 'Religious Musings', the two poems can be read as different
moments within the same poetic mode, a mode which can incorporate
both Coleridge's radicalism and his withdrawal from political
concerns. What both poems share is a form of idealism which permits
Coleridge to discover and name the spiritual principle that
underlies sensory phenomena. The poet moves to a position of
intuitive certainty about the nature of a spiritual reality,
although the development of Coleridge's poetry from 1794-8 suggests
that this spiritual reality inhabits an increasingly limited domain.
As in 'France, an Ode' there may be temporary obstructions to
vision, but the poet can still win through to a sense of 'the beauty
of the inanimate impregnated, as with a living soul, by the presence
of Life'.

  If we turn to the most celebrated part of Coleridge's poetic
production, the mystery poems, we can see that, read in relation
to the conversation poems, they constitute a significant but short-
lived mutation in Coleridge's idealism. For all their differences,
'Kubla Khan', 'Christabel', and 'The Ancient Mariner' share an
idealist sense of a spiritual reality underlying and governing
the appearances of the material world. But it is a spiritual
reality which refuses any conventionally pious translation, least
of all in terms of the enlightened optimism indicated by 'the one
omnipresent mind/Omnific'. (17) In this respect, the mystery poems
can be read as a reaction against both the theodicy and the poetic
mode exemplified by 'Religious Musings' and the conversation poems.
Whereas these latter poems seek some revelation of the harmonious
relation between spiritual forces and the material world, the
mystery poems present the relation between matter and spirit as

obscure and disruptive. The Mariner moves from extremes of
dereliction to extremes of joy by virtue of a spiritual power whose
workings he can scarcely comprehend, let alone predict. Christabel
glimpses a reality in Geraldine which contradicts the evidence of
waking sense, but it is a reality that she cannot name; 'Kubla Khan'
mingles images of terror and bliss without reference to a single
governing idea, such as theodicy, as a unifying principle. Another
mark of the mystery poems' difference lies in Coleridge's break
from the discursive mode of the conversation poems. The conversa-
tional intimacy of 'This Lime Tree Bower', moving between
introspection and dialogue, is replaced in the mystery poems by
forms, and fragments of forms, which are either deliberately archaic
or exotic. Coleridge's engagement with these forms means that the
mystery poems push to a far and obscure distance that order of
reference which pretends to make ultimate sense of experience.

What is remarkable is that Coleridge could be writing such
different kinds of poetry at the same time. Read together, the
conversation poems and the mystery poems reveal a particular dilemma
in Coleridge's writing between 1796-8. One poetic mode, the mode
of the conversation poems, moves toward a reconciliation of opposites,
although, as we have argued, Coleridge's resolutions often result
from an abstract, desocialized understanding of the tensions the
poet tries to resolve. The poems do not give a full realization of
the contradictory pressures they claim to transcend. By contrast,
the mystery poems give a peculiarly powerful form to contradiction:
things can turn into their opposites in startling ways. Thus in
'Kubla Khan' the daemonic 'woman wailing for her demon lover' is
transformed into the sublime 'damsel with a dulcimer' without
Coleridge seeking to moralize the connection between the two
('Kubla Khan', 16, 37). The conclusion to Part II of 'Christabel'
explores the contradictory relation between emotions of intense
pleasure and love and the language of hatred through which they find
expression. The little child

     Makes such a vision to the sight
     As fills a father's eyes with light
     And pleasures flow in so thick and fast
     Upon his heart, that he at last
     Must needs express his love's excess
     With words of unmeant bitterness.
                    ('Christabel', 660-5)

The poetry allows the contradiction to stand without recourse to
theodicy as an escape route. Nor is there any sense in the mystery
poems of what new forms can emerge out of contradiction. As a
result, the Mariner is forced into a compulsive retelling of his
story as if that endless repetition might stand in for an explanation of what has happened to him. He remains locked within a
cycle of guilt and expiation, a cycle which invests him with the
contradictory identities of criminal and scapegoat. With 'Christabel'
and 'Kubla Khan', it seems that Coleridge cannot imagine how the
forces represented in the poems could possibly find any form of
resolution. Both remain unfinished experiments in writing.

The dilemma, then, is between a poetic form which achieves

synthesis and resolution but only at the cost of reducing the power
of contradiction, and a poetic form which gives expression to the
violence of contradiction but without moving to a perspective which
would make contradiction intelligible. To argue that Coleridge's
belief in original sin is the explanatory principle of the mystery
poems seems inadequate. The Mariner's voyage may lead him to a
new-found piety and a craving for religious conformity in some
'goodly company' at 'the kirk'. But this vision of obedient
community is, literally, no resting place for the Mariner. Whatever
his story means, it cannot be easily reconciled with piety toward
the 'great Father'. What looks like a 'great Father' to a 'goodly
company' can look like a capricious monster to the Mariner:

> Alone, alone all all alone
> Alone on a wide, wide sea.
> And never a saint took pity on
> My soul in agony.
>   ('Ancient Mariner', 232-5)

If, in the conclusion to Part II of 'Christabel', Coleridge invokes
the notion of a 'world of sin' as an hypothesis to explain contradictory states, it seems, none the less, that the poet's central
concern is with presenting the dialectical relations between
pleasure and pain, love and cruelty, rather than with using these
relations as evidence of man's fallen condition, within a coherent
orthodox theological scheme.

In summary then, the mystery poems question the confidence in a
theodicy which informs 'Religious Musings' and the conversation
poems alike. In doing this they also question the kind of idealism
carried by a poetic mode which can so readily perceive the workings
of a beneficent supra-human force beneath the apparent contradictions
of history and individual experience. They represent the possibility
of a break with idealist notions of form altogether but the
possibility remains largely unrealized. They move into a world of
powerful contradictions but in a way that condemns Coleridge to
the creation of forms that are either incomplete or, in the case
of 'The Ancient Mariner', obsessively circular - contraries without
progression.

At no point does Coleridge seem able to envisage human agency
untrammelled by desocializing abstractions of metaphysics and
theology, whether these are doctrines of necessity or original sin.
His later thought discloses important continuities with the unsolved
dilemmas of the earlier work.

To grasp the significance of Coleridge's later thought it is
essential to focus on his idealism. Deeply changeable as were many
of his attitudes and theories, in this respect he was unwavering:
for him there was a world higher than the material, whether, as
in his pantheistic phase, he regarded the connections between that
world and the realm of nature as extremely close, or, as in his
later more theologically orthodox phase, he saw the spiritual in
terms of a conventional deity. Intellectually, the idealism which
he professed was a complex one, and this was at least partly
because its provenance was complex. The problematic of his thought

was composed of a number of discrete elements, and many of his
speculations were parts of a continuing attempt to reconcile the
different traditions of which he regarded himself as the representative. We can list the most important ones: Platonism, and many of
its more modern variants; orthodox Christian theology; the heterodox
mystical tradition represented by Eckhart, Boehme and others; and,
probably most vitally, the contemporary Germanic idealism represented
for him chiefly by Kant, Fichte and Schelling. (18)

A major part of Coleridge's thinking consists in the identification of that type of thought which he refers to as 'the philosophy
of death', (19) and by which he means to refer to both empiricism
and abstract rationalism. When he refers to reason as man's guiding
faculty, it is important to him to point out that he means 'not the
abstract reason, not the reason as the mere organ of science, or as
the faculty of scientific principles and schemes a priori' but
'reason ... as the integral spirit of the regenerated man, reason
substantiated and vital'; this reason, 'without being either the
Sense, the Understanding or the Imagination, contains all three
within itself, even as the mind contains its thoughts, and is present
in and through them all'. (20) The worst aspect of this
philosophy of death is expressed in a dry adherence to formal logic;
syllogistic reasoning, Coleridge says, is a 'mere Farrago of hard
Names, a list of Classification where Classification can answer not
one wise purpose, where in short Class itself can never be mistaken
while the logical exponents or technical phrases expressive of the
Classification will never be remembered'. (21) No kind of thought
can be truly reasonable if it cuts itself off from nature; for in
doing so it loses sight of its real objects, and, further, actually
damages the life of those objects by attempting to conceive of them
as static, fixed, dead. To reduce life to a mere matter of cause
and effect is to refuse to recognize the richness, the diversity,
the unpredictability of the natural world, and thus Coleridge
devotes himself to propounding arguments 'against the system of
Calculation of Consequences'; (22) calculation, again, is a
reduction to number, a refusal to recognise freedom in the natural
and consequently in the human world.

Thus far, however, it would be fair to put the 'mature' Coleridge
down as a simple organicist, and to ask how these general trends in
his thought can possibly be made concrete without the presence of
any sense of the mediating role of social structures. Coleridge,
we could reasonably say, became yet another naive romantic believer
in the 'natural life', lacking in any sense of the power of economic
determinants or of their effects on human freedom. And yet there
is, of course, more in the later Coleridge. There is, for instance,
an insistent, and Germanically inspired, demand for 'system'.
Fichte he praises for providing the idea for 'a metaphysique truly
systematic', (23) and elsewhere he explicitly separates this concept
of system from anything which might relate to the dreaded 'calculation'. (24) And in theory at least, Coleridge does show some
consciousness that the only way of providing system without falling
back into abstraction is by studying the concrete facts of human
history. 'I wish', he writes, 'to connect by a moral "copula"
natural history with political history; or, in other words, to make
history scientific, and science historical - to take from history

its accidentality, and from science its fatalism'. (25) Considered
purely as a programme, such a statement makes a good deal of sense,
as does his other well-known comment on the intellectual importance
of history:

> The directing Idea of History is to weave a Chain of Necessity
> the particular Links in which are free acts - or - to present
> that which is necessary, as a Whole, consistently with the moral
> freedom of each particular act - or - to exhibit the moral
> necessity of the Whole in the freedom of the Components - the
> resulting chain as necessary, each particular Link remaining
> free.
>
> (Snyder, 'Coleridge on Logic and Learning', p.137)

Although Coleridge once said that history as such held no appeal for
him, in the context of his works as a whole this is not entirely
true: he was concerned with the theoretical problem which concrete
historical facts present to the purely speculative mind. 'The
theorising habit in a sound mind', he says, 'can counteract only
for a short time the love of seeing things in their real light'
(Snyder, p.30): the problem, however, is that so often having
achieved that real vision, the theorizing habit disappears completely,
and reality ends up standing merely over against theory in
irreconcilable contradiction. Realities 'are not objects of Logic
and therefore cannot be submitted to a discussion or reasoning
purely logical.... The first source therefore of falsehood in Logic
is the abuse and misapplication of Logic itself' (Snyder, p.87).
While this may well be true in itself, as far as Coleridge is
concerned there seems to be a continuing danger that distrust of
this specific mode of 'discussion or reasoning' might become
distrust of any kind of discussion or reasoning; that reality might
become only apprehensible through intuition.
    There is a term which Coleridge uses to suggest the way in which
one might escape this danger, and evolve a systematic mode of
discourse which would not reduce and kill its own objects, and that
is the 'Science of Realities'; but significantly, the only place
where he finds this science operant is in the Bible, which, he
says, (26)

> alone contains a Science of Realities: and therefore each of
> its Elements is at the same time a living Germ, in which the
> Present involves the Future, and in the Finite the Infinite
> exists potentially. That hidden mystery in every, the minutest,
> form of existence, which contemplated under the relations of
> time presents itself to the understanding retrospectively, as an
> infinite ascent of Causes, and prospectively as an interminable
> progression of Effects ... this same mystery freed from the
> phenomena of Time and Space, and seen in the depth of real
> Being, reveals itself to the pure Reason as the actual immanence
> of All in Each.

What seems to begin as a demand for a concrete science of the
historical ends up looking something like a theory of myth; the
concern with 'Realities' is sidestepped and replaced with a concern

for the historical structure of metaphor, an interesting field
undoubtedly, but hardly adequate for the purposes Coleridge claims
to have in mind. The dissatisfaction with empiricist and rationalist
accounts of the world is present and genuine, but it turns back upon
itself and leaves Coleridge worrying away at concepts of tradition,
rather than seeing through the pretensions of idealism.

At this point it is worth saying a little more about the structure
of his idealism; for, compared with views which go under the same
banner, Coleridge's opinions may seem to acknowledge the importance
of establishing the historical roots of forms of consciousness.
Theoretically, Coleridge at least believes that these forms of
consciousness have precise and locatable origins in human life, as
he says in introducing his 'Philosophical Lectures' (1818), where
he announces his intention to consider philosophy: (27)

> historically, as an essential part of the history of man, and
> as if it were the striving of a single mind, under very different
> circumstances indeed, and at different periods of its own growth
> and developement; but so that each change and every new direction
> should have its cause and its explanation in the errors,
> insufficiency, or prematurity of the preceding, while all by
> reference to a common object is reduced to harmony of impression
> and total result.

And, indeed, this general tendency permits Coleridge some very
specific insights into the relations between ideology and the real,
on occasions even some quite startling ones:

> When Euclid or Pythagoras promised his pupils or followers to
> teach them to construct the circle and to deduce its astonishing
> properties independently of all outward experience, he neither
> denied nor meant to deny that the very words in which he expressed
> his promise might have conveyed neither meaning nor inducement
> but for the empirical necessities, discoveries and technical
> inventions occasioned by the overflowing of the Nile (Snyder,
> p.134).

This is the kind of tortuous and suggestive formulation which
reassures the reader of the scope and originality of Coleridge's
mind; the reactionary trinitarian theologian was also capable of
tracing 'the origin of Moral Philosophy out of the talkativeness
incident to petty Republics in a cheerful climate', and of describing
the specific form of logic appropriate to a democracy. (28)

But if Coleridge was aware of the importance of historical
formations, he also referred this back at root to the third level
of his system, an immaterial level of 'spirit', of which events
and processes in the material world were, as in orthodox Platonic
theory, mere emanations. The mode of existence which history has
for Coleridge is continually moving from the concrete back into the
abstract, from history as a science to 'History' with a capital
letter, a portentous teleological concept which only impedes actual
study. Thus overall we would be right in discerning in Coleridge's
writing a repeated process whereby the concrete turns back into the
abstract, a process which is in itself essentially reactionary.

Coleridge's yearning for a historical past is actually considerably
less intense than that expressed by other romantics (Keats, Carlyle,
Scott), but this is because so crude a formulation of reaction is to
him unnecessary; his intellectual methods are their own reaction,
continually forcing the concrete and the actual back out of sight,
subsuming them beneath the anachronistic concepts which mystify
their origins.

And yet it is also important to note that there are, submerged in
Coleridge's thought like sunken wrecks, facets which demonstrate
resistance to this sequence of conservative naturalizations. One
such is a pervasive concern with the nature of contradiction. The
whole structure of 'Biographia Literaria' (1817) can be seen as
unified – and this is perhaps the only way in which it can be seen
as unified – if one takes its paramount tendency as the transcendence
of contradiction, and, more broadly, of dualism in all its forms.
(29)   Coleridge is fascinated by 'the universal Law of Polarity
or essential Dualism, first promulgated by Heraclitus, 2000 years
afterwards republished, and made the foundation both of Logic, of
Physics, and of Metaphysics by Giordano Bruno'; (30)   indeed, his
attitude towards dualistic philosophy is very much one of 'dreadful
pleasure'. (31)   On the one hand, he senses a vampiristic quality
in philosophies which attempt to separate the subject from the
object, as though he is aware that in doing so they suck the living
blood from the connecting 'copula'; on the other, he is fatally
attracted to speculation on divisiveness, even when this feels
psychologically harmful: 'Has every finite being the temptation
to become intensely and wholly conscious of its distinctness and,
as a result, to be betrayed into the wretchedness of division?'
('Anima Poetae', p.184). It would seem from his strongly imaged
distinction in 'Biographia' between the transcendent and the
transcendental (32) that he ought to be all too well aware of the
different possible versions of the political significance of dualism,
but his speculations seem always to circle around such a distinction,
rather than clinching it.

Perhaps the strongest resistance to false consciousness in
Coleridge resides in his grapplings with psychology. 'What a swarm
of Thoughts & Feelings, endlessly minute fragments & as it were
representations of all preceding & embryos of all future Thought
lie compact in any one moment', (33) he remarks in a notebook,
thereby filling out the point made in 'Kubla Khan': and although
it would be an exaggeration to refer to Coleridge as a systematic
psychologist, none the less there are some startling comments to be
found scattered through his work. He notes the importance of 'a
full sharp distinction of Mind from Consciousness – the Consciousness being the narrow Neck of the Bottle', (34) and also draws
attention to the importance of conditioning in respect of 'the
nature and necessary limits of human Consciousness. For the same
impossibility exists as to the first acts and movements of our own
will' ('Inquiring Spirit', p.45), he remarks, emphasizing his strong
sense of the influence of material factors on the conduct of life.

With these concerns personally and intellectually central, it is
hardly surprising that many of his most perceptive comments concern
childhood and adolescence, times which he clearly sees as those
when the neck of the bottle closes in. (35)   There is a recurrent

interest in the concept of the self, and in the stages of the
formation of that concept: (36)

> I know few questions more delicate in Education than this:
> How shall we manage that ordinary but in its indefinite extent
> vicious assurance/if you will tell the truth, I will never be
> angry - I will never punish you - without bribing the mind &
> inserting inward falsehood & Selfishness in order to produce a
> verbal veracity.

The internalization of repression is a social device about which
Coleridge feels very strongly:

> Two things we may learn from little children from 3 to 6 years
> old ...
> The first lesson, that innocent Childhood affords me, is - that
> it is an instinct of my Nature to pass out of myself, and to
> exist in the form of others.
> The second is - not to suffer any one form to pass into me and
> to become a usurping Self in the disguise of what the German
> pathologists call a fixed Idea ('Inquiring Spirit', p.68).

This is essentially a brief account of the genesis of obsession,
and its relations with the romantic concept of negative capability,
which Keats after all may have found in Coleridge, are complex.
(37) Negative capability, we may say, is a pathological form of
sociability, the form into which the social is displaced under
conditions which emphasize the isolated and the lonely. Absence
of real communication, evidenced in the solitude of the poet, is
sublimated into an internal discourse, which may well be between
different parts of the fragmented mind. 'Poetry', Coleridge says,
in a strikingly disorganized note, is 'a rationalized dream dealing
to manifold Forms our own Feelings, that never perhaps were attached
by us consciously to our own personal Selves'. (38) Not consciously,
perhaps, but Coleridge has no doubts about the reality of that
which is less than conscious, or about the real identities which
socialization puts asunder: (39)

> remark the seeming identity of body and mind in infants, and
> thence the loveliness of the former; the commencing separation
> in boyhood, and the struggle of equilibrium in youth: thence
> onward the body is first simply indifferent; then demanding the
> translucency of the mind not to be worse than indifferent; and
> finally all that presents the body as body becoming almost of
> an excremental nature.

What he cannot do, of course, is to connect this vision of anal
decay with specific features of bourgeois society, and the same is
true of his perception of alienation. 'Power without Strength' is,
in various different words, a persistent Coleridgean formulation:
(40) if it is, on the one hand, an attempt at description of dream
experience, it is also clearly a reflection of the powerlessness
of the intelligentsia at the beginning of the nineteenth century.
But Coleridge's perceptions of psychological damage are constantly

deflected: instead of serving as guidelines to identify specific
social ills, they serve as the bases for a set of fearful speculations about the internal strife of the mind, some of which are
highly reminiscent terminologically of Blake: (41)

> in its utmost abstraction and consequent state of reprobation,
> the Will becomes satanic pride and rebellious self-idolatry in
> the relations of the spirit to itself, and remorseless despotism
> relatively to others; the more hopeless as the more obdurate by
> its subjugation of sensual impulses, by its superiority to toil
> and pain and pleasure; in short, by the fearful resolve to find
> in itself alone the one absolute motive of action, under which
> all other motives from within and from without must be either
> subordinated or crushed.

As a description of a pseudo-permanent condition of the psyche,
this sounds unhelpful; as an account of specific features of class-
divided society and its attitude to love and work, it makes a great
deal of sense, although of course once that has been grasped it is
perfectly possible to make the further transition into a socio-
logically informed psychology, and to see obsession in its social
context, the deformed mechanisms of the will as outcroppings of
the economic deformity of acquisitive individualism.

Where Coleridge does choose to see psychology and social life
in the same lens, he is generally content to let them lie
suggestively side by side and to avoid, puritanically, actually
describing their relationship. There is a curious passage from the
fragmentary 'Opus Maximum' (c. 1815-28) which summarizes this
tendency by actually omitting the verb which alone could give us
the secret of organization: 'Among the consequences of the overbalance of the commercial spirit', he writes, 'the long eclipse of
philosophy, the transfer of that name to physical and psychological
empyricism [sic]' (Snyder, p.121). The connection seems entirely
reasonable; but are these intellectual phenomena the consequence of
the 'overbalance of the commercial spirit', or are they, along
with the economic factors, the origin of a phenomenon yet to be
named? Yet as evidence for Coleridge's percipience we would want
to lay alongside this displaced comment one of his analyses of
what he diagnosed as a contemporary lack of 'principle'. This
results, he claims, from:

> the pressure of our ranks on each other up the whole ascent of
> the social ladder ... the extent and systematic movements of
> trade and the interdependence of every species of property (and
> in this age what is not property? - all things and all powers,
> nay the very passions, prejudices, and vices of mankind are
> modes of property or the raw material out of which it is
> formed; nay the man values himself chiefly as a part in the
> machine), and lastly the evidentness of the fact that in such
> a state of things every deviation from outward integrity must
> find its speedy if not immediate punishment from its mere
> commercial effect as obstruction and irregularity, so that ere
> the profit have been received the heavier loss is nigh at hand
> (Snyder, p.130).

In passages of this kind, we sense the thrust *against* residing in personal guilt, the insistence that the very cycle of offence and punishment which is so basic to the poetry, from 'The Ancient Mariner' outwards, is itself referrable to the pseudo-science of 'calculation', which is in turn consequent on the hypostasization of the profit motive.

Coleridge's idealism cannot be avoided; nor can we even call it an open idealism which, like Hegel's, leaves many questions about primacy and determination carefully unanswered. What we can say, however, is that it was a capacious idealism, because Coleridge the thinker needed a lot of room in which to move around. The insistence on an unspecifiable 'system' is, of course, the reverse side of intellectual disorder; and this same disorder, itself the result of trying to operate as Renaissance all-purpose thinker in an age of divided intellectual and material labour, means that Coleridge is engaged on a constant search for agency. In broad terms, this search is not a particularly interesting one, since the only solutions he nominally adopts for any length of time are super-natural ones; but this assessment of broad trends in his philosophical development does not really account for the moment-by-moment experience of reading his work, during which one becomes aware that there were many more possibilities than that in his mind, however fleetingly. The lesson of 'The Ancient Mariner', surely, is that the mere killing of an albatross is not enough to provoke this frightful vengeance: in more immediate terms, Coleridge seems to have been often aware that his personal troubles were not adequate as originators of the vengeance he found visited upon himself: but if not, then what?

Coleridge's literary and intellectual career may most usefully be seen, not in terms of a set of biographical changes, but as a series of articulations of a continuing central structure. The drive towards action - whether this be practical, political action; the action of forming a closed writing; or the action of working concretely on intellectual problems and contradictions - is continually bent back upon itself. Nothing can proceed without a prior investigation of the grounds for proceeding; yet, to change the metaphor, the wounds which Coleridge believes he discovers in his exposed psyche are so painful that they are rarely susceptible of generalization into symptoms of a wider social condition. Under these circumstances, powerfully evasive abstractions - 'system' - 'life' - 'interdependence' - act in the texts to shield concrete analysis, and we are thus presented with a structure in which the fountain moment by moment bursts forth, only to have the full weight of German idealism and/or trinitarian Christian orthodoxy dumped on top of it; and then again, perhaps that is close to a paradigm of the romantic predicament and strategy. What in the end remains most distinctive about Coleridge is less the plight than the accompanying self-awareness present throughout the vast bulk of work, and expressed as well as anywhere in his letter to Collins in December, 1818: (42)

Poetry is out of the question. The attempt would only hurry me into that sphere of acute feelings, from which abstruse research, the mother of self-oblivion, presents an asylum.

Chapter 6

Social Relations of Gothic Fiction

David Punter

The phenomenon of Gothic fiction is of considerable cultural importance. It is not often that a literature of terror attains the popularity which this fiction attained, and it is remarkable that such a literature should be able, as Gothic has been, to dominate a culture's imagery of fear for a century and a half after its ostensible supersession. Ostensible, because the Gothic has in fact lived on: through the nineteenth century in the works of Dickens, Poe, Sheridan LeFanu and Bram Stoker, and into the twentieth in the short stories and novels of, for instance, Wells, Conan Doyle and Peake, and, above all, in the horror film. A thorough interrogation of Gothic would need to take account of its history and of its survival, and this is a massive topic: (1) what I intend to do here is rather to examine a group of key texts written between 1764 and 1797 and to discuss the social relations visible within them. I do not mean to demonstrate social themes or ideas: the notion that Gothic is a form of escapism has long since been exploded. (2) My concern is not with content but with literary and social role: we know now that Gothic is not unconcerned with society, but to understand its meaning and purpose we have to move beyond the conventional categories, according to which Gothic simply provides comment on religious practices, sexual manners, social hypocrisy. We need rather to take seriously the fact that Gothic is a distinctive fictional mode, (3) quite different from realistic or naturalistic modes; although the characteristics of this mode are, of course, largely determined by the social problems with which Gothic tries to deal, and may indeed be defined as a series of strategies for dealing with tabooed material. Of necessity these strategies are partly revelatory and partly evasive, and they are also deeply fissured by class and social relations. But the strategies cannot be isolated purely within the texts: in so far as the texts are sustained acts of communication, they need to be looked at as parts of a web of social relations, in which author, narrator, characters and reader all play a part. Furthermore, Gothic is deeply concerned with fantasy, and this also plays an important role within this web of relations: that is to say, it has always been known that Gothic attends to a set of problems concerning relations between bourgeoisie and aristocracy, but what

also needs to be grasped is that the portrayal of this relation
which Gothic offers is a fantasy one, and that the roles which the
writers enjoin us to adopt may bear a relation to social reality
which is at best tangential. (4) I shall begin with some prefatory
remarks on 'The Castle of Otranto' (1764), and then move on to
consider 'The Mysteries of Udolpho' (1794), 'The Monk' (1795) and
'The Italian' (1797).

'The Castle of Otranto' seems at first glance to belie its Gothic
attribution by being, not a dark or heavy text, but light, airy, a
fairy-tale rather than a nightmare even when it ostensibly strives
for the horrific. It was a significant manifestation of the late
eighteenth-century revival of romance, that is, of the older
traditions of prose literature which had been supplanted by the rise
of the bourgeois novel. Walpole himself spoke of his book as an
attempt to combine both modes, (5) and if we describe this as an
attempt to reconcile characteristics of feudal and bourgeois
literature we are merely discerning the discriminations operant in
Walpole's mind without committing ourselves to the correctness of
the implied literary-historical view. But Walpole's claim to 'blend
the two kinds of romance, the ancient and the modern' ('Otranto',
p.7), remained practically unrealized, in that it was the anti-
realist tendency in the text which stood out at the time and which
still stands out now. The story is set in the twelfth century, in
and around a castle clearly modelled on Walpole's own Strawberry
Hill, and the plot is a joyous compilation of absurdities including
many traditional romance ingredients: a tyrannical baron and his
machinations, complicated revelations about paternity, and most
important a panoply of supernatural portents and appearances. It
was vastly popular; from the outset, Walpole deliberately, and in
a way reminiscent on the surface of popular cultural modes like
pantomime, sets out to flout realist conventions, in his insistence
on the supernatural, in his depiction of physical settings, in the
casual slightness of his character portrayal. Like a child
appealing to indulgent grandparents to shore up a minor domestic
revolt, Walpole appeals to the example of Shakespeare in precisely
the area which the Augustans had condemned, that is, in his mixing
of kinds and genres, and provocatively uses and exaggerates devices
of which the Augustans could not have approved, notably the
interspersal of scenes of 'high life' and 'low life' and the
presentation of buffoon and servant figures in the same continuum
as their betters and masters.

Walpole's affinities with pre-eighteenth-century writers hinge
not on any wish on his part to write like them but on his need to
use their example to give himself licence forbidden by realism.
Contentual and formal taboos merge. But there is in the text a
distinct problem of tone caused by the mixing of harmlessness and
transgression, a problem the illustration of which unfortunately
requires a lengthy quotation. Manfred, tired of his wife, attempts
to seduce his daughter-in-law. He apprises her of his intentions,
whereupon she shrieks and runs:

    Manfred rose to pursue her; when the moon, which was now up,
    and gleamed in at the opposite casement, presented to his sight
    the plumes of the fatal helmet, which rose to the height of the

windows, waving backwards and forwards in a tempestuous manner,
and accompanied with a hollow and rustling sound. Isabella, who
gathered courage from her situation, and who dreaded nothing so
much as Manfred's pursuit of his declaration, cried, Look, my
lord! see heaven itself declares against your impious intentions! -
Heaven nor hell shall impede my designs, said Manfred, advancing
again to seize the princess. At that instant the portrait of his
grandfather, which hung over the bench where they had been sitting,
uttered a deep sigh and heaved its breast.... Manfred, distracted
between the flight of Isabella, who had now reached the stairs,
and his inability to keep his eyes from the picture, which began
to move, had however advanced some steps after her, still looking
backwards on the portrait, when he saw it quit its pannel, and
descend on the floor with a grave and melancholy air. Do I
dream? cried Manfred returning, or are the devils themselves in
league against me? Speak, infernal spectre! Or, if thou art
my grandsire, why dost thou too conspire against thy wretched
descendant, who too dearly pays for - Ere he could finish the
sentence the vision sighed again, and made a sign for Manfred
to follow him. Lead on! cried Manfred; I will follow thee to
the gulph of perdition. The spectre marched sedately, but
dejected, to the end of the gallery, and turned into a chamber
on the right hand. Manfred accompanied him at a little distance,
full of anxiety and horror, but resolved. As he would have
entered the chamber, the door was clapped-to with violence by
an invisible hand. The prince, collecting courage from this
delay, would have forcibly burst open the door with his foot,
but found that it resisted his utmost efforts. Since hell will
not satisfy my curiosity, said Manfred, I will use the human
means in my power for preserving my race; Isabella shall not
escape me   ('Otranto', pp.23-4).

Clearly this passage operates in terms of irony, and this irony is
revelatory of the audience determinants according to which Walpole
is siting his text. The use of the supernatural is not, we become
aware, intended to terrify but to interest and amuse by its self-
conscious quaintness; similarly, the contrast between sudden action
and long-winded, elegant phraseology is an irony not only, or
principally, in terms of character, but in terms of form, designed
to suggest to a middle-class audience the absurdity of a certain
kind of formal discourse. Manfred's behaviour reminds us of
Hamlet's only in order that we may smile at its comparative
inadequacy and, indeed, at the insignificance and small gestural
repertoire of the ghost. The descents into the matter-of-fact and
the prosaic have the paradoxical effect of calling into question
the overall texture of the narrative, and enjoin us to look upon
it as a virtuoso performance in novelty and the exotic rather than
as an attempt at character creation.
   And the same is true of the historical content of 'Otranto'.
Walpole is comparatively unconcerned with the details of life in
the Middle Ages; what he is concerned with is conjuring a general
sense of 'past-ness' by the occasional insertion of costume detail
or its equivalents. And yet, in another sense, 'Otranto' is serious
about history, for whatever its shortcomings and infelicities, it

does give evidence of an eighteenth-century view of feudalism and the aristocracy, and in doing so originates what was to become one of the most prevalent themes in Gothic fiction, the visiting of the sins of the fathers on their children. When this is placed in a contemporaneous setting, it is a simple theme; but it becomes altogether more complex when the very location of crime and social disorder is thrust back into the past. The figure of Manfred, laden with primal crime, is larger than 'Otranto' itself: his violence, his bullying, his impatience with convention and sensibility mark him out partly as feudal baron, but also partly as irrepressible villain who merely mocks at socialization, who remains unassimilable.

What is interesting is the conjunction in Manfred, as in many other Gothic villains, of the baron and the figure of antisocial power. The widespread appearance of these figures in the closing years of the eighteenth century signifies historical anxiety: threat to convention was seen as coming from the past, out of the memory of previous social and psychological orders. In other words, it was embodied in images of the atrophying aristocracy; and if one thing can be said of all the different kinds of fiction which were popular in the later eighteenth century, it is that they all played upon the remarkably clear urge of the middle class to read about aristocrats. 'Otranto's' strength and resonance derive largely from the fact that in it Walpole evolved a primitive symbolic structure in which to represent uncertainties about the past: its attitude to feudal domination is a blend of admiration, fear and curiosity.

Realistic depiction of everyday life and a rational approach to nature were indissolubly linked in the novels of the mid-eighteenth century; (6) Walpole originates a genre in which the attractions of the past and of the supernatural become similarly connected, and in which the supernatural becomes a symbol of our past rising against us, whether it be the psychological past - the realm of those primitive desires repressed by the demands of a closely organized society - or the historical past, the realm of a social order characterized by absolute power and servitude. But we are again sliding back towards a criticism centred on content, whereas it is the form of 'Otranto' which is important for our purposes. The early Gothic novels are usually regarded as having close affinities with the emergent historical novel, and this proximity may be theorized thus: Gothic was in itself a mode of history, a way of articulating an obscure and shadowy past and interpreting it. During the 1770s and 1780s several different kinds of fiction were arising to challenge the realist tradition; but what they all had in common was a drive to come to terms with the barbaric, with those realms which had been excluded from the Augustan synthesis, and the primary focus of that drive was the past itself. Walpole treats this problem by producing a narrator as small child, demonstrating new toys to other children: as readers we are enjoined to *play*, even though we know, and from time to time suspect that the narrator knows, that these specific toys may be dangerous. Walpole produces on stage - and the metaphor is deliberate - the materials which the later Gothic novelists proceed to negotiate, but the text itself can also be considered as a defensive strategy, whereby irony shields us from the full impact of its materials.

Thus there is present a significant contradiction: like a child
using adult-sized furniture as the props of a private, miniaturized
world, Walpole simultaneously naturalizes and distantiates his
subject matter (anxieties about the past, images of the aristocracy,
sexual transgressions). This is most clearly evidenced in the
gigantism of his motifs. The model of society offered is one in
which the audience can lead a charmed life, playing unmolested amid
the threatening symbols of change in the social order.

'Otranto', however, was a fairly isolated text: it was later, in
the mid-1790s, that the Gothic novel reached its major peak in terms
of quantity and popularity. (7) These were chaotic years in which
domestic unrest, counter-revolution and fears of invasion from
abroad shaped political and cultural life, and the literary market
turned very largely on fiction which rejected direct engagement
with the practices of contemporary society in favour of historically
and geographically remote settings and actions; but these two facts
need to be positively connected. Within the Gothic which succeeds
Walpole we find an intense if displaced engagement with political
and social problems, the difficulty of negotiating these problems
being precisely reflected in Gothic's stylistic conventions. The
interrogation of these problems takes place within an identifiable
and changing constellation of social roles, involving author,
narrator, characters and reader, and it is these roles which we
need to probe in the major Gothic works. Radcliffe and Lewis
attempted more complex historical tasks than had Walpole: whereas
he was on the whole content to display the oddness of the past,
the writers of the 1790s are concerned with connections between
past and present: with, on the one hand, what the violence and
crudity of past economic and social relations can reveal about
those relations in the present, and with, on the other hand, the
possibility that present 'civilization' can tell us something about
the barbarity of the past, and especially about the extent to which
it might be still inside us. Before looking in more detail,
however, at how Radcliffe and Lewis deal with these issues, it may
be as well to make some simpler descriptive points about the texts.

'The Mysteries of Udolpho' is by far the longest of the three
novels with which we are concerned, and it relates the simplest
narrative, fundamentally a single story structured around the
experience of a single character. Emily St Aubert is imprisoned in
a decaying castle during the central and most memorable part of the
book, and it is a mark of Radcliffe's skill that the many and
terrifying dangers which threaten her while at Udolpho are never
clear. At one moment, it seems to be forced marriage, at another
rape, at another the theft of her remaining estates, at another
supernatural terrors, but none of these come to pass. Eventually,
after many nights of horror and after her aunt has been done to death
she escapes to the chateau of Le Blanc, which proves to have sinister
connections with her own family and an assembly of ghosts of its own.
These, however, are duly exposed, as were the phantoms of Udolpho,
and Emily rediscovers her 'true love' Valancourt; he repents of the
moral decline which has overtaken him since their parting, and the
lovers are married.

Despite Coleridge's very high opinion of 'Udolpho' and its
suspense techniques, (8) there are certain problems in the narrative.

The incidents at Le Blanc are pallid beside the richly coloured and
terrifying Udolpho scenes, and Radcliffe fails in her apparent
design of using them to show how Emily has recovered from the over-
credulity which has caused her such misery earlier. The removal of
the villainous Montoni from the action and his subsequent death
leave a regrettable space which is never filled; and the attempt to
introduce the Villefort family as a further centre of narrative
interest is too cursory to succeed. But the technical strengths of
'Udolpho' lie less in narrative than in other areas: character
psychology, symbolic intensification, and an extraordinary use of
suspense and doubt which constantly blurs the boundaries of reality
and fantasy. In terms of character, not only is Montoni an
excellent and sometimes subtle version of the attractively cruel
villain, but Emily herself, although she emerges as a highly
conventional eighteenth-century heroine, is given to us clearly
and in enormous, moment-by-moment detail. Her fearful plight is
continually referred back to the other stories and legends of
cruelty and murder which lurk, half-told and threatening, in the
background: the mysterious disappearance of the former owner of
Udolpho, the murder of the Marchioness de Villeroi, the fate of
Madame Cheron, are interesting not in themselves, but for the
terrifying parallels they offer of the various dooms which Emily
barely avoids. This kind of symbolism reaches a high point in the
scene at Le Blanc where the servant, Ludovico, locked for a night
in a haunted room, reads a ghost story which eventually shades
into reality; the celebrated fact that Radcliffe in the end explains
all her apparently supernatural machinery in no way removes the
power which her ghosts have over Emily or over the reader.
   There is a significant point, halfway through the second book,
when Emily is on the eve of being married to the undesirable
Morano: alone, friendless, fearful of the malignity of Montoni,
'her mind, long harassed by distress, now yielded to imaginary
terrors; she trembled to look into the obscurity of her spacious
chamber, and feared she knew not what'. (9) It is possible to read
the whole of the rest of the work as the nightmare which follows
that eve of terror, as the poetic and symbolic correlative of the
state of Emily's overwrought imagination; and no explanation can
destroy the potency of dreams. The inhabitants of Udolpho may be
ghosts, bandits or devils: to Emily they are the incarnation of
evil, and their reality can only be read through the medium offered
by her dislocated mind.
   'The Monk' is two stories in one, and although there seems
little narrative connection between them, their co-presence allows
Lewis scope for the dramatic alternations which give the book a
pace and energy quite foreign to the langorous, opiated mood of
Radcliffe. The major story concerns the monk Ambrosio, a paragon
of virtue and famous throughout Madrid for his powerful, 'sublime'
sermons. His closest associate in the abbey, a young and virtuous
novice, reveals himself to be a woman, Matilda by name, and proceeds
to seduce him, a deed which releases Ambrosio's pent-up passions
and sets him on a course of violence and self-destruction. Unlike
Radcliffe, Lewis makes no excuses for the supernatural. Interwoven
among the main stories are elements of many of the fearsome legends
most dear to the romantics: the Wandering Jew, Faustus, the Water-

King, the pact with the devil. There are also lesser-known legends,
like that of the Bleeding Nun, which Lewis found in the German
writers and happily wove into his fabric. But although these are
materials which Radcliffe would have found sensationalist and
implausible, they contribute in 'The Monk' to a textual density not
unlike that of 'Udolpho': the sufferings of the heroines are
situated against a background of legend which both substantiates and
intensifies their plight. Lewis, in fact, manages to take materials
far more arcane and improbable than Radcliffe's and, by the terse
naturalism of his style, to make them seem oppressively solid.
We are not really required to believe in the supernatural by Lewis -
this is assumed: rather, we are required to see it before us, lurid
and gory as a stage ghost.

Although Lewis's methods are sometimes crude, 'The Monk' is a
very self-conscious book, much more so than 'Udolpho', and delights
in complicating the narratively simple. The reader is made to move
through a series of stories, and stories within stories: we
experience Raymond's history as told by himself to his friend
Lorenzo, and within it is a further tale of banditry. Also within
Raymond's narration, Agnes relates the tale of the Bleeding Nun,
'in a tone of burlesqued gravity'. (10) But a little later, the
story of the Bleeding Nun is told again, all too seriously, by the
Wandering Jew, who has come to exorcise her; and the Nun herself
gives a brief account of her plight, which is basically the same
as the Provençal Tale in 'Udolpho'. Agnes eventually gets round
to completing her own history; and, as if Lewis were precociously
determined to show us how conscious his methods were, the servant
Theodore is made to spend a couple of happy hours frightening the
nuns of the convent with ridiculous tales and songs. In 'Udolpho',
the boundaries of reality and fantasy were blurred and softened:
Lewis, taking the anti-realist process a step further, begins the
essentially Gothic construction of a world of mutually self-
validating fictions which are texturally more 'real' than reality
itself.

Seen in these terms, 'The Italian' is a cogent response to the
decadence which Lewis's procedure suggests; it is at least partly a
kind of de-parodization of 'The Monk', especially, for instance, in
the opening scene in the church of San Lorenzo. It is a far more
complex book than either of the others, for Radcliffe has become,
rather unexpectedly and perhaps partly because of further reading
in French and German (d'Arnaud, Schiller, Naubert, Grosse), able to
handle sophisticated alternations, not only between scenes but,
more significantly, between different characters as centres of
interest and feeling; but it is also far more insistent in its
bending of a typically Gothic multiplicity of tales and half-
remembered details towards a complex central plot. The central
pair of lovers, Ellena and Vivaldi, are no more interesting in
themselves than were Emily and Valancourt, but Radcliffe seems to
realize this, and instead of describing them exhaustively gives
most of her attention to her villains, Schedoni and the Marchesa;
the conversations between them are masterpieces of mutual guilt and
hypocrisy, cast in veiled utterance and half-confidences. The
investigation of their psychology is thorough and convincing, largely
because we are in no doubt about their overall purposes and motives,

which, although changeable, are always clear and brutal. The scenes
in the Inquisition, partly derived from Lewis but described largely
in terms of dialogue, are almost impressionistic in their manner:
mysterious voices in the gloom, flitting figures and unknown
instruments of torture create a picture of fear which reduces
Udolpho to a toy castle. Radcliffe responds to the blatancy of
Lewis and the earlier Gothic writers with a virtuoso demonstration
of the imaginative power of the half-seen and half-explained, as if
to show that there are kinds of vividness which depend less on
concrete authorial depiction than on releasing the springs of the
reader's fantasy.

Again, 'The Italian' is a work which, like many other Gothic
works, plays with story. Like 'Otranto' it is 'framed', as a book
read by later English visitors to Naples, the scene of most of the
action; and the revelations at the end rely on the piecing together
of further stories, each of which contains a different aspect of
the essential information. Radcliffe even throws in tales which
turn out to be totally irrelevant, including one about a Baróne di
Cambrusca, whom we are supposed to conceive as an earlier incarnation of Schedoni but who turns out not to be. The high point of
Radcliffe's manipulative technique comes in the third book, when
Schedoni encounters a peasant who may or may not know facts about
the past which the monk wants concealed: on the one hand, he needs
to know the peasant's story, in case it threatens him with exposure,
while on the other he does not want the peasant to think he is
interested. The story is thus thwarted at every turn by Schedoni's
interruptions and anticipations, but the peasant struggles through,
adhering to his determination to tell what he knows clearly and in
the right order, while Schedoni continually tries to claim that it
is all nonsense, even saying towards the end that 'the narrative
resembles a delirious dream, more than a reality', (11) which opens
up a whole range of speculations about Radcliffe's opinions of her
own art. The episode is a masterly parody of the twists and turns
of Gothic fiction itself.

The social themes with which Radcliffe and Lewis were both
concerned can be simply listed. They were concerned with the
problems of sensibility and its tendency to unfit the individual
for life in the real social world. They were concerned with the
superstitious end of religion; or, perhaps more accurately, with
religion considered under the category of superstition. They were
concerned with the dialectical relations between the distortion of
perception caused by excessive sensibility and the further
distortion occasioned by actual social isolation - an isolation
attributed to the upper classes, but imaged as isolation in prisons,
convents and so forth. They were concerned with the contradiction
and strain produced in individuals by sexual hypocrisy and its
elevation into a code of conduct, the fictional world to which
these perceptions refer being, of course, primarily the world of
Richardson, characterized by Watt as 'a universe where the calm
surface of repressive convention and ingrown hypocrisy is
momentarily - but only momentarily - threatened by the irruption
of the secret violences which it provokes but conceals' (Watt,
'The Rise of the Novel', p.211): this moment of disruption is
considerably prolonged by Radcliffe and Lewis, and is further

emphasized by their characters' inefficient handling of the
conventions themselves. And hindered on the one hand by the
complexities of hypocrisy and on the other by the paradoxically
superior intellectual powers of stony-hearted villains, Radcliffe's
and Lewis's variously persecuted heroines are martyrs also to the
repressed parts of their own psyches.

It is by reference to these features of the novels that their
symbolic structure needs to be assessed, for this structure hinges
on a particular set of relations between psychological tendencies
and the social conditions which encourage these tendencies. Radcliffe
and Lewis clearly share anxieties about social institutions, in
particular the family and the Church. But these anxieties are only
really about the extent to which these institutions confirm the
'deeper' problems of hypocrisy, lack of communication and the
bondage of convention. In the case of the family, for instance,
the tragic situations through which Ellena and Vivaldi pass in
'The Italian' can be seen as the direct result of the aristocratic
pride of the Marchese and his wife; but in fact, the Marchese becomes
towards the end a figure of fun, and his wife repents movingly on
her deathbed. Similarly, 'The Monk' is obviously antagonistic
towards monastic life, but it is a curious feature of the book that
the part the Inquisition plays is actually beneficent, while
Radcliffe takes up a consistently ambiguous attitude towards
religious institutions, evidenced principally in the parallel but
opposing qualities of San Stefano and Santa della Pieta, one convent
being seen as horrific, the other as a refuge and a place of safety.
In this sense both Radcliffe and Lewis see ideology underlying
institutions rather than produced by them: their diagnosis of social
problems begins with general ideas and individuals' acceptances,
and only then proceeds to the analysis of institutions and social
structures.

Thus far, Radcliffe and Lewis have much in common, but their
stances and tonal problems differ. In 'Udolpho', the principal
tonal problems centre on Emily. The attitude which Radcliffe seems
to want to encourage towards her heroine is a kind of indulgence:
she is perfect in many of her attitudes and feelings, yet she is
too perfect for a profane world, which causes an occasional odd
irascibility in the writing. When, leaving La Vallée, Emily finds
that one of her books has been removed and replaced with Valancourt's
volume of Petrarch, Radcliffe notes that she 'hesitated in believing,
what would have been sufficiently apparent to almost any other
person' ('Udolpho', p.58); her moral perfection is, like her
sensibility, sometimes inappropriate to the social world in which
she is constrained to move; confronted with the harder exigencies
of life, it looks merely silly. Radcliffe wants us, however, to
believe that there is no reason why Emily herself should know that
in order to survive reality she must 'downgrade' her behaviour; but
she expects us, as readers, to know that the middle-class world
will ceaselessly require her, acting as a displaced aristocrat, to
do that. As readers, therefore, we experience both a superiority
and an inferiority to Emily, as we would to a marvellous child;
and our sense of her as a delightful but ingenuous daughter is
reinforced generally by her lack of sexuality and locally by, for
instance, her inability to think of the obvious reason why her

father should have preserved his memento of the Marchioness of
Villeroi. It is perhaps because of these tendencies and attitudes
that the author has come down to us through history as 'Mother
Radcliffe'; (12) and while reading we find that we are constantly
expected to collaborate with her as wise but worldly parents, are
invited to share with her a consoling and pitying tone.

With Montoni, however, the situation is very different, for in
certain important ways Radcliffe fails to present him as a consistent
character. The novel requires that he be depicted, at least
potentially, as evil incarnate, but he constantly becomes assimilated to a less extreme model of the adult male, and even his dubious
behaviour cannot prevent Radcliffe from also showing him as a
protective and stable figure. His wickedness comes over not as a
positive force but as a kind of unfeelingness, laziness or
irresponsibility; he cannot even be bothered to do his own courting
of Madame Cheron, but retains a useful friend to do it for him.
Yet alongside these faults, and despite his ferocious and threatening
demeanour, he retains many qualities intended as admirable –
strength, loyalty, courage – and he is not even a particularly
ruthless criminal; the reader feels that he could surely have
obtained Cheron's estates much more easily if he had really tried,
and in fact it even turns out that he did not commit some of the
nastier crimes – for instance, the murder of Laurentini – with
which the narrative at times appears to charge him.

Radcliffe's protective attitude towards Emily, and her ambiguity
about Montoni, which sometimes verges on covert admiration, fit
together if we suggest that the social model in which 'Udolpho'
enjoins its readers to participate, and by means of which Radcliffe
seeks to naturalize and thus neutralize the threat of the past, is
largely familial. The kind of anxiety felt about Montoni is reduced
to the kind felt about the proverbial 'black sheep': he may betray
his family responsibilities, but at heart he is aware of them, and,
like a rather tame wicked uncle, his fire and splutter are much
more impressive than his actual capacity for violence. It is
important in this context that St Aubert and his wife are removed
so quickly and easily from the scene, because their continuing
presence would interfere with the distribution of palliative,
quasi-parental roles among the readers, and because it is their
place which the readers are required to fill, as a counterbalance
to the perverted family life of the castle itself.

Condemnation of Montoni is limited by the fact that, for better
or worse, he has been given a role in the bourgeois family of the
novel; it is forces and influences outside the family which draw
down Radcliffe's more whole-hearted disapproval. Underlings and
servants are mostly malicious in 'Udolpho', and when they are not,
they are foolish and presumptuous. City life, as in the works of
so many of Radcliffe's contemporaries, is portrayed as wholly
destructive of real, familial virtue: (13) it is from a sojourn in
the city that all Valancourt's moral difficulties stem, and the
whole book is framed within an essentially conservative rural
idyll, centred on the transcendent moral virtue of 'retirement'.
Even the more unpleasant aristocrats, like Count Morano, are
allowed to despise those, like Monsieur Quesnel, whose fortune and
status are connected with the city and with commerce: we thus see

in Radcliffe, transmuted into the stuff of fantasy, the familiar
spectacle of a bourgeois stratum assimilating to itself those
elements which it requires from the class which it has superseded,
while simultaneously refusing to acknowledge the economic base which
has in fact brought it to power. The family of 'Udolpho' itself
stands as a multivalent symbol for these suspect acts of inclusion
and exclusion, the nostalgic emphasis on the family unit as sacred
and inviolable being all too often in direct contradiction with the
themes of claustrophobia and confinement; and this configuration is
reflected in Radcliffe's style, which is based on a very direct
relationship between narrator and reader and on an immediacy of
description which belies the supposed historical dimension of the
novel.

By contrast, the social world of 'The Monk' is a much wider and
more public one. Unlike Radcliffe, Lewis places considerable
emphasis on crowd scenes and on the civic ramifications of disaster
and tragedy: Ambrosio's fate is not merely his own, but simultaneously an aspect of the wider decadence and hypocrisy of a mythical
Madrid. The reader is given no family role to fill, and is thus
forbidden the intimacy with the past which Radcliffe appears to
proffer; rather, he or she is required to occupy the position of
spectator at a dramatic entertainment. Lewis is deeply conscious
of the exposed position in which this puts the writer, (14) but he
is, of course, not really worried by this: the public eminence of
Ambrosio and the importance of his reputation - factors which have
no clear analogues under the rule of the bourgeoisie - should be
seen as analogies of the location of the writer, but only according
to Lewis's own fantasies: clearly he was more concerned with the
pleasures of public idolization than with its dubious moral causes
and effects. There are risks in sensationalism, as there are risks
in the exposed position of the spiritual or actual aristocrat, but
they are risks which Lewis was happy to run for the sake of
admiration.

And in 'The Monk', the reader's admiration is deflected from
the characters, even from the virtuous Antonia, on to Lewis's own
sleight of hand. Many of the lurid qualities and sensational
oppositions in the text are calculated more to show us the range of
the author's abilities than to provide any profound comment on
life: Lewis is his own melodramatic villain. Satan's 'explanation'
of Ambrosio's worst crimes at the end of the book has not the
slightest narrative justification; it is a piece of deliberate
extremism, and the same is true of Lewis's juggling with Matilda's
human-ness or otherwise. Lewis tries constantly to challenge his
audience, to upset its security, to give the reader a moment of
doubt about whether he may not himself be guilty of the complicated
faults attributed to Ambrosio. Where Radcliffe brings her
aristocrats to the fireside and domesticates them, Lewis tries to
take us out into the wilderness where they now prowl, donning for
the purpose his own lordly disguise.

It is consistent with Lewis's designs on his audience that
nothing in 'The Monk' is what it seems, for any state can equally
easily be considered as the repression of its opposite. The more
attractive and suitable a man or woman may seem as a sexual partner,
the more 'dangerous' he or she is; the sexual roles of Ambrosio

and Matilda even become reversed as Matilda gains more and more
ascendancy over the monk and threatens to change back into the man
she had once pretended to be. The motif of this process is, of
course, the double appearance of the demon at different points in
the book: in his transformation from beauty to savagery is
summarized the disturbing trickery Lewis cheerfully practises on
his audience.

Lewis is too egocentric a narrator to want our participation;
he wants his reader to be impressionable, admiring, spectatorial,
and open to sudden doubt about whether the author's paradoxes do
not in fact undermine his own moral pretensions and show him
unwholesome and repressed aspects of his own psyche. Where
Radcliffe welcomes us into a slightly odd middle-class family,
Lewis exposes us to his vision of the barbarities of feudal social
life, a world dependent on force and violence rather than collaboration, and sneers at our repressions. Lewis survives as credible
narrator through sheer bravado; at all points, he tries to be more
cynical than his audience, and to dominate it by means of this
cynicism. The reader can cope easily when the author says - and
shows - that 'nobody dies of mere grief' ('Monk', p.243), and
that 'men have died, and worms have ate them, but not for love!'
('Monk', p.314); (15) it is harder to cope with the remarkable
viciousness of that part of the denouement in which the unfortunate
Antonia gets not only murdered but also replaced in her erstwhile
lover's affections, at the wave of a magic wand, by a girl who has
hardly taken any previous part in the story. It is not merely the
content of 'The Monk' which makes it a disturbing book, and which
has caused it to be censored almost continuously since the time it
was written; it is also the unnerving mixture of inadequacy and
revulsion in the reader which Lewis deliberately sets out to
produce, and the sense the reader gets that he is himself the main
object of Lewis's animosity, the vassal who is totally in the power
of the narrator as lord.

In some ways, the world of 'The Italian' is as familial,
parochial and conservative as that of 'Udolpho': looking for a
way of describing the real joy which comes to the protagonists at
the end, Radcliffe can find no better way than by conjuring an
'English' ambience ('Italian', p.412), and so strong is her sense
of natural justice that even the dreaded Inquisition is portrayed
as essentially virtuous in its workings. But there are significant
differences between 'Udolpho' and 'The Italian', some of which
relate to Lewis's technique and stance, and all of which combine
to render the later text considerably less reassuring than the
earlier, and to suggest that Radcliffe did not find the apparent
accommodation of bourgeois and aristocratic values which
characterized 'Udolpho' entirely easy.

Schedoni is covertly admired, as was Montoni, and is granted a
kind of harsh approbation: like the earlier villain, he has
extraordinary strength, and a natural and aristocratic superiority
to lesser criminals. But he has a dimension of introspection
which Montoni entirely lacked, and indeed the whole book shows a
much greater psychological sophistication than did 'Udolpho'.
The debt to Lewis's less familial, more individualistic stance
shows itself particularly in obsessional matters; the nightmares,

for instance, which the minor villain Spalatro suffers and which
cause him to shudder before the undertaking of new crimes are
reminiscent of the frenzied vacillations of Ambrosio, and the
convent death cell to which Ellena is nearly confined is a close
reproduction of Agnes's crypt in 'The Monk'. The evil Marchesa
too seems to display much of the perverse strength of Matilda, and
to rest rather uneasily within the conventional sexual boundaries
which otherwise characterize Radcliffe's world.

But the most important development in 'The Italian' lies in
Radcliffe's movement away from the familial model. Much more than
either 'Udolpho' or 'The Monk', 'The Italian' is a book about
conspiracy, and about the complex social relations between
conspirators, and this becomes the dominant image of society
available in the text. It is in this context that Schedoni and the
Marchesa come most startlingly alive. There was an anticipation of
this in 'Udolpho'; often, when Emily thought Montoni was engaged on
some horrible crime or other, Radcliffe tells us that in fact he has
been occupied in political discussion with his cohorts. In fact,
the picture one gets of the castle of Udolpho is very much of the
ladies 'retired' in their rooms upstairs while Montoni and the
other men discuss the affairs of the world over port and cigars.
It is true that they are actually concerned with practical and
violent interventions in the affairs of their country; but except
for this factor, which Radcliffe is unable or unwilling to describe
in any detail, this is obviously a grotesquely exaggerated but
thoroughly recognizable picture of eighteenth-century bourgeois
domestic life. In 'The Italian' the conversations between Schedoni
and the Marchesa, the Inquisition scene, the final battle of wills
between Schedoni and Nicola, are all grotesque extensions of a
discourse of power which is simultaneously a discourse of masculinity,
and the world of 'The Italian' is built partly on a stronger pressure
on Radcliffe's part to deal with her fear of, and alienation from,
this discourse and the corresponding powerlessness which such
alienation entails. (16)

The 'women's world' which Radcliffe and many other female
novelists of the time depict may be said to be 'dependent on an
obscure male world of action and business, which its occupants can
seldom envisage, but of which they feel the reverberations'
(Tompkins, 'The Popular Novel in England, 1770-1800', p.128).
Tompkins goes on to analyse the general consequences of this
perception in the fiction of the 1790s, pointing out that one
frightening and repeated aspect is that while the 'henpecked husband'
and the 'presumptuous wooer' are frequently ridiculed, the tyrant
and the seducer are not, 'for to be a victim, as these women saw
it, is to gain rather than lose in dignity' (Tompkins, p.134).
Essentially, the point goes back again to the issue of sexual
hypocrisy. As has been well-known since the work of Christopher
Hill and others, a significant marriage crisis occurred in the
eighteenth century, largely due to problems of inheritance, problems
which figure very largely in novelists from Richardson to Jane
Austen. (17) The crisis appears to have been caused by contradictions between patriarchal and individualistic family structures,
and to have been partly responsible for the worship of concealment
of feeling. Hill suggests that financial and status considerations

contributed to making it a crime against the social code for any woman to admit her real feelings or to confess to passion, and the main purpose of the education of 'ladies of condition' becomes this suppression of feelings and passion. This was clearly one factor in the separateness of male and female discourses, insulated from each other by the different interests of the sexes in relation to the maintenance of the social order. At the end of the century, some of this disparity was forced out into the open, precisely because it was then that women started writing themselves; it was hardly surprising that their main themes were 'pursuit and endurance' (Tompkins, p.138). This is not to say, of course, that one can derive a wholesale analysis of the problems of sexual division from Radcliffe or from any of her contemporaries: but in 'The Italian' the problem is certainly present, and there is a strong connection between the Gothic novel in general and the evolution of perceptions about the subjection of women and the covert social purposes of marriage and marital fidelity.

In 'The Italian', the unitary discourse of 'Udolpho' has degenerated, and much play is made with the potentially delusive power of words in class- and sex-divided situations. The reader is cast as a kind of detective, placed within a closely knit social situation but not fully of it, trying to find truth amid the multiple hypocrisies and deceptions of conspirators. Radcliffe is less socially confident than she had been in 'Udolpho', even though she has greater technical mastery: she often implies limits to her own knowledge, which renders the reader's task all the more difficult. We are required neither to collaborate nor to marvel, but to discover a path through a maze of half-heard and half-understood conversations: in relation to the narrator, we are cast neither as family member nor as serf, but as social observer: and Radcliffe no longer forestalls our interpretations, but suspends judgments and even deliberately withholds important evidence to ensure that the reader's attention can never be relaxed.

The books we have discussed have two obvious features in common, the fact that they were written for middle-class audiences, and the fact that they all deal primarily in images of the aristocracy. We may theorize this into a statement that Gothic was a mode of writing in which middle-class audiences and writers attempt to come to grips with their changing relations to a myth of aristocracy, and simultaneously try to invent myths to justify their own dominance. The kinds of fear in which Gothic deals are, from one aspect, general psychological forces: fear of isolation, claustrophobia, paranoia. But they are consistently presented as connected with a world of feudal class relations in which baron, priest and monk are seen as the principal agents of evil, thus displacing evil from the everyday. Most of the major Gothic works are fables of persecution, in which heroes and heroines with largely middle-class values, not always underwritten by the authors, are haunted and pursued by these agents, but on the whole emerge, presumably to the relief of the reader, untainted by the crude social violence which they represent.

Thus the social significance of Gothic is ambivalent: the texts operate through a blending of threat and relief. In 'Udolpho', the narrator on the whole reassures the audience of its stability

and safety by treating the past as socially unexceptional. In
'The Monk' and 'The Italian', the narrative voice is more threatening,
and 'The Italian' in particular looks towards the later Gothic
masterpiece, 'Melmoth the Wanderer' (1820), in the doubts it
expresses about narrative veracity and social stability. (18) In one
sense, the high point of early Gothic is the Inquisition scene in
'The Italian', in which the comforting narrator, guarantor of our
social relation to the text, effectually disappears from the page,
leaving the reader isolated in a world of hints, innuendo and
incomprehensible danger. Walpole's toys have begun to come to life.
Archaism becomes, not a mere reminder of what is past, but a return
of repressed ways of feeling and behaving: the world of hierarchical
domination becomes an image for the skull beneath the skin of
bourgeois politeness and decency.

These books are all variations on a single theme: the problem of
how to reach out and understand the past without simultaneously
disturbing that which is best not disturbed. Looked at from this
point of view, they are not merely fictions but also attempts at the
representation of history. It is hardly surprising that Coleridge,
Shelley, Keats were interested in Gothic, because like them the
Gothic writers were trying to comprehend the relations between
historical present and past, trying to assess what had been gained
and what lost in the transition to the emergent capitalist state.
(19) But these representations of history simultaneously embody
evasions, evident in the roles to which the reader is enjoined:
playmate, admirer, spectator or detective, in no case are we
empowered to construct adult judgments from a position of knowledge.
We are shown either a version of events which appears to be largely
a disguise for the narrator (a Punch and Judy show) or a collection
of half-observed events which suggests narrative gnosticism. Gothic
veers between blatancy and reserve, but in neither case are we
allowed to feel much trust, and it is this challenge of the reader's
role which causes much of the difficulty of coming at the texts.
No less than realist fiction, Gothic was a middle-class literature,
but it was a peculiarly embattled one: where realism was appropriate
for dealing with those areas of social life which were regarded as
securely under bougeois control, Gothic occupied a borderguard
position, forever on the lookout for threats from without, whether
from the un-dead aristocracy or simply from the past, or even from
within the bourgeois order itself, from those aspects of reality,
psychological and social, which threatened to break through the
thin web of ideological conformism and disrupt conservative
synthesis. The concern of the authors is to produce fear in a form
in which it can be immediately neutralized: to act as lightning
conductors for social transition. The fantasization, the making
strange, finds its culmination in making the reader feel more at
home; yet where our comfort is to be purchased only through an
extensive suspension of disbelief, or through the obvious withholding
of narrative information, the roles in which we are placed end by
seeming inadequate, by in fact revealing what the Gothic writers try
to conceal, the jaggedness of social change and the unsatisfactori-
ness of attempts to domesticate the violent. Gothic as inoculation
ends by failing to control the disease it seeks to circumvent.

Chapter 7

Community and Morality:
Towards Reading Jane Austen

David Aers

> Take notice, That *England* is not a Free
> People, till the Poor that have no Land,
> have a free allowance to dig and labour
> the Commons, and so live as Comfortably
> as the Landlords that live in their
> Inclosures.
> (Gerrard Winstanley, 1649)

[Emma] delineates with great accuracy the habits and manners of
a middle class of gentry; and of the inhabitants of a country
village at one degree of rank and gentility beneath them ...
instead of the splendid scenes of an imaginary world, *[she gives]*
a correct and striking representation of that which is daily
taking place ... her *dramatis personae* conduct themselves upon
the motives and principles which the readers may recognize as
ruling their own and that of most of their acquaintances. The
kind of moral, also, which these novels inculcate, applies
equally to the paths of common life ... (1)

So wrote two reviewers of 'Emma' in 'The Gentleman's Magazine' and
the Tory 'Quarterly Review' in 1816. The reviewers can take for
granted that one's 'acquaintances' will not include English jacobins,
the many agricultural labourers who carried on a constant struggle
against the gentry's expropriation of land, game and gentry justice;
nor will they include women with views such as those held by Mary
Wollstonecraft or radical intellectuals such as Blake or Shelley.
Their 'acquaintances' would not write letters such as the following
anonymous ones to 'the Gentlemen of Ashill' in 1816 and to Oliver
Cromwell, Esquire, of Cheshunt Park: (2)

It is too hard for us to bear *[the enclosures[*, you have often
times blinded us by saying that the fault was all in the Place-
men of Parliament, but ... they have nothing to do with the
regulation of this parish.
    You do as you like, you rob the poor of their Commons Right,
plough the grass up that God send to grow, that a poor man may
feed a Cow, Pig, Horse nor Ass; lay muck and stones on the road
to prevent the grass growing.... There is 5 or 6 of you have
gotten all the whole of the Land in this parish in your own
hands & you would wish to be rich and starve all other part of
the poor.... We have counted up that we have gotten about 60 of

us to 1 of you: therefore should you govern, so many to 1?
We right these lines to you who are the Combin'd of the Parish
of Cheshunt in the Defence of our Parrish rights which you
unlawfully are about to disinherit us of...
Resolutions is maid by the aforesaid Combind that if you intend
of inclosing Our Common fields Lammas Meads Marshes &c Whe
Resolve before ... that bloudy and unlawful act [it] is finished
to have your hearts bloud if you proceede in the aforesaid bloudy
act Whe like horse leaches will cry give, give until whe have
spilt the bloud of every one that wishes to rob the Inosent
unborn.

Nor would the reviewers and their readers share the same views
about morality, justice or religion with the writers of these
letters, any more than they would share the social and economic
situation of the vast majority of English rural people. Yet the
continuities between the highly partial standpoint of Jane Austen's
admiring reviewers and the social and literary assumptions of such
a representative modern admirer and scholar as Professor Bradbury
are plain enough: (3)

> The constraints of a fixed society are firmly felt, and Jane
> Austen never tests the values that arise within this world
> outside the area in which they are possible (in industrial cities
> or in the lower social brackets); there is no need to; in the
> agrarian and hierarchical world, subscribing by assent to a
> stylized system of properties and duties, she finds a context in
> which they can yield their full resources ... it is true that
> class attitudes are of the greatest importance; but it is in
> evaluation of these attitudes and the building up of a scale
> of them for the proper conduct of the moral life that she
> excels.

These assertions about early nineteenth century agrarian England,
in which everyone was 'subscribing by assent' to gentry social
practices in a harmonious organic community, are common enough in
the writings of twentieth-century literary critics. Nevertheless,
they manifest a quite unnecessary ignorance about the history of
agrarian England from the thirteenth century to the early nineteenth.
Here there is only space to recommend some remedial and basic
reading to correct such irresponsible myth-making concerning our
past. (4) What interests me at the moment in the continuity between
the gentlemen reviewers of 1816 and the modern scholar is the
acknowledgment that Jane Austen's art is very closely bound up
with the partial viewpoint of one social group, combined with the
assumption that this partisan viewpoint provides an unquestionably
adequate foundation for an imaginative exploration and exemplification of what Bradbury calls 'the proper conduct of the moral life'.
It is characteristic of such criticism to pass easily from statements
about the 'great accuracy' with which Jane Austen portrays 'the
habits and manners of a middle class of gentry' to claims about her
'representation' of 'universal nature' and a convincing moral
vision. The present chapter attempts to encourage reflection about
such moves by looking at some of the ideological and social

dimensions of the way Jane Austen hopes to educate the understanding
and feelings of her characters and readers. This task is much
helped by a growing awareness among scholars that Austen was not the
naturalistic, objective portrayer of a segment of the contemporary
social reality on which she appears to bestow such attention, nor a
psychological 'realist' concerned to follow the subtle movements of
individual motivation and consciousness. In her outstanding study,
'Jane Austen and the War of Ideas', Marilyn Butler demonstrated
how, (5)

> The crucial action of her novels is in itself expressive of the
> conservative side in an active war of ideas.... Jane Austen's
> fable carries her partisan meaning farther than it could be
> carried in reasoned argument, even by Burke.... Jane Austen's
> plots express a typical conservative middle-class ethic of the
> day. When her principal characters experience an inward
> reformation - as, in each of the novels, some of them do - it is
> so that they can see their way to a marriage promising continued
> self-discipline, and a higher commitment than ever before to
> service of the community.

Although Marilyn Butler has little to say about 'the community'
that existed in Jane Austen's England she carefully situates the
novelist in her intellectual and ideological contexts. Jane Austen
emerges as a polemical tory ideologist, a most accomplished partisan
in a period of open and intense ideological controversy in which
novelists played a significant role. A contemporary of Blake, and
one for whom, as Alistair Duncan claims in his recent study of Jane
Austen's novels, Burke himself, the leading ideologist of the English
counter-revolution, may sometimes serve as 'a useful gloss'. (6)

Following suggestions of Alistair Duncan and Marilyn Butler, I
think it is worth looking at a passage from the counter-revolutionary
ideologist whom they both align with Jane Austen, one from
'Reflections on the Revolution in France' (1790). (7) It is a
representative enough passage and brings out a central contradiction
in Burke's ideology which has been overlooked by both Duncan and
Butler. The contradiction is important here because it is not
peculiar to Burke. On the contrary it is at the heart of the neo-
feudal ideology so favoured by the class to which Austen is, in the
last resort, utterly committed, the one identified by the 'Gentleman's
Magazine' as the 'middle class of gentry'. The contradiction appears
in many works of the time, from moral tracts to judges' speeches,
and it has been succinctly identified by E.J. Hobsbawm and G. Rudé
in their study of agrarian conflict in early nineteenth-century
England: (8)

> [England's] Rulers wanted it to be both capitalist and stable,
> traditional and hierarchical. In other words they wanted it to
> be governed by the universal free market of the liberal economist
> (which was inevitably a market for land and men as well as for
> goods), but only to the extent that suited nobles, squires and
> farmers; they advocated an economy which implied mutually
> antagonistic classes, but did not want it to disrupt a society
> of ordered ranks.

This is a vital insight which students of late eighteenth- and early
nineteenth-century literature do well to remember. Burke argues in
this way:

> ... Good order is the foundation of all good things. To be
> enabled to acquire, the people, without being servile, must be
> tractable and obedient. The magistrate must have his reverence
> the laws their authority. The body of the people must not find
> the principles of natural subordination by art rooted out of
> their minds. They must respect that property of which they
> cannot partake. They must labour to obtain what by labour can
> be obtained; and when they find, as they commonly do, the success
> disproportioned to the endeavour, they must be taught their
> consolation in the final proportions of eternal justice. Of
> this consolation, whoever deprives them deadens their industry,
> and strikes at the root of all acquisition as of all conservation.
> He that does this is the cruel oppressor, the merciless enemy of
> the poor and wretched; at the same time that by his wicked
> speculations he exposes the fruits of successful industry, and
> the accumulations of fortune, to the plunder of the negligent,
> the disappointed, and the unprosperous.

The passage opens with a seeming truism, a truism which discourages
the reader from asking the concrete and objective questions, 'good'
for whom? The aphoristic mode implies a consensus. But the very
same passage reveals this to be unwarranted. The second sentence
muffles the fact that it is 'the people' who transform nature into
human subsistence, and humanized nature, by introducing them with a
passive, 'To be enabled'; this passive is matched by the sentence's
close, 'tractable and obedient' - not, of course, 'tractable and
obedient' to themselves, but to the magistrate and the laws. But
who appoints the magistrates? And what are the magistrates'
relations to the means of production? Whose interests does he defend,
and for whose benefit are 'the laws', and who made them? The rhetoric
conceals such questions, but they were answered clearly enough in
contemporary England. The following sentence immediately invokes
the image of society as an organic human figure, 'The body of the
people'. This is a popular conservative metaphor because the body
is 'naturally' subordinated to its head, who in this tradition is
either the ruling class or Christ, depending on where the sermon is
delivered. Burke claims that hierarchy is 'natural', (9) whereas
social and critical analysis of the status quo and its ideology is
unnatural 'art'. No defence of the metaphor is made and so sure is
the writer of its potency that he does not even notice the internal
contradiction between 'the body' and 'their minds', a contradiction
which in fact reflects the incoherence of the metaphor and its
political content. Burke then moves on to assertion, to command -
'They must.... They must ... they must'. Property is for the few,
and the rhetoric implies that the exclusion of 'the people' from
land and productive means has the status of a natural immutable law.
In the second line of the passage Burke implied that 'the people'
should be able to acquire, but now we see that this merely muted his
total acceptance of vast disproportion in the distribution of goods
in his society. Since the first mention of acquiring (in the second

line), the passage has moved on to disclose how it is actually the
few who are to acquire by the labour of the many, urged on by 'the
magistrate', 'the law' and neo-feudal Christian ideology. Just how
important Burke takes the latter to be in propping up the status quo
can be seen in the sentence where he contemplates its undermining
(beginning 'Of this consolation ...'): when he offers the generalization 'strikes at the root of all acquisition' he actually means, as
we have seen, 'strikes at the root of the dominant class's free and
irresponsible appropriation of the labour of the many'. By now the
mystifying shell has been discarded and we see the kernel of market
ideology, of early capitalism. The final sentence is utterly frank
in its defence of arbitrary and limitless exploitation, while the
critic of social exploitation and alienation is made the enemy of
the exploited.

It is worth looking at a representative passage of later Burke
in detail because his work is at the centre of dominant ideology
in Austen's period, and served as a model. There is not space here
to do more than refer the reader to places where one can study
Burke's 'magistrate' and 'the law' in action, where magistrates
claim the impersonality and eternity of the 'market' in the face of
hungry labourers and the impoverished unemployed, deploy moralistic-
paternal rhetoric combined with the use of religion we have just
seen, and hand out sentences which embody the brutality underpinning
gentry law, order and morality. (10) But Austen could not simply
present society as a stable hierarchy governed by mutual duties and
responsibilities. She was far too aware of contest and conflict in
her world. In fact, she positively wanted to acknowledge the
existence of the capitalist market, with its specific values and
relations, while, at the same time, 'cashing' the neo-feudal
rhetoric of hierarchy with its claims about the 'assent' of the
lower ranks to the upper. This aspiration was characteristic of
a dominant ideology and I shall argue that Jane Austen's art and
morality reveals contradictions whose roots are in this dominant
ideology. In this chapter I shall focus the argument on 'Emma',
with occasional reference to 'Mansfield Park'.

Marilyn Butler commences her chapter on 'Emma' with some
fundamental observations about its plot and its relation to fiction
in the later eighteenth century: (11)

> The plot to which the language harmoniously relates is the
> classic plot of the conservative novel. Essentially a young
> protagonist is poised at the outset of life, with two missions
> to perform: to survey society, distinguishing the true values
> from the false, and in the light of this new knowledge of
> 'reality', to school what is selfish, immature, or fallible in
> herself. Where a heroine is concerned rather than a hero, the
> social range is inevitably narrower, though often the personal
> moral lessons appear compensatingly more acute. Nevertheless,
> the heroine's classic task, of choosing a husband, takes her out
> of any unduly narrow or solipsistic concern with her own
> happiness. What she is about includes a criticism of what
> values her class is to live by, the men as well as the women.

In the following discussion I will illustrate the way Jane Austen

fulfils this process, and the way she mediates social reality. I
begin with a part of the novel where she deploys her famous 'irony'
in launching Emma's 'moral' education. Emma makes an impetuous and
self-centred judgment about her friend Harriet Smith, deciding that
Harriet's deferential and distinctly uneducated lower-middle class
charms, (12)

> should not be wasted on the inferior society of Highbury and
> its connections ... the friends from whom she had just parted,
> though very good sort of people, must be doing her harm. They
> were a family of the name of Martin, whom Emma well knew by
> character as renting a large farm of Mr Knightley, and residing
> in the parish of Donwell - very creditably she believed - she
> knew Mr Knightley thought highly of them - but they must be
> coarse and unpolished, and very unfit to be the intimates of a
> girl who wanted only a little more knowledge and elegance to be
> quite perfect. *She* would notice her; she would improve her;
> she would detach her from her bad acquaintances, and introduce
> her into good society.

Most readers, disapproving of overt 'snobbery', readily admire Jane
Austen's ironic criticism of the heroine. Neither reader nor Jane
Austen could possibly make such an elementary blunder as Emma does
in correlating 'inferior society' and moral delinquency, especially
when the 'inferior', 'bad' acquaintances are called 'very good sort
of people'. Readers feel assured that Emma's 'snobbery' is a
personal aberration, and one which is firmly judged by the humane
author, who will educate her. We are certainly not encouraged even
to ask whether Emma's obnoxious attitudes might be necessary products
of her place in that specific, very divided society. Quite the
contrary, the reader is invited to assume that there is an acceptable norm, acceptable to all classes, from which Emma, personally,
deviates.
    Jane Austen will attempt to exemplify this assumed norm, but
already her reader might begin to suspect that there is something of
the ideologue about his guide. The novelist isolates individual
aberration in a way designed to prevent any critical questions being
asked about the total social structure. Furthermore, it is striking
that Emma is being attacked by Jane Austen for exaggerating the
class differentials within respectable middle-class society. Emma
thinks that Martin is a yeoman and says, 'The yeomanry are precisely
the order of people with whom I feel I can have nothing to do' (p.59).
Professor Trilling was upset at this remark because he sees the
'yeomanry' as virtually 'gentlemen', supporters of what he calls
'the best - safest - tendency of English social life'. However
briefly, we need to recall that Trilling misrepresents the social
realities and forces in Jane Austen's England: the 'yeomanry' he
envisages was, in most of England, in an advanced stage of
disintegration, forced into the ranks of the rural wage-labourer.
This 'yeomanry' tended, if anything, to be aligned against the
bigger landowners (as the agrarian riots of 1816, 1830 may suggest).
(13) So if the Martins were in this group Emma would be correct to
claim that Martin was one of that 'order of people' with whom she
'can have nothing to do'. But the real, and educative irony is that

Emma has failed to register how Martin is a large tenant farmer,
even though Jane Austen tells us that Emma knew him 'by character,
as renting a large farm' (p.54).   Since he rents a large farm we,
and Austen's audience even more readily, can tell that he has
survived the intense acceleration of enclosures, prospered in the
inflated wartime prices, and despite spiralling rents is going to
survive the post-war economic crisis.   He is safely and firmly
aligned with agrarian capitalists, the big, very respectable gentry.
     Austen wants us to get this clear, and she shows how Martin
studies the reports of the Board of Agriculture, has two large
parlours, a maid, a shepherd, and 'a very fine flock'.   Harriet,
herself 'the daughter of a tradesman' (p.462), tells us excitedly
that 'he has been bid more for his wool than anybody in the country'
(p.58).   Disapprovingly Emma comments, 'How much his business
engrosses him already', and objects that he is 'a great deal too
full of the market to think of anything else'. (14)   Jane Austen
shows that Emma has a vague sense of this 'market' which 'engrosses'
Martin.   She notes that, 'whatever his share of the family property,
it is ... all afloat, all employed in his stock, and so forth; and
though, with diligence and good luck, he may be rich in time, it is
next to impossible that he should have realized anything yet' (p.59).
But, a sign of how teachable Emma is, she does realize that he '*will*
thrive and be a very rich man in time' (p.62).   Indeed, the
similarities between Martin, the large tenant, and Mr Knightley,
capitalist farmer, are already striking.   Both are committed to the
'market', its values and its 'luck'.   But Emma is not; her consciousness is not yet fully initiated into the norms and ideology of her
class.   Unlike Jane Austen, she fails to discern that Martin's
commitment to 'the market' and his success within it makes him an
utterly reliable and admirable gentleman-in-the-making.   Her
'education' will teach her not to make such errors.   So the artist's
irony undermines Emma's anachronistic neo-feudal stratifications
and at this point defends a bourgeois society whose forms and
valuations are based on the capitalist market.   To enforce the
irony's judgment the reader is further reassured about Martin by
hearing Mr Knightley himself refer to Martin as 'a respectable,
intelligent gentleman farmer' (pp.54, 88).   To Knightley Martin pays
his rent, so who could be a more appropriate person to assess his
respectability in such a society?
     Nevertheless, tory ideologues, following Burke, did not offer a
straightforward defence of existing market relations.   They wished
to secure the benefits that agrarian capitalist production and
social relations had secured for their class but they wanted a far
more elevated, sanctimonious and selfless legitimation for this mode
of production and social control than had been offered by the
irreligious Hobbes, the sharp satires of Mandeville or the work of
Smith and the later eighteenth-century economists.   How, in the
words of Joan Robinson, 'justify the ways of Mammon to man'? (15)
One answer, we saw, was in the neo-feudal vocabulary of hierarchic
but harmonious, mutually responsible orders in an organic totality.
(16)   But when tories used such a model in Austen's world the aim
was legitimation of their own position rather than analysis of the
realities of social practices, conflicts and structures.   Despite
criticizing Emma in the manner just described, Austen herself evades

or blurs the realities of market society, and in her treatment of
Mr Knightley we find her support of the Burkian neo-feudal ideology.
This clashes with the version of Mr Knightly whose own definition of
acting 'rationally' is to know 'the value of a good income' (p.92),
but such contradictions are inherent in the ideology and her
aesthetic form does not make them vanish.

Far from it, the contradictions are manifested by her hero Mr
Knightley. The enthusiastic reception of this character in the
scholarly literature on Austen seems to have overlooked this fact,
happy to embrace and applaud the way, in Alistair Duncan's words,
he 'exemplifies the kind of behaviour Jane Austen considers necessary
for the maintenance of a morally founded society'. Critics have
on the whole accepted his practice and stance as an utterly
unproblematic reflection of the author's coherent moral and social
views. (17) Yet while Mr Knightley is certainly Jane Austen's
standard of male excellence (without being infallible), (18) she
does present him as an agrarian capitalist, not as some kind of
pseudo-feudal magnate. He is prospering well, like his capitalist
tenant, Robert Martin, and yet despite his relatively modest lifestyle
we are told that he has 'little spare money' (p.223). This is
because he re-invests his profits, accumulating in good capitalist
fashion. Miss Bates notes that Knightley's bailiff-manager 'thinks
more about his master's profits than anything' (p.246), and Knightley
himself confesses, 'I would rather be at home looking over William
Larkin's week's account' than out dancing (p.262). He shows his
respect for Martin (pp.56, 88), whose values he shares, attacks
Emma's misconception of Martin's position in the class structure
and calls this tenant his 'friend'.

Alongside this, however, Mr Knightley also deploys the Burkian
ideology of an organic but fixed, stable, stratified and coherent
social order. For example, he comments about Harriet, to Emma:

Till you chose to turn her into a friend, her mind had no
distaste for her own set, nor any ambition beyond it ... *she*
cannot gain by the acquaintance. Hartfield will only put her
out of conceit with all the other places she belongs to. She
will grow just refined enough to be uncomfortable with those
among whom birth and circumstances have placed her home. (pp.89,
67)

With this Jane Austen tends to agree: '[Harriet] was less and less
at Hartfield; which was not to be regretted' (p.463). She emphatically accepts the imperatives of social stratification in determining
the possibilities of human relationships and simultaneously supports
Mr Knightley's anachronistic view of society as a static neo-feudal
order where identity is a function of fixed social occupation and
place. Mr Knightley also perceives Martin's position through the
glasses of neo-feudal stratification. Whereas the allegedly
unregenerate Emma had grasped the way Martin invested his economic
means and so '*will* thrive and be a very rich man in time' (p.62),
when Mr Knightly himself tells Emma that Harriet has accepted
Martin's proposal he adds:

His situation is an evil - but you must consider it as what

> satisfies your friend; and I will answer for your thinking better
> and better of him as you know him more.... His rank in society
> I would alter if I could; which is saying a great deal I assure
> you, Emma. You laugh at me about William Larkins; but I could
> quite as ill spare Robert Martin. (p.454)

Again Mr Knightley seems to imply that his world is one where 'rank'
is fixed and totally controlled by family status and original
circumstances. Yet when, and if, Martin does 'thrive' in the
agrarian market, as Emma foresees, his social and political position
will shift, however gradually - irrespective of Mr Knightley's
paternalistic attitudes. Furthermore, as we have seen, both Mr
Knightley and his tenant are as firmly grounded in the world of
late eighteenth-century agrarian capitalism as their author. Mr
Knightley in fact manifests practices and perceptions which reflect
contradictions in his creator's consciousness and the tory ideology
she represents.
Awareness of the contradiction in question, with its social and
ideological contexts, will affect our reading of more than 'Emma'.
For example, one might start to reassess those scenes in 'Mansfield
Park' (1814, revised 1816), so characteristically replete with
decisive moral and social judgments - ones such as that in which
Mary Crawford tries to arrange for her harp to be brought from
Northampton to Mansfield. She recounts her great difficulties in
hiring a horse and cart: (19)

> I found that I had been asking the most unreasonable, most
> impossible thing in the world, had offended all the farmers, all
> the labourers, all the hay in the parish. (p.89)

Edmund reminds her that they are 'in the middle of a very late hay
harvest' and observes:

> you must see the importance of getting in the grass. The hire
> of a cart at any time, might not be so easy as you suppose; our
> farmers are not in the habit of letting them out; but in harvest,
> it must be quite out of their power to spare a horse. (p.89)

Mary Crawford makes a reply which Austen intended to illustrate just
how corrupt and finally unteachable she is. For Mary explains
without any sense of guilt that 'coming down with the true London
maxim, that everything is to be got with money, I was a little
embarrassed at first by the sturdy independence of your country
customs' (p.90). But Austen's condemnation of 'urban' money values
exemplifies ideological schematism rather than imaginative
engagement with agrarian social relations. For the agrarian world
of the part of England in which she chose to set Mansfield Park,
'seventy miles from London' (p.89) had long since been involved in
production for profit and indeed for urban markets, rather than in
peasant production for 'use value'. (20) Mr Knightley and Martin
represent landowner-tenant relations in the world of capitalist
farming, but Austen screens its realities when she puts down Mary
Crawford and the commodity world of 'London'. She encourages
simple-minded social judgments (grounded in neo-feudal ideology)

about town and country and uses these to help her enforce an equally
simple moral judgment against one of her 'urban' characters.
Morality here is thus informed by schematic ideology devoid of
imaginative engagement with the relevant communities and the texture
of growing up within them.

Once a reader is detached enough from Austen's polemic to notice
such features he may well also start to see some double-think and
ideological obfuscation in the whole topic of 'improvement'. For
instance, Jane Austen makes much of the fact that already at
Sotherton, 'There have been two or three fine old trees cut down'
and Fanny quotes from Cowper, one of the author's favourite poets,
'Ye fallen avenues, once more I mourn your fate unmerited' (p.87).
Such 'improvement' and the landscaping planned by Henry Crawford
here and later in the book are obvious symbols of the immoral,
depraved energies of those who sponsor it, while those who oppose
it are, as Duckworth says, like Fanny, 'the representative of
Austen's own fundamental commitment to an inherited culture'. (21)
But what Austen, Fanny, Edmund and now Duckworth fail to consider
is that this 'inherited culture' of the gentry is one actually
grounded in the coercive 'improvement' and transformation of rural
England in the triumph of agrarian capitalism and increased
profitability of production for the market, enabled by a Parliament
solely composed of substantial property-owners. (22) The point to
grasp here is that Jane Austen's symbolism and judgment, working
so effectively on readers like Duckworth, functions to inculcate a
distorted version of 'inherited culture' and an ideologically
falsified version of the present foundations of the gentry forms of
life to which she is committed. Here the neo-feudal, static
ideology conceals the class's immersion in the practices and values
of agrarian capitalism pursued so decorously by Mr Knightley and
Martin in 'Emma'.

Readers of 'Mansfield Park' may also recall that despite such
ideology, Jane Austen does make the baronet owner of Mansfield Park
a man whose 'large income' is bound up with investment in the West
Indies. Indeed his absence from Mansfield Park is actually to do
with 'some recent losses on his West India Estate' (pp.59, 65, 66),
and when he comes back it is because 'His business in Antigua had
latterly been prosperously rapid, and he came directly from
Liverpool' (p.195). Once home his first morning at least is centred
on 'his steward and his bailiff - to examine and compute ... active
and methodical' (p.206). It is not surprising that his first
adverse judgment of Mr Rushworth includes the fact that his putative
son-in-law is 'ignorant in business' (p.214). His estate in the
West Indies would doubtless be made profitable through the labour
of black slaves, whose appalling treatment by Europeans was well
known in Austen's England. (23) Indeed, Fanny actually asks Sir
Thomas 'about the slave trade' (p.213), but having acknowledged the
existence of slaves, Jane Austen drops the subject without examining
the links it has with the baronet's affluence in England or its
morality. The glimpses Jane Austen allows us of Sir Thomas's
economic foundations suggest, quite as much as her presentation of
Mr Knightley and Martin, the centrality of the capitalist market in
agrarian England. Sir Thomas, as much as Mr Knightley, is an
example of what the historian Lawrence Stone described as 'the

extraordinary homogeneity of English elite society, and the ease
of cultural and social connections between the landed classes and
the wealthy bourgeoisie from the late seventeenth century'. Stone
also notes in this context the 'high degree of intermarriage'
between the squirarchy and 'the bourgeoisie', and its basis in
shared cultural and social values as well as in common economic
motivations. (24) Jane Austen recognized this, and it is one of the
facts Emma must accept. Nevertheless, as we have also observed, the
novelist still imposes anachronistic neo-feudal ideology on to these
presentations, and perhaps it is time that those who believe that we
can learn from Austen about 'the proper conduct of the moral life'
paid some attention to the moral implications of such ideological
impositions on the world she is mediating in her fiction.

The present limitations of space demand that we leave 'Mansfield
Park' and return to 'Emma'. In the present context it seems
appropriate to mention Jane Austen's depiction of the Coles, for
they play a small but revealing part in Emma's education. In
handling this family the author directs our attention from capitalist
farmers to specialist traders. She states that the Coles, 'were of
low origin in trade' but that 'the last year or two had brought them
a considerable increase of means ... in fortune and style of living'
(pp.217-18). She outlines how the Coles have 'arrived' through trade,
while the Martins are in the process of 'arriving' through capitalist
farming. Their success in the market economy is similar and so is
their social movement. It is important to notice that Austen's
irony in this chapter (XXV) is again aimed at Emma's failure to
judge correctly who are respectable people, acceptable to the
country elite. Capitalist relations and mobility must be embraced
by the consciousness of leading squirarchy as well as bourgeoisie,
and Emma must learn not to misrepresent her class's true interests.
Indeed Mr (!) Cole and Mr Knightley are explicitly aligned in
organizing 'parish business' (p.223): that is, in supervising and
controlling the working classes, poor law, and so on. Here again,
Jane Austen is 'educating' Emma, but the education is for a particular and narrow social class, in a specific historical situation.
Emma must learn what Defoe had been preaching a hundred years before:
'the tradesmen in *England* fill the lists of our nobility and gentry;
no wonder that the gentlemen of the best families marry tradesmen's
daughters ... trade in *England* makes Gentlemen'. (25)

As we move through Emma's social world it cannot be amiss to make
a few observations about the treatment of working people. The
normal attitude of the literary establishment here is that as Austen
handles the middle segment of the gentry there is no reason why she
should pay any attention to the other social groups comprising the
majority of the population on whose existence the life-style of the
gentry depended. Yet Jane Austen herself sensed the impossibility
of presenting middle class life in what she calls a 'large and
populous village almost amounting to a town' (p.39), without at
least some glances towards 'lower' social life and groups with which
her own was in antagonistic relation. It is true that her favoured
strategy is as simple as the one used by those who extol her moral
and social wisdom. She waves a magic wand and the mass of the
population vanishes into thin air, leaving only the fruits of their
labour for the likes of Mr Knightley to appropriate. You can walk

around 'large and populous' Highbury, or walk around Mr Knightley's
estate and never see a labourer. The system of production is so
natural, we are persuaded that it needs no workers. (26) But this
nature is the human world of early nineteenth-century agrarian
capitalism, involving a specific social and cultural organization to
which Mr Knightley's class is committed and one which depends on a
specific form of exploiting other peoples' labour. And ideology
which only deals with a central phenomenon (the working classes) by
pretending it does not exist is exceptionally vulnerable. Jane
Austen senses this fact, and on two separate occasions in 'Emma'
she gives us her mediation of the agricultural proletariat, the
labour-side of agrarian capitalism. The form of the mediation, we
shall see, is itself affected by the author's ideology, rather than
a triumph of imaginative insight and aesthetic power.

The first of these scenes is Emma's visit to 'the poor'. If we
are to pinpoint Jane Austen's own position it is necessary to
consider just where the irony in this chapter resides. The two
young ladies, Emma and Harriet, are described walking 'down Vicarage-
lane ... containing the blessed abode of Mr Elton'. This is typical
of Austen's overt irony: Mr Elton's house and company are the
opposite of blessed and the irony is made more spicy by the play
on blessed (heavenly). Later, after the visit to the poor, Jane
Austen again exposes Emma and Harriet to irony:

> 'These are sights Harriet, to do one good. How trifling they
> make everything else appear! - I feel now as if I could think of
> nothing but these poor creatures all the rest of the day; and
> yet, who can say how soon it may all vanish from my mind?'
>   'Very true' said Harriet. 'Poor creatures! one can think of
> nothing else'.

The conversation goes on in this vein, repeating that the sight
will not slip from their minds. Besides Emma's complacent egocen-
tricity, in this passage the irony is located in the fact that a
few lines later the pair meet the Reverend Mr Elton, and Emma's
attention becomes fixed on the means of leaving Harriet and the
priest alone together. So the author shows a discrepancy between
Emma's real and her avowed interest. The irony is very straight-
forward. Having located the irony we can perceive Jane Austen's
norm, the ideal response against which deviations are to be
assessed. Her own normative values are expressed in this passage:

> Emma was very compassionate; and the distresses of the poor were
> as sure of relief from her personal attention and kindness, her
> counsel and patience, as from her purse. She understood their
> ways, could allow for their ignorance and their temptations, had
> no romantic expectations of extraordinary virtue from those,
> for whom education had done so little; entered into their
> troubles with ready sympathy, and always gave her assistance
> with as much intelligence as good-will. (p.111)

This assures the reader that the well-to-do lady is capable of
providing material relief for 'the poor'. But certain evasions
become apparent, despite the novelist's magisterial tone. By

selecting the generalized noun, 'the poor', does Jane Austen mean
all 'poor' in the village, that 'large and populous village almost
amounting to a town'? No answer emerges. One can also see that the
criteria used in deciding who qualifies as 'the poor' Emma should
visit and who should be given 'relief' are also not even mentioned.
Will the 'relief' still leave them poor and if so exactly what kind
of 'relief' is it? Indeed, one may notice that Jane Austen does not
begin to wonder why 'they' are so poor when the groups of Emma,
Mr Knightley and Sir Thomas Bertram or Henry Crawford are so
immensely affluent. But such questions should be taken seriously,
for Jane Austen was actually alluding to one of the most discussed
social and moral problems in her world. In the most recent major
study of poverty in 'pre-industrial' Europe, Catharine Lis and
Hugo Soly have shown in considerable detail how through the
seventeenth century and later the 'Development of agrarian capitalism
worked hand in glove with the impoverishment process of rural
England'. They find that 'The triumph of agrarian capitalism' was
inseparable from 'the proletarianization of broad strata of the
populance'.(27) Such research reminds one that the wealth of those
like Mr Knightley, Martin or Sir Thomas Bertram should be understood
as dialectically related to the impoverishment of the mass of working
people. While Blake explored such connections, (28) Austen's
ideology hinders her from even suggesting any connection. Yet the
presence of 'the poor' in 'Emma', however vaguely figured as a
function of Emma's activities, is itself a muted response to the
way that, 'From the mid-eighteenth century poverty became one of
the main subjects of concern to governments, ecclesiastics, learned
societies, and middle-class circles throughout Europe'. Lis and
Soly note that eighteenth-century philosophers such as Godwin,
Price and Wolff 'all acknowledged the dehumanizing living conditions
of the lower classes and the tyranny of the poor-law administration.
Most agreed that destitution was not the result of laziness or
individual misfortunes but arose through economic and social abuses.
Some even emphasized the *right* of the poor to claim assistance,
since the rich had unlawfully appropriated for themselves all
material goods.' For Austen, these issues are ideologically
screened, although their moral relevance to her culture and
standpoint are plain. They are so plain that a contemporary rural
dean, one who was to become a bishop, asked by what moral or
political right did the wealthy (29)

> take upon themselves to enact certain laws (for the rich compose
> the legislative body in every civilized country) which compelled
> that man to become a member of their society; which precluded
> him from any share in the land where he was born; any use of its
> spontaneous fruits, or any dominion over the beasts of the
> field, on pain of stripes, imprisonment, or death? How can they
> justify their exclusive property in the *common heritage* of
> mankind unless they consent, in return, for the subsistence of
> the poor, who were excluded from those common rights by the
> laws of the rich, to whom they were never parties?

One could, of course, quote Blake, Winstanley or medieval Christian
radicals like John Ball on these lines, but the fact that this is

Richard Woodward, dean and bishop-to-be may help modern readers see just how severely constrained is Austen's ethical imagination. Her attitudes in the passage from Emma are those of a class whose national and local officials concentrated on social control of the poor labourers and many unemployed while they confined their acts of charity to the 'respectable' poor, those who could obviously present no threat to their own possessions and power.

I must now pass on to a place where Jane Austen mediates her class's fear of the lower orders loosened from particular ties to land and its gentry. Harriet and her friend are walking along the Richmond road the morning after the ball when they suddenly come across 'a party of gipsies', a group who provide a perfect symbol for the masses of uprooted people who were dispossessed, landless, without regular employment and economic resources. (30)

> A child on the watch came towards them to beg; and Miss Bickerton, excessively frightened, gave a great scream, and calling on Harriet to follow her, ran up a steep bank, cleared a slight hedge .... But poor Harriet could not follow. She had suffered very much from cramp after dancing, and her first attempt to mount the bank brought on such a return of it as made her absolutely powerless - and in this state, and exceedingly terrified, she had been obliged to remain ... Harriet was soon assailed by half a dozen children, headed by a stout woman and a great boy. (p.330)

Gipsies, of course, are not literally the labourers who work the land around Highbury, not those who are organized by local overseers of the poor. They represent those who are escaping from 'the iron discipline of the factory' and of the workhouse, and Austen tempts the reader to treat them simply as classless vagrants. They seem a negligible minority barely ruffling the novelist's social ideas and ideology about a coherent society with ranks 'subscribing by assent'. But whereas the visit to 'a poor sick family' mediated her vision of poverty in her society, presenting 'the poor' merely as tame objects for gentry patronage and 'counsel', this scene mediates the worry that below the surface order all is not under control, a fear about the threatening aspect of 'the poor'. (31) To Harriet and her friend, however, they are purely the source of a hysteria which breaks out before any physical challenge whatsoever is offered. This suggests how the hysteria is grounded in the ladies' unarticulated consciousness of a social world composed of dangerous antagonistic groups, their fear and hatred for those not duly respectful of gentry rule and not holding a fixed place in the local community.

But Jane Austen herself is confident of the triumph of law-and-order. First of all she reassures the reader by banishing any adult masculine presence from the gipsies. Then she implies that had the ladies stood firm the threat would have dissolved. But even though they surrender, the mere presence of Frank Churchill inspires the gipsies with 'terror' (significantly this is Austen's word). He leaves them 'completely frightened' (p.331). This is a personalized and genteel symbol of the role of terror in gentry law, so illuminatingly discussed in a recent essay by Douglas Hay. (32) Jane

Austen makes it clear that the gipsies' 'terror' is not simply
inspired by an individual, Churchill: she shows him setting off
to give 'notice of there being such a set of people in the neighbourhood to Mr Knightley' (p.331). Mr Knightly is a JP, the magistrate
and landowner who could judge and sentence these people, and Jane
Austen, without any specific comment writes: 'The gipsies did not
wait for the operations of justice; they took themselves off in a
hurry' (p.333). Now knowing something of what contemporaries knew
about the 'operations' (!) of gentry 'justice' against any social
challenge, we are not surprised that the gipsies run away. But here
Austen discourages us from probing the implications of landed
property's 'justice', from asking how the mass of uprooted rural
people could survive within gentry and bourgeois 'justice'. Instead
she encourages us to feel relieved at their terrified disappearance
as soon as confronted by the representation of Mr Knightley's
'justice'. Our 'moral' education continues, certainly. But we
should not overlook the way the novelist's treatment of the gipsies
is a small and mild part of a long, profoundly ignorant and vicious
tradition in which landless and uprooted social groups have been
described as enemies and treated as subhuman aliens.

But in one of the most sensitive passages in 'Emma' Jane Austen
does mediate the vital relationship between individual abilities,
fulfilment and work. She handles it from the aspect with which she
is most familiar, focusing on Jane Fairfax (chapters XXXIV and
XXXV). In the following quotation Jane is speaking to Mrs Elton
about finding work:

> 'I am not at all afraid of being long unemployed. There are
> places in town, offices, where inquiry would soon produce
> something - Offices for the sale - not quite of human flesh -
> but of human intellect.'
>
> 'Oh! my dear, human flesh! You quite shock me; if you mean
> a fling at the slave-trade, I assure you Mr Suckling was always
> rather a friend to the abolition'.
>
> 'I did not mean, I was not thinking of the slave trade',
> replied Jane; 'governess trade, I assure you, was all that I
> had in view.' (p.300)

This reflects the most specific encounter of Jane Austen's class
with the role enacted by most people in her society - wage labour.
The intelligent, sensitive, educated Jane Fairfax has no capital and
no property. She is thus forced to sell her powers on to a 'free'
market which will in fact control and deform them. She envisages
herself as a commodity she would be 'glad to dispose of', and the
analogy of the slave market is a vivid one to reflect the realities
of the contemporary situation endured by so many governesses. This
occupation does not fit the neo-feudal ideological model at all,
and Lawrence Stone notes that it was one developed in the later
eighteenth century, a rare chance of employment for 'well-educated
spinsters' from gentry families who lacked the necessary land and
money to attract 'respectable' marriage offers. He describes the
job as a particularly isolated and exploited kind of female wage
labour. (33) Jane Fairfax's response is intense, and the intensity
is unequivocally Jane Austen's own. Jane Fairfax has the credentials

demanded by the cultured middle class for acceptance and success.
As Mrs Elton says, 'with your superior talents you have a right to
move in the first circle' (p.301). But in reality (as opposed to
ideology) her class has little to do with rewarding 'talents' and a
very great deal to do with property, money, and material comforts.
Jane Austen knew enough of this to realize what a distressing problem
confronts her: the tory artist finds the social group she supports
turning even one of its own moral and intellectual paragons into a
mental and psychological cripple. (34) This is a powerful reflection
of life within gentry society from a perspective Jane Austen seldom
chose to take up. But while the ensuing piece of writing offers a
moving perception of the individual alienation generated by a
specific set of social relations and attitudes within her class, one
must also acknowledge that the author makes absolutely no attempt to
explore the psychic consequences of such social relations as they
affected employees such as Jane Fairfax, let alone those in more
typical forms of wage labour - indeed the very last thing she does
is wish the reader to connect and compare Jane's situation with the
conditions of wage labour occupied by the majority of women in her
society. And even while she shows us central features of the
destructive effects such conditions have on a gifted individual,
she still fully accepts the existing social relations and values
which generate this miserable and wasteful situation. So she
retreats into the comforting ideology that informs her basic trust
in her class. She attacks Jane Fairfax for concealing the relationship with Churchill without attacking the social norms which drove
Jane to this concealment, and she finally 'solves' the vital problem
of wage labour by waving her magic wand to acquire capital and
property for Jane Fairfax. This, of course, delivers Jane from
the 'destiny' of wage labour and allows the novelist hastily to
cover over the extremely unpleasant features of her class's normal
social organization which her imagination has momentarily disclosed.
Ideology triumphs, yet the fact that Jane Austen encourages the
reader simply to dissolve an intractable social phenomena she herself
has disclosed points to major problems in the ideology and its
relation to the contemporary world; as well as to its effect on her
vision and fiction.
     The final topic I shall raise is the rather unpromising one of
the treatment of sex by this contemporary of Blake and Shelley.
Jane Austen's self-consciously tory and counter-revolutionary stance
in her presentation of the most intimate areas of human life has been
well documented and situated by Marily Butler. (35) Austen's art in
these areas is quite unequivocally a part of the pattern of
increasing repression within middle-class familial and sexual
relations which Lawrence Stone has traced in his study, 'The Family,
Sex and Marriage in England 1500-1800'. It is in this context of
increasing sexual repression and patriarchal domination that the
famous passivity of Fanny Price and the education, and marriage, of
Emma should be viewed. Stone describes the increasingly 'authori-
tarian tendencies within the family' and the increasing and 'general
hostility towards sexuality' in respectable society which culminated
in 'extraordinary heights' of prudery. Discussing the 'causes' of
this tide of repression, or 'moral' regeneration, Stone notes, (36)

There was a sense of social and political crisis, a fear that the
whole structure of social hierarchy and political order was in
danger ... the fear was that under the inspiration of 1789 the
impoverished and alienated masses in the industrial cities would
rise up in bloody revolution. Secondly, two rival religious
factions, one established and one non-conformist, were in
competition for the allegiance of the population ... the
Evangelicals and the Methodists. In each case, both sides
stressed the enforcement of patriarchy and obedience, and the
crushing of the libido.

Jane Austen's affinities with 'the Evangelicals' are no coincidence,
and as she issues her punishments at the end of 'Mansfield Park' we
meet the increasingly widespread norms of a conventional Christianity
which 'exalted a stern and unforgiving masculine God whose vengeance
fell inexorably on all sinners' and whose ideas of virtue included
'puritanical sexual codes'. (37) Typically of this brand of
Christianity (there are others, as Blake pointed out), the greatest
sins are those against middle-class sexual norms and the patriarchal
authority indissolubly bound up with these norms. For Jane Austen
does not choose to focus on, let alone punish, the orientation of
life, spirit and intellect, towards the habitual pursuit of affluence
and material gain that pervades the lives of those in her class.
Her morality is one in which the gospels and Christian ethics have
been conveniently circumscribed to the repression of eros in the
sphere of personal relations and to the exercise of social and
political control over what Stone calls 'the impoverished and
alienated masses' in the public sphere. As Lucy Aikin shrewdly
observed, 'the precepts of Christianity have been pressed into the
service of a base submission to all established power'. The
Christianity that at least included for Langland critical scrutiny
of the normative social and economic practices of the powerful and
wealthy (38) has been moulded to reflect the social and ideological
needs of the middle classes in the early nineteenth century. It is
thus hardly surprising that at the conclusion of 'Mansfield Park'
the young, adulterous Maria is condemned to a lifetime's internment
in isolation with Mrs Norris and that to Austen adultery is 'too
gross a complication of evil, for human nature, not in a state of
utter barbarism, to be capable of' (p.430), one that, typically,
makes her sympathy go not to the miserable, frustrated and destroyed
Maria but to the offended patriarch - 'Fanny felt for him most
acutely' because the event was a social 'disgrace never to be wiped
off' (pp.438, 436). And Fanny definitely has Austen's support here
as the author comments, 'poor Sir Thomas ... was the longest to
suffer' (p.446). Her clergyman hero, Edmund, judges his sister's
behaviour in similar vein as 'the dreadful crime' (p.443) for which
forgiveness is not even considered, and Jane Austen herself sanctions
Sir Thomas's refusal to allow his daughter to be 'received at home',
as this would apparently comprise too 'great an insult to the
neighbourhood'. This is a kind of conventional Christianity which
makes a most revealing contrast not only with Blake's heterodoxy,
but also with the analogous episode in the gospels where Jesus freed
a woman taken in adultery from the orthodox religionists of his day,
who were ready to stone her (John, 8.7, 9-11). The qualities of

love and forgiveness manifested by Christ here are not ones found in Austen's brand of Christianity. The Christian Austen hardly takes Christ's admonition seriously; 'He that is without sin amongst you let him cast the first stone'. Indeed, she is quite unhesitating in her casting of stones at deviancy from public sexual norms. She fails to consider what Jesus reminds moralists to take seriously: namely, the ways they may participate in what they condemn.

Rather than pursuing these important moral and religious issues I will conclude by pointing towards the manner in which Jane Austen's fundamental commitment to market values and practices incoherently clashing with the neo-feudal ideology, is manifested in the way sexual relations are absorbed by the market. (39) The point that is often obscured here is Jane Austen's aesthetic and moral complicity in this situation. Here there is room for one example from 'Emma': 'Captain Weston, who had been considered ... as making such an amazing match, was proved to have much the worst of the bargain; for when his wife died after a three year's marriage, he was rather a poorer man than at first' (pp.46-7). After entering 'trade' for twenty years and owning a 'small house' in Highbury, he 'realized an easy competence - enough to marry a woman as portionless even as Miss Taylor', though he sensibly determines on 'never settling (i.e. marrying) till he could purchase Randall ... [and had] made his fortune' (p.47). So total is the acceptance of market values that there seems no need for any defensive justificatory moves. But with Jane Fairfax's predicament in mind, Jane Austen decides to protect Emma from the bourgeois nexus of cash payment and exchange value. She hopes in this way to explore the individual in liberated isolation from the mundane situation, but to achieve this approach she resorts to rather crude economic magic. She produces £30,000 for Emma from unspecified sources, 'liberating' her from the deforming social structure. The novelist again dissolves the reality of the market, and the normal position of gentry females, on behalf of her heroine's 'personal' development. This is an evasion of any imaginative exploration of the interactions between the market contexts, in which women are commodities for exchange, and their real pressures on individual consciousness and development. Of course, it is perfectly true that Jane Austen objects to Maria Bertram marrying Mr Rushworth purely for his wealth and to escape from the oppressive presence of her father, one who was all too understandably 'no object of love' to either of his daughters (p.66). (40) But the novelist's emphatic objections against Maria do not go on to examine just how Maria's position and values are representative within the class. Instead, she treats the young woman as a gross deviant against norms which she assumes are themselves satisfactory; yet, as we see from Sir Thomas (41) and Jane Austen's own striking emphasis on the exact financial and class basis of marriage settlements, together with her condemnation of financially 'imprudent' marriage (for example 'Mansfield Park', p.41), these norms themselves absorb marriage and sexuality into the nexus of economic exchange values and patriarchal controls. Jane Austen is fundamentally committed to the market norms as long as they are pursued in moderation and under strict male authority. One of the consequences in her works can be seen in the prevalence of sexless and socio-economically decorous marriages stamped with authorial approval - like the marriage of Emma and

Mr Knightley, justly depicted by Angus Wilson in these terms: 'His
[Mr Knightley's] manliness consists in the looming spectre of a
Victorian paterfamilias.... It is a sad sort of father-daughter
marriage that has been achieved'. (42)

Many critics continue to venerate Jane Austen as a great artist
who is also and inseparably a great 'moralist', while doggedly
refusing to discuss the way her work mediates contemporary ideological,
moral and social conflicts, unwilling or unable to discuss the way it
is informed by a peculiarly tory ideology and its incoherence. The
consequence of this ideology is that instead of her art opening out
gentry/middle-class reality and assumptions to a genuinely exploratory fiction which takes alternative forms of life and aspiration
seriously, Jane Austen systematically closes up her imagination
against critical alternatives. In doing so, her art, her religion,
her morality and her version of the individual and community quite
fail to transcend the narrow limitations of her historical class,
albeit a class whose dominant role in English society is still very
evident.

Chapter 8

Hazlitt: Criticism and Ideology

Jonathan Cook

Despite some valuable attempts to reinstate Hazlitt as a central
figure in English romantic writing, he still remains on the margins
of debate about the relations between literature and society in the
early nineteenth century. (1) Hazlitt's lack of recognition can be
explained in part by the way this debate has been founded. In his
seminal work, 'Culture and Society', Raymond Williams makes one
passing reference to Hazlitt. When Williams considers the formative
moment of English cultural criticism, Hazlitt is not amongst the
contrasting figures - Burke and Cobbett, Southey and Owen - used to
structure the account. (2) Yet, as I want to argue in this essay,
it is there, in the contrast with Burke, that Hazlitt should be
placed because it is in his writing that we find some of the earliest
and the most trenchant criticisms of Burke, a figure who became a
formidable ideologue of reaction and a model of political intellect
for Wordsworth and Coleridge alike.
  There are other reasons for Hazlitt's relative anonymity. One
of these is the nature of his work itself, dispersed across a wide
range of topics - painting, drama, literature, politics, philosophy,
social reportage, biography - and written in journalistic forms which
do not encourage the kind of meditation and debate on a single 'great'
work or a recognizable oeuvre that is so often necessary to the
making of a critical reputation. One consequence both of the range
of Hazlitt's writing and of its characteristic form, the essay, is
that he is generally available today only in anthologies. Of these,
one of the largest, the selection edited by Geoffrey Keynes, gives
a strangely lop-sided view of Hazlitt because it omits much of his
political writing. But in a study such as this, concerned with the
relations between literature and ideology, it is precisely some of
the political writing that becomes central because it is in pieces
like 'What is the People?' that we find Hazlitt engaged in the
exposure of those forms of distortion which constitute an important
part of ideology.
  In what follows I want to show something of Hazlitt's distinctive
understanding of his own society. This demands an engagement with
the political dimension of his work because it is the pressure of a
political conjuncture - the French Revolution and its aftermath -
which gives Hazlitt's writings their distinctive accent. This does

137

not mean, in Hazlitt's case, that familiar disillusionment with the course of the Revolution, accompanied by a general rejection of political radicalism, which characterizes the careers of Wordsworth and Coleridge. For Hazlitt, the French Revolution signalled a potential for democratic social change which is then betrayed again and again through the agency of a powerful English establishment capable of stifling radical initiatives at home and defeating them abroad.

The development of democracy was, in Hazlitt's view, the product of expanded means of communication. The invention of printing was an event of immense political consequence: (3)

> The French Revolution might be described as a remote but inevitable result of the invention of the art of printing. The gift of speech, or the communication of thought by words, is that which distinguishes man from other animals. But this faculty is limited and imperfect without the intervention of books, which render the knowledge possessed by everyone in the community accessible to all. There is no doubt, then, that the press (as it has existed in modern times) is a great organ of intellectual improvement and civilisation.

The 'invention of books' brings about the exposure of tyranny and a revulsion from it, 'Who in reading history, where the characters are laid open and the circumstances fairly stated, and where he himself has no false lies to mislead him, does not take part with the oppressed against the oppressor?' (4) In one respect Hazlitt's discussion of the French Revolution in his 'Life of Napoleon' is based upon a commonplace of Enlightenment thought, that historical progress consists in the diffusion of rational knowledge and the erosion of superstition. But this commonplace is given a particular nuance by Hazlitt, in his constant stress upon the relation between a material process, printing, and the new forms of consciousness to which it gives rise: (5)

> From the moment that the press opens the eyes of the community beyond the actual sphere in which each moves, there is from that time inevitably formed the germ of a body of opinion directly at variance with the selfish and servile code that before reigned paramount.

This is a repeated emphasis. The change in quantity that print brings about, making 'the knowledge possessed by everyone in the community accessible to all', is accompanied by changes in quality, new forms of consciousness and knowledge, what Hazlitt calls 'This new sense', or, in another formulation, 'public opinion'. But Hazlitt's version of public opinion needs to be distinguished from the conservative appropriation of the concept that occurred later on in the nineteenth century, in the works of Comte and George Eliot. (6) In Hazlitt's account 'public opinion' necessarily comes into conflict with the feudal order, and if this conflict becomes peculiarly stubborn and protracted, as it did in eighteenth-century France, then 'public opinion' necessarily becomes a revolutionary force: (7)

> Why then should there be an individual in a nation privileged
> to do what no other individual in the nation can be found to
> approve? But he has the power, and will not part with it in
> spite of public opinion. Then that public opinion must become
> active, and break the moulds of prescription in which his right
> derived from his ancestors is cast, and this will be a Revolution.

These sentences allude to a persistent debate, one that took on
a renewed intensity in Hazlitt's lifetime, about the propriety of a
revolution or popular uprising against an established government.
But this general context has a specific application because Hazlitt
is trying here to assert the logicality of revolution, and to do
this he has to free the word from that charge of contempt and fear
which had been one result of the work of Burke, Southey, Wordsworth
and Coleridge. Hazlitt wants to establish 'Revolution' as the
necessary outcome of a certain sequence of events and thereby to
counteract the effects of Burke's influential description: (8)

> All circumstances taken together, the French Revolution is the
> most astonishing thing that has hitherto happened in the world....
> Everything seems out of nature in this strange chaos of levity
> and ferocity, and all sorts of crimes jumbled together with all
> sorts of follies. In viewing this monstrous tragicomic scene,
> the most opposite passions necessarily succeed and sometimes
> mix with each other in the mind.

What Hazlitt sees as a proper means of resolving a political dispute
Burke sees as a violation of natural order; what Hazlitt wants to
make acceptable to the mind of his reader Burke wants to make
virtually unthinkable; revolution is a threat to mental as well as
social order, 'the most opposite passions necessarily succeed and
sometimes mix with each other in the mind'.
Hazlitt's dialogue with Burke will be a recurrent theme in this
essay. But 'The Life of Napoleon', and the account of the French
Revolution that it contains, evidences more than this dialogue
Written in the final years of Hazlitt's life, 'The Life of Napoleon'
gives, in retrospect, a clarity to themes and pre-occupations
implicit in his earlier work. Given his understanding of one
important source of the French Revolution in the 'intervention of
books', the literary intellectual becomes for Hazlitt a key figure
in a process of intellectual enlightenment which had also become,
in historical fact, a political struggle. Hazlitt states what that
political struggle was in the preface to 'The Life of Napoleon', as
part of his defence of Napoleon's reputation: (9)

> He [Napoleon] kept off that last indignity and wrong offered to
> a whole people (and through them to the rest of the world) of
> being handed over, like a herd of cattle, to a particular family,
> and chained to the foot of a legitimate throne. This was the
> chief point at issue ... whether mankind were, from the beginning
> to the end of time, born slaves or not?

The language of this description places Hazlitt in the radical
tradition which construed the political and social conflicts of the

late eighteenth and early nineteenth centuries as a struggle between
tyranny and liberty. (10) But the writer is not so placed as to be
one who simply reports and comments on this struggle. Writing, the
printed word, and the forms of communication and consciousness
enabled by print, are themselves sites of the struggle between
liberty and tyranny: (11)

> This new sense acquired by the people ... is like bringing a
> battering-train to bear upon some old Gothic castle, long the den
> of rapine and crime, and must finally prevail against all absurd
> and antiquated institutions, unless it is violently suppressed,
> and this engine of political reform turned by bribery and terror
> against itself.

By the time these sentences from 'The Life of Napoleon' were
published, in 1828, Hazlitt knew well enough that 'this engine of
political reform' could be 'turned by bribery and terror against
itself'. 'The Spirit of the Age' published in 1825 is, amongst
other things, a record of that process and its consequences. Given
so much evidence to the contrary, what is remarkable is Hazlitt's
persistent belief in the progressive role of public opinion and the
literate culture that sustains it. Writing after the defeat of
Napoleon and the restoration of the Bourbon dynasty, Hazlitt can
still see the conflicts of 1789 as part of an historical process
which continues in the 1820s. The reflex of his style places those
conflicts not in the past tense but in the present and thus preserves
the possibility of the triumph of democratic enlightenment over a
decayed feudal order. Why it remains a possibility rather than an
inevitability can be measured in the development of a single
sentence, where the confidence of 'must finally prevail against
all absurd and antiquated institutions' meets with a major
qualifying condition 'unless it is violently suppressed, and this
engine of political reform turned by bribery and terror against
itself'. For Hazlitt, the principal example of obstruction on the
part of the old order to the triumph of enlightenment lay in the
career and writing of Edmund Burke.
   Hazlitt's relation to Burke was not one of simple antagonism.
In his essay, 'On the Prose Style of Poets', Hazlitt judged him the
unparalleled master of English prose, and, as we shall see, this
admiration for Burke's style was important to the formation of
Hazlitt's own writing. (12) But it is equally clear that his
admiration for Burke could become a source of embarrassment to
Hazlitt. When he published his character of Burke from 'The
Eloquence of the British Senate' in the 'Political Essays' of 1819,
Hazlitt added a footnote by way of apology: 'This character was
written in a fit of extravagant candour, at a time when I thought
I could do justice, or more than justice, to an enemy, without
betraying a cause'. (13) In an essay written in 1817 Hazlitt is
more confident in his condemnation of Burke: (14)

> It is not without reluctance that we speak of the vices and
> infirmities of such a mind as Burke's: but the poison of high
> example has by far the widest range of destruction: and ... we
> think it right to say that however it may be defended upon other

grounds, the political career of that individual has no right
to the praise of consistency. Mr Burke, the opponent of the
American War, and Mr Burke the opponent of the French Revolution,
are not the same person, but opposite persons - not opposite
persons only but deadly enemies.

Burke was the prototype of Wordsworth, Coleridge and Southey, the
literary intellectual who moved from the side of revolution to the
side of reaction. Moreover, he is for Hazlitt the main source of
reactionary ideology in the age, a writer who sacrificed a concern
for truth to the promotion of the Court interest: (15)

he represented the French priests and nobles under the old
regime as excellent moral people, very charitable and very
religious, in the teeth of notorious facts - to answer to the
handsome things he had to say in favour of priesthood and
nobility in general.

Burke is the master of unprincipled abstractions and, as such,
the head of a school of politics and political journalism which
draws the full weight of Hazlitt's sarcasm: 'and it is perhaps to
his [Burke's] example ... that we owe the prevailing tone of many
of those newspaper paragraphs which Mr Coleridge thinks so invaluable
an accession to our political philosophy'. (16)
Burke was an enemy then, but Hazlitt did not find him an enemy
who could be easily laid to rest. It was as though Hazlitt intuited
what Gramsci was later to theorize, that a dominant ideology, if it
was to be overthrown, had to be attacked at its strongest point. (17)
How complex the antagonism was between the two writers can be judged
through the analysis of an article, 'What is the People?' written
by Hazlitt in 1817. (18)
Burke is not explicitly named as the target of Hazlitt's attack
in 'What is the People?' but his presence is constantly summoned
through Hazlitt's irony. The title of the article recalls Burke's
attempts to define the people in his 'First Letter on a Regicide
Peace' and 'Appeal from the New to the Old Whigs'. (19) In the
opening paragraph of 'What is the People?' Hazlitt quotes ironically
from 'Reflections on the Revolution in France', and in the second
paragraph he emphasizes the term 'abdication' because he is there
alluding to Burke's claim in the 'Reflections' that James II was
not deposed in 1688, but abdicated. (20) Again, Hazlitt's ironic
invocation of Burke's writing can be detected in his selection of
metaphor. Thus Burke's evocation of the 'spectre' of revolution
in the 'First Letter on a Regicide Peace' - 'out of the tomb of
the murdered monarchy in France has arisen a vast, tremendous,
unformed spectre' (21) - finds its riposte in Hazlitt's 'spectre'
of Legitimacy: 'that haunts the understanding like a frightful
spectre, and oppresses the very air with a weight that is not to
be borne'. (22) Indeed, the linguistic extravagance of Hazlitt's
diatribe against Legitimacy, developing through some twenty-five
lines in the opening paragraph of 'What is the People?' can be read
as a counter to the equally extravagant diatribes against Revolution
to be found in Burke. Hazlitt adopts Burke's manner but transfers
the charge of loathing away from the word Revolution and toward the
word Legitimacy.

A more complex example of Hazlitt's appropriation of Burke comes
in his account of the source of the idea and the term 'Legitimacy'.
Hazlitt begins by sardonically rehearsing the possibility that it is
something which English kings leave as part of their inheritance: (23)

Is it an echo from the tomb of the martyred monarch Charles the
First? Or was it the last word which his son, James the Second,
left behind him in his flight, and bequeathed with his *abdication*,
to his legitimate successors?

Here again we can see how Hazlitt's style is formed out of
Burke's text: 'an echo from the tomb of the martyred monarch'
paralleling 'out of the tomb of the murdered monarchy' from the
'First Letter on a Regicide Peace'. More generally, Hazlitt's
questions mock the pious stance of Burke's writing towards the
belief that monarchy rules by inherited right.
   Hazlitt answers the questions about the source of the doctrine
of legitimacy in the following way: (24)

By taking root in the soil of France, from which it was expelled
(not quite so long as from our own) it may in time stretch out
its feelers and strong suckers to this country; and present an
altogether curious and novel aspect, by engrafting the principles
of the House of Stuart on the illustrious stock of the House of
Brunswick.

Here Hazlitt takes one of the most notorious metaphors deployed
by Burke in his attack on the revolution and makes it mean something
that the latter never intended. The relevant passage from Burke's
writing is in 'Reflections on the Revolution in France' and comes
in the context of his attack on the right of a people 'to form a
government for ourselves': (25)

The very idea of the fabrication of a new government is enough
to fill us with disgust and horror. We wished at the period of
Revolution, and do now wish, to derive all we possess as an
inheritance from our forefathers. Upon that body and stock of
inheritance we have taken care not to innoculate any cyon alien
to the nature of the original plant.

In this passage from 'Reflections', Burke has recourse to an
organic metaphor which counterposes 'natural' growth to 'unnatural'
grafting and he does so in order to defend his doctrine that
political arrangements can only be justified by appeal to what is
customary. Hazlitt uses precisely the same form of the metaphor
to suggest that Burke's doctrine and those justifications of
hereditary rule derived from it are themselves alien grafts on the
nature of English political life: 'by engrafting the principles of
the House of Stuart on the illustrious stock of the House of
Brunswick'.
   This is one instance of Hazlitt's subversion of the role of
organic metaphor in Burke's apologia for political and social
conservatism. Hazlitt's technique is to draw out an implication of
the metaphor which disturbs its conservative applications. Thus,

if Burke can use a language of organicism to persuade his reader
that the continuity of the state, like some healthy tree, must be
defended against the threat of revolution, Hazlitt can draw on the
same resource to denote not healthy but parasitic growth, as in this
attack on privilege: (26)

> [privileges] are the deadly nightshade of the commonwealth, near
> which no wholesome plant can thrive, - the ivy clinging around
> the trunk of the British oak, blighting its verdure, drying up
> its sap, and oppressing its stately growth.

One could multiply examples of Hazlitt's contention with Burke
in the text of 'What is the People?'. For the purposes of the
present analysis I want to draw on two more examples. The first
illustrates the importance of Hazlitt's writing to an understanding
of the early stages of the nineteenth-century debate about the
relations between culture and society. What Hazlitt opposes is an
account of the origins and maintenance of culture which has one
authoritative source in Burke's 'Reflections': (27)

> Nothing is more certain, than that our manners, our civilisation,
> and all the good things which are connected with manners, and
> with civilisation, have, in this European world of ours,
> depended for ages upon two principles; and were indeed the result
> of both combined; I mean the spirit of a gentleman, and the
> spirit of religion. The nobility and the clergy ... kept learning
> in existence even in the midst of arms and confusions.... Happy
> if learning, not debauched by ambition, had been satisfied to
> continue the instructor and not aspired to be the master! Along
> with its natural protectors and guardians, learning will be cast
> into the mire, and trodden down under the hoofs of a swinish
> multitude.

The central proposition, advanced by this rhetoric, that culture
depends upon elites for its existence, was to become a standard
item in the line of conservative, cultural criticism traced by
Williams in 'Culture and Society'. (28) By contrast Hazlitt's
account stresses the origins of culture in the activity of a whole
society: (29)

> Where are we to find the intellect of the people? Why, all the
> intellect that ever was is theirs. The public opinion expresses
> not only the collective sense of the whole people, but of all
> ages and nations, of all those minds that have devoted themselves
> to the love of truth and the good of mankind ... who have thought,
> spoke, written, acted and suffered in the name and on the behalf
> of our common nature. All the greatest poets, sages, heroes, are
> ours originally and by right.... All that has ever been done for
> society has, however, been done for it by this [the people's]
> intellect, before it was cheapened to be a cat's paw of divine
> right.

Again, we can notice the hidden presence of Burke's argument
structuring Hazlitt's reply. Like Burke, Hazlitt's celebration of

the sources of culture refers to what threatens it with corruption;
but whereas Burke sees the sources of this corruption in the 'swinish
multitude', Hazlitt finds its source precisely in Burke and others
like him who have cheapened intellect 'to be a cat's paw of divine
right'.

It has been necessary to quote at some length from both Burke
and Hazlitt because this helps to illuminate the aspect of their
contest that has to do with sheer rhetorical staying-power. In
'What is the People?', Hazlitt seeks to match, and even outbid the
virtuosity of Burke's prose style. Through their contest, we can
glimpse a topic that is well beyond the confines of this essay, the
role of eloquence in the political culture of which Hazlitt was a
part. But we can note Hazlitt's awareness of the importance of
eloquence in establishing politically loaded associations in the
mind of a reader or listener and then see how this adds further
evidence for what this analysis seeks to establish, that for Hazlitt
a satisfactory refutation of Burke and the conservative ideology he
represented was importantly a matter of discovering a style as
powerful as his opponent's. (30)

For Hazlitt, the refutation of Burke is achieved by changing the
meanings of metaphor, by developing an eloquence which can parallel
his opponent's and by providing alternative descriptions of
ideologically loaded topics. Thus the commitment to one kind of
description, of the sources of culture, for instance, carries with
it a commitment to other kinds of description. Taken in its
entirety, 'What is the People?' is a refutation of that contemptuous
phrase 'the swinish multitude', originated by Burke and repeated by
Coleridge and others. It is evident that describing the people as
'the swinish multitude' is not likely to connect with a description
of them as the source of culture. What it will connect with,
though, is a glorification of the aristocracy, of the sort that we
find in this passage from Burke's 'Appeal from the New to the Old
Whigs': (31)

> A true natural aristocracy is not a separate interest in the
> state, or separate from it. It is an essential integrant part
> of any large body rightly constituted. It is formed out of a
> class of legitimate presumptions, which, taken as generalities
> must be admitted for actual truths. To be bred in a place of
> estimation; to see nothing low and sordid from one's infancy;
> to be taught to respect one's self; to be habituated to the
> censorial inspection of a public eye; to look early to public
> opinion ... these are the circumstances of men that form what
> I should call a *natural* aristocracy, without which there is no
> nation.

What I have omitted from this quotation is some eighteen lines
in which Burke continues to itemize the virtues of a natural
aristocracy. It seems that Burke felt that one way to defeat an
opposition was by a multitude of examples. But it is important to
see what kind of examples they are because in this passage from the
'Appeal' Burke is constructing an imaginary aristocracy as part of
an exercise in political theory. The examples are there not because
they refer to known facts but because they give detail to Burke's

imaginary ideal, 'natural aristocracy', and, in so doing, possess
the reader's mind with an image of the aristocrat so compelling and
so attractive that it will, indeed, seem that aristocracy, and its
corollary, social inequality, are natural and, therefore, right.
It is, then, a short step from extolling an imaginary aristocracy in
theory to defending historically existing aristocracies in fact.

Hazlitt's riposte is to give Burke's kind of sentiment about the
aristocracy the title of myth that it does not want to acknowledge,
and then to contrast the myth with the facts: (32)

> The great and the powerful in order to be what they aspire to be ...
> perfectly independent of the will of the people, ought also to be
> perfectly independent of the assistance of the people. To be
> formally invested with the attributes of Gods upon earth, they
> ought first to be raised above its petty wants and appetites....
> But Legitimate Governments (flatter them as we will) are not
> another Heathen mythology. They are neither so cheap nor so
> splendid as the Delphin edition of Ovid's Metamorphoses. They
> are indeed 'Gods to punish', but in other respects 'men of our
> infirmity'. They do not feed on ambrosia or drink nectar; but
> they live on the common fruits of the earth, of which they get
> the largest share, and the best. The wine they drink is made of
> grapes: the blood they shed is that of their subjects: the laws
> they make are not against themselves: the taxes they vote, they
> afterwards devour. They have the same wants that we have.

In this passage, Hazlitt attacks a conservative mythology of
leadership by various means. One is simply to give the same thing
a different name: 'Legitimate Government' for 'natural aristocracy'.
Another is to stress what Burke's descriptions of a natural
aristocracy omit: the material needs which human beings have in
common. A third brings together two related techniques, metaphor
and description. Thus, Burke's rhapsody on the 'natural aristocracy'
leads him on to consider their role in society in terms of a metaphor
of the soul's relation to a body: (33)

> Men, qualified in the manner I have just described, form in
> Nature, as she operates in the common modifications of society,
> the leading, guiding and governing part. It is the soul to the
> body, without which man does not exist.

The metaphor sustains an argument that the governing class, 'the
natural aristocracy', is essential to the very identity of a social
order. To depose a governing class is therefore to dissolve the
social order. Under such circumstances, according to Burke, it
becomes impossible to claim a right to political power by virtue of
representing the people's will, because the people have ceased to
exist with the overthrow of their rulers.

Hazlitt opposes casuistry of this kind by switching metaphors.
The governing class are not in the relation of a soul to a body but
of a parasite to a tree: 'the ivy clinging round the trunk of the
British oak, blighting its verdure'. The metaphor of parasitism
shapes the subsequent description of the great and powerful: 'They
do not feed on ambrosia or drink nectar; but live on the common

fruits of the earth, of which they get the largest share and the best ... the taxes they vote, they afterwards devour'. The metaphor of parasitism melds into another kind of metaphoric implication governing Hazlitt's description, that of the ruling class as a selfish, voracious child, always consuming, never producing: (34)

> They have the same wants that we have: and having the option, very naturally help themselves first, out of the common stock, without thinking that others are to come after them.... Our state paupers have their hands in every man's dish, and fare sumptuously every day. They live in palaces, and loll in coaches....

As with Burke, the explicit and implied metaphors in Hazlitt's writing contribute to the argument about what constitutes legitimate political action. To destroy a parasite does not dissolve the identity of a people, but contributes towards the realization of freedom. It is a step towards Hazlitt's version of the ideal state in which individual and general interests are in a direct and reciprocal relation: (35)

> If we could suppose society to be transformed into one great animal (like Hobbes's Leviathan), each member of which had an intimate connection with the head or Government, so that every individual in it could be made known and have its due weight, the state would have the same consciousness of its own wants and feelings, and the same interest in providing for them, as an individual has with respect to his own welfare.... But such a Government would be the precise idea of a truly popular or *representative* Government. The opposite existence is the purely hereditary and despotic form of Government, where the people are an inert, torpid mass, without the power, scarcely with the will to make its wants or wishes known.

Characteristically, Hazlitt's hope for 'a truly popular or representative Government' is haunted by a sense of the powers that oppose it. As we have seen, Hazlitt believed the press to be a central mechanism in the development of democracy. But his political writings of 1817 give abundant evidence of a conviction that this central mechanism had long since been disrupted by a dominant conservative ideology fathered by Burke. Although evident in 'What is the People?', this conviction finds one of its fiercest expressions in Hazlitt's articles in 'The Times' newspaper, written in the same year. (36)

> We grant to our ingenious and romantic friend [Robert Owen] that the progress of knowledge and civilization is itself favourable to liberty and equality, and that the general stream of thought and opinion constantly sets in this way, till power finds the tide of public feeling becoming too strong for it, ready to sap its rotten foundations and 'bore through its castle walls', and then it contrives to turn the tide of knowledge and sentiment clean the contrary way.... Thus, in the year 1792, Mr. Burke became a pensioner for writing his book on the French Revolution, and Mr. Thomas Paine was outlawed for his *Rights of Man*. Since that period, the press has been the great enemy of freedom.

Written under the shadow of the conservative domination described in this quotation, 'What is the People?' is an act of definition which is also and necessarily an act of criticism. What it criticizes is, of course, Burke, but it is important to understand what form this criticism takes because at no point in the article does Hazlitt attack Burke's writings directly. As I have argued, the presence of these writings is a central force determining Hazlitt's text, but they are not present in an explicit form. What Hazlitt criticizes is the dispersed evidences of Burke's writing in the literary and journalistic culture of his time, a presence signalled by one kind of repeated phrase, or a certain kind of metaphor or rhetorical structure. Hazlitt is, in effect, criticizing Burke not as a writer but as an ideology, and with a peculiarly acute sense of the form that ideology can take as a body of ideas and language whose particular, human authorship has either been forgotten or ceased to matter.

Hazlitt could grapple with Burke as ideology because he understood his own times so insistently, and even obsessively, in terms of a political struggle between tyranny and liberty. In Hazlitt's view, by 1815, the outcome of this struggle had been decided largely in favour of tyranny. Burke's apostasy of 1792, followed by that of Wordsworth, Coleridge, and Southey, the final defeat of Napoleon in 1815, all signalled tyranny's triumph. Under such conditions, one task for writing was to keep liberty alive and we can see Hazlitt doing this in a variety of ways: by debunking conservative mythology in 'What is the People?', by commemorating the principles of the French Revolution in 'The Life of Napoleon', by arguing for the validity of democratic government in essays such as 'Project for a New Theory of Civil and Criminal Legislation', and simply by maintaining an oppositional tone in much of what he wrote. (37) But it also meant trying to understand why tyranny had defeated liberty. Hazlitt's energies were repeatedly drawn out in the effort to understand this problem and it is here that we can find evidence of incoherence and strain in his writing.

Tyranny was a compelling fact to Hazlitt's imagination, as can be evidenced by this passage from the Preface to his 'Political Essays' written in 1819: (38)

But there are persons of that low and inordinate appetite for servility, that they cannot be satisfied with anything short of that sort of tyranny that has lasted for ever, and is likely to last for ever; that is strengthened and made desperate by the superstitions and prejudices of ages; that is enshrined in traditions, in laws, in usages, in the outward symbols of power, in the very idioms of language; that has struck its roots into the human heart, and clings round the human understanding like a nightshade; that overawes the imagination and disarms the will to resist it, by the very enormity of the evil; that is cemented with gold and blood; guarded by reverence, guarded by power; linked in endless succession to the principle by which life is transmitted to the generations of tyrants and slaves, and destroying liberty with the first breath of life; that is absolute, unceasing, unerring, fatal, unutterable, abominable, monstrous.

We can trace an effort to understand the sources of a human
desire for and acceptance of domination in Hazlitt's protracted
description of tyranny. His starting point is a relatively crude
kind of psychology, 'that low and inordinate desire for servility',
which presupposes the existence of a drive within 'persons' which
finds its gratification in tyranny, but this is rapidly replaced by
a more subtle understanding of the part played by ostensibly
apolitical forms of culture - 'traditions', 'laws', 'usages', 'the
outward symbols of power', 'the very idioms of language' - in the
perpetuation of a specifically political form of domination. The
more subtle understanding brings with it an unrecognized reversal
of the place of human subjectivity vis à vis tyranny. Tyranny
ceases to be the passive object of a debased desire for subjection
and becomes instead an agent infecting human emotion and intellect
like a poisonous plant. The surface unity of the passage, supplied
as much by the sheer force of Hazlitt's indignation as anything
else, masks a radical incoherence within it over the relative power
of individual will and impersonal political forces in determining
the course of history. One consequence of this incoherence is that
the attempt at explanation tends to break down as the passage
continues. Hazlitt's preoccupation is less and less with the
operations of tyranny and more and more with giving vent to his own
anger at the very existence of political domination. Unsupported
by any attempt at explanation, Hazlitt's emotion exhausts itself
in a series of indignant adjectives: 'absolute, unceasing, unerring,
fatal, unutterable, abominable, monstrous'.

The problem revealed by this analysis of Hazlitt's prose can be
stated another way, as a problem of the relation between ethical
and political idioms in his writing. Was the defeat of democracy
to be understood principally as the outcome of an unequal political
battle in which the English state had marshalled the forces of
reaction against the revolution in France? Had the English literary
and political intelligentsia been swept on to the side of reaction
in this battle by forces that were beyond their control? Or was
the explanation to be found in the ethical character of Hazlitt's
fellow intellectuals, in a fatal bias of the will which led them
to desire fame, comfort and the protection of the powerful rather
than the continued articulation and defence of the cause of the
people?

The intensely difficult relation between an ethical and a
political understanding of culture is evident in the text of 'The
Spirit of the Age'. First published in 1825, the work proceeds
by way of a series of character sketches. One can assume from the
book's title that each one of these is intended to evoke some aspect
of the 'Spirit of the Age', although Hazlitt neither starts with nor
moves towards any general commentary on the state of English culture
in the early nineteenth century. One central problem in reading
'The Spirit of the Age' is then to infer from the aggregate of
character sketches what the nature of Hazlitt's general commentary
is.

Roy Park, in his book 'Hazlitt and the Spirit of the Age', has
argued that Hazlitt's compositional method is quite deliberate:
'it enables Hazlitt to do justice to the uniqueness of the
individual without distorting his analysis in the interest of some

more general pattern or theme'. (39) Hazlitt himself provides some
support for this judgment. In the essay 'On Depth and Superficiality'
he describes 'the way in which I work out some of my conclusions
underground, before throwing them up on the surface.... Depth consists
then in tracing any number of particular effects to a general
principle.... It is in fact resolving the concrete into the abstract.'
(40) The problem with applying this description to 'The Spirit of the
Age' is that Hazlitt's conclusions never come to the surface of the
text - certainly not in a form which would make them recognizable as
conclusions. Hazlitt's general comments on his age are scattered
through the text as appendages to his descriptions of individuals,
but they are never brought together in the form of a concluding
summary.
     If we read 'The Spirit of the Age' in the light of Hazlitt's
insistent preoccupation with the defeat of 'liberty' by 'tyranny',
it suggests that the coherence of the work is not as evident as Roy
Park contends. In one respect 'The Spirit of the Age' is a brilliant
piece of reportage, tracing the effects in personality, in intellectual work and political life of an historical change - the triumph
of 'liberty' - that failed to occur. Hazlitt's presentation of
cultural life is resonant with the defeat of the French Revolution
and of the equivalent political radicalism in England. The
evidences are there in particular lives, in Southey's apostasy,
starting out as a democrat, ending up as a conservative Poet
Laureate: 'He wooed Liberty as a youthful lover, but it was perhaps
more as a mistress than a bride; and he has since wedded with an
elderly and not very reputable lady, called Legitimacy.' (41)
     The same pattern is evident in Hazlitt's sketch of Coleridge,
although the spectacle of Coleridge's life engages Hazlitt's sympathy
as much as his sarcasm: (42)

> It was a misfortune to any man of talent to be born in the
> latter end of the last century. Genius stopped the way of
> Legitimacy, and therefore it was to be abated, crushed or set
> aside as a nuisance.... The flame of liberty, the light of
> intellect was to be extinguished with the sword - or with slander,
> whose edge is sharper than the sword. The war between power and
> reason was carried on by the first of these abroad, by the last
> at home. No quarter was given (then or now) by the Government-
> critics, the authorized censors of the press, to those who
> followed the dictates of independence, who listened to the voice
> of the tempter Fancy.

Coleridge is presented by Hazlitt as the principal victim of the
political and cultural reaction described in this quotation. In
this perspective, the causes that distorted Coleridge's creativity
are to be found in a determining historical condition, one, moreover,
to which Coleridge was peculiarly vulnerable as a poet because, in
Hazlitt's view, 'the poets, the creatures of sympathy, could not
stand the frowns both of king and people. They did not like to be
shut out when places and pensions, when the critic's praises, and
the laurel wreath were about to be distributed'. (43) But the
anger and the irony in these sentences is ambivalent. It is
difficult to know whether Hazlitt is attacking a cultural condition -

the damaging effects of political repression upon a crucial and
sustaining relation between poet and audience - or whether he is
attacking poets for their moral weakness, their excessive dependency
upon an audience which makes them fold when the political going gets
tough. What in one sentence looks like a legitimate need for
'sympathy' becomes in the next a morally reprehensible desire for the
comforts of patronage and the rewards of fame: 'places and pensions',
'the critic's praises, and the laurel wreath'.

The uncertainty of focus revealed in Hazlitt's essay on Coleridge
is indicative of the transitional nature of 'The Spirit of the Age'.
In one respect the work is written out of an eighteenth-century mode,
the essay, whose predominant concerns are with moral satire, with
judgment in ethical and aesthetic matters. The social function of
the mode was to patrol and define the shifting boundaries of 'polite'
culture during the eighteenth century. (44) It was one instrument in
promoting the alliance between aristocracy and bourgeoisie, an
alliance whose importance in Jane Austen's work has already been
discussed by David Aers. (45) Yet in 'The Spirit of the Age' this
mode is used by Hazlitt to carry a consciousness of historical change,
of the impact of political forces upon individual lives, and this is
a strain which it can hardly bear.

The same difficulty can be defined in a different way. In 'The
Spirit of the Age' Hazlitt is constrained to write in the mode of a
culture whose historical failure it is one of his purposes to
criticize and condemn. One consequence of this has already been
noted in the confused relation between attacks on a particular
individual and a criticism of the culture that he represents. Another
consequence is in the sudden shifts of attention within a single
essay. Thus the essay on Sir Walter Scott begins as a conventional
exercise in literary taste. Hazlitt discriminates the weakness of
Scott's poetry from the strength of his novels. He seems to be
working within the terms of the culture that read Scott's fiction in
such quantity. But Hazlitt's praise of Scott's novels - 'He is the
only amanuensis of truth and history' - unexpectedly turns into a
political critique of his fiction, and, by implication, of its
audience: (46)

> The political bearings of the Scotch Novels has been a considerable
> recommendation to them. They are a relief to the mind, rarefied
> as it has been with modern philosophy, and heated with ultra-
> radicalism. At a time also, when we bid fair to revive the
> principles of the Stuarts, it is interesting to bring us acquainted
> with their persons and misfortunes....
>
> Sir Walter is a professed *clarifier* of the age from the vulgar
> and still lurking old-English antipathy to Popery and Slavery.
> Through some odd process of *servile* logice, it should seem, that
> in restoring the claims of the Stuarts by the courtesy of romance,
> the House of Brunswick are more firmly seated in point of fact
> and the Bourbons, by collateral reasoning, become legitimate!

The emphasis which Hazlitt gives to the word 'clarifier' in this
passage is an index to the nature of its irony. The project of the
Enlightenment, to dispel superstition through the operations of
reason, finds its reversal in the work of Scott which puts supersti-

tion in the place of reason and identifies what is reasonable as superstitious. Hence a rational objection to Catholicism (which Hazlitt consistently identifies as the religion of feudalism, and, therefore, tyranny) and to slavery is ironically phrased as 'the vulgar and still lurking old-English antipathy to Popery and Slavery'.

Hazlitt's judgment of Scott identifies the latter as part of that process of co-operation and accommodation with political reaction which Hazlitt saw as the leading characteristic of the English intelligentsia in the early nineteenth century. The problem is that a hostile judgment of the ideological tendency of Scott's work is juxtaposed with a more conventional praise of his literary merits in an essay which can relate the two kinds of judgment only by means of a vitriolic attack on Scott's character culminating in a generalized lament on the degradation of 'genius'. This is simply to restate the co-existence of Hazlitt's opposed responses to Scott's work without engaging with the problem they imply, that what is good as literature can be bad as politics. One could analyse Hazlitt's failure to relate his contradictory judgments of Scott's work as, again, a matter of the constraints of the essay form. But there is another kind of explanation which needs to be set alongside an analysis of the constraints imposed by a particular form, and it has to do with the obsessional nature of Hazlitt's thought. Hazlitt's preoccupation with the struggle between liberty and tyranny in his own time, and the defeat of the former by the latter, has the quality of an obsession because of its insistent repetition in his writing; because, as in the essay on Scott, it can co-exist, quite unconsciously, with seemingly opposed responses, and because it provides a displaced form of expression for a sense of personal grievance and frustration in Hazlitt himself. This is not to argue that because Hazlitt's reading of his own time was obsessional it was therefore untrue. He was a prescient and acute critic of the repressive and politically conservative culture that was to become increasingly dominant during the nineteenth century. Hazlitt saw this culture in the making and he had an exacerbated perception that what he saw was not an inevitability of English life but the outcome of a particular historical period in which forces of revolution and reaction came into an acute and decisive conflict.

But to see an obsessional character in Hazlitt's thought confronts us with some of its limitations. Thus, the defeat of Napoleon in 1815 added to Hazlitt's conviction that the cause of radicalism had been defeated. Although his political writings of the period show him responding to the crisis in British society brought on by the end of the Napoleonic war, he did not read that crisis as a renewal of radical politics in England, as what E.P. Thompson has described as the 'heroic age of popular Radicalism'. (47) For Hazlitt the 'heroic age' ended rather than began with 1815. His formation as a political radical had occurred long before. He was brought up in an atmosphere of dissent, the son of a Unitarian minister who had strongly supported the American cause in the War of Independence, and was educated at Hackney College, a place which in its brief existence became notorious as a centre of atheism and radical politics. (48) The outbreak of the French Revolution in 1789 rather than events in England after 1815 had confirmed Hazlitt in his radical convictions. Hazlitt's political formation disposed him to

make two kinds of identification. One caused him to see the
principal source of a politically radical culture in a relatively
small circle of intellectuals, men like his father, or Priestley, or
the young Coleridge. The other was to make him identify the fate of
the radical cause with the outcome of events in France. Given these
circumstances, and given, too, the intensity of Hazlitt's identifications, the way for example, in which he could view the young
Coleridge as the harbinger of a new age, it is not surprising that
he failed to respond to a radicalism whose source was in mass
insurgency and not in the espousal of the cause of liberty by small
groups of intellectuals and religious dissenters. (49)

Thus, the defeat of liberty became for Hazlitt not only a way of
understanding events after 1789 but a myth about his own relation
to culture. If it was a myth which could set limits to his
perception of history, it could also give him a sharp awareness of
the ideological bearings of thought in early nineteenth-century
England. It can tell us, too, about the particular character of
Hazlitt's romanticism. If we apply to Hazlitt Frederic Jameson's
description of romanticism 'as a coming to consciousness of some
fundamental loss in shock and rage, a kind of furious rattling of
the bars of the prison, a helpless attempt to recuperate lost being
by posing and assuming one's fatality in "interesting" ways', then
the sense of 'fundamental loss' in Hazlitt's writing does not
consist in the projection of what the writer takes to be a lost
historical world but in the reference to an historical eventuality
that failed to occur: the realization of a new civilization in
England and France after 1789. (50) Thus, although Hazlitt's work
contains Wordsworthian recollections of childhood and speculations
about the importance of memory to personal identity, memory does
not lead on, as it does in Wordsworth, to the imagination of a
social world threatened by historical change. The sense of loss in
Hazlitt's writing is figured less in terms of what has ceased to be
than in terms of what might have been.

The political basis of Hazlitt's sensibility has a number of
consequences for his thinking on art and literature, and here I
only have room to mention two of them. Hazlitt discerned and
responded to a utopian content in art. Art could preserve and
sustain the hopes that history had failed to realize. The result
was that Hazlitt responded to the works of art gathered in the
Louvre with a particular intensity: (51)

> Instead of robbery and sacrilege, it was the crowning and
> consecration of art; there was a dream and a glory like the
> coming of the Millenium.... Art, no longer a bondswoman, was
> seated on a throne, and her sons were kings. The spirit of man
> walked erect, and found its true level in the triumph of real
> over factitious claims. Whoever felt the sense of beauty or
> the yearning after excellence haunt his breast, was amply avenged
> on the injustice of fortune, and might boldly answer those who
> asked what there was but birth and title in the world that was
> not base and sordid - 'Look around! These are my inheritance;
> this is the class to which I belong.'

For Hazlitt, the Louvre is a setting which releases art from its

association with tyranny. This new setting permits a new kind of
response, one which sustains an energy that drives against the
arguments of privilege. It is characteristic of Hazlitt's sensibility
that aesthetic response should lead on to an argument with a
reactionary conservatism; it is an index of his sense of isolation
that, by the late 1820s, he should be finding his principal kinship
with art.

Politics inform Hazlitt's contribution to the romantic concern
with the faculty of imagination. In his discussion of 'Coriolanus'
Hazlitt opposes the 'aristocratic' imagination to a 'republican'
faculty of understanding: (52)

> The language of poetry naturally falls in with the language of
> power. The imagination is an exaggerating and exclusive faculty:
> it takes from one thing to add to another: it accumulates
> circumstances together to give the greatest possible effect to a
> favourite object. The understanding is a dividing and measuring
> faculty. It judges of things not according to their immediate
> impression on the mind, but according to their relations to one
> another. The one is a monopolising faculty which seeks the
> greatest quantity of present excitement by inequality and dispro-
> portion; the other is a distributive faculty, which seeks the
> greatest quantity of ultimate good, by justice and proportion.
> The one is an aristocratical, the other a republican faculty.
> The principle of poetry is a very anti-levelling principle. It
> aims at effect, it exists by contrast.... Poetry is right-royal.

Hazlitt's politically grounded definitions contrast strongly
with Coleridge's metaphysically based account of imagination in
'Biographia Literaria'. (53) Where Coleridge emphasizes the
synthesizing power of imagaination, Hazlitt's stress falls upon the
imagination as an 'exaggerating and exclusive faculty'. Indeed,
what Hazlitt calls imagination could be seen, in other terms, as an
obsessional mode of perception.

Starting in politics rather than metaphysics, Hazlitt sees a
problem about the relation between imagination and democracy which
is simply not there for the Coleridge of the 'Biographia Literaria'.
Writing in 1816, Hazlitt seems to have arrived at a final judgment
on the opposition between the forces that lead to poetry and those
that lead to democracy. But in the same year, Hazlitt could write
in another place that the 'spirit of poetry is in itself favourable
to humanity and liberty: but, we suspect, not in times like these -
not in the present reign'. (54) This suggests that the opposition
between poetry and democracy is not absolute but contingent. With
this in mind, we can return to Hazlitt's distinction between
imagination and understanding in his essay on 'Coriolanus' and
recognize that what is being opposed is not imagination to democracy
as such. Rather the opposition is between imagination and Jacobinism.
This latter Hazlitt regarded as a vital, but essentially negative,
moment in the formation of democracy. Jacobinism was a state of
mind which dispelled illusions about the ancien régime: 'A person
who is what is called a Jacobin ... who has shaken off certain well-
known prejudices with respect to kings or priests, or nobles, cannot
so easily resume them again'. In its necessary work of destruction

'it levels all distinctions of art and nature'. (55) The negativity of Jacobinism opposed what Hazlitt saw as the affirmative powers of art. What art foregrounded was the specific and the particular in objects and people, and it was at odds with a Jacobin understanding which saw objects and people in terms of their abstract equality.

This reading supplies a coherence to Hazlitt's understanding of the relation between imagination and politics by connecting together the disparate evidences of the essay on 'Coriolanus' with the discussion of poetry and Jacobinism in his 'Illustrations of "The Times" Newspaper'. Hazlitt does not make the connection himself, does not make clear to the reader of the essay on 'Coriolanus' that the opposition between imagination and understanding can be equated with the opposition between poetry and Jacobinism. The tendency of the essay on 'Coriolanus', proceeding by way of an analysis of faculties, is to make art and democracy seem absolute opponents; the historically based commentary in the 'Illustrations of "The Times" Newspaper' allows us to see the opposition as contingent, a matter determined by the particular phase of a historical culture rather than an absolute of perception. Supplying coherence in this way can draw our attention to another source of limitation in Hazlitt's work, in the fragmenting pressure exercised upon his thought by the demands of writing for a literary market. These demands dictated a form which, as we have seen, Hazlitt could put to effective, radical use. But they also set a limit to the kinds of connection that Hazlitt could make between his political and artistic writings. Thus, what we find in Hazlitt's work is a series of brilliant but dispersed criticisms of his culture rather than a sustained critique of it. He perceived problems which remain crucial to radical criticism: the relation between art and politics and between language and ideology, the predominance of conservatism within English culture. But he did so in forms which prevented a sustained reflection on the meaning of what he saw. In this way, perhaps, the culture which he could criticize with such vehemence and insight exacted its revenge upon him.

Chapter 9

Shelley: Poetry and Politics

David Punter

Shelley, like Blake, has a reputation as a difficult poet: erudite, imagistically complex, full of classical and mythological allusions. But the acts of reading Blake and Shelley, and the problems we encounter in reading, are very different; both writers make high demands on our interpretative powers, but they do so in quite distinct ways. We can usefully summarize these differences by beginning from the 'received idea', the general critical opinion which surrounds all writers like an aura. The received idea about Blake is bifurcated: on the one hand there is the image of the mystic, the visionary cut off from the affairs of men, on the other the image of the working-class social revolutionary; we have already seen that neither image retains much force when we actually examine the texts. The received idea with which Shelley is surrounded is also bifurcated, but in a way which reminds us more strongly of Coleridge: it is summarized in the well-known passage from Mary Shelley, where she describes what she thought of as the battle which took place in her husband's mind and in his writing: (1)

> Shelley possessed two remarkable qualities of intellect - a
> brilliant imagination and a logical exactness of reason. His
> inclination led him (he fancied) almost alike to poetry and
> metaphysical discussions. I say 'he fancied', because I believe
> the former to have been paramount, and that it would have gained
> the mastery even had he struggled against it. However, he said
> that he deliberated at one time whether he should dedicate himself
> to poetry or metaphysics, and resolving the former, he educated
> himself for it, discarding in a great measure his philosophical
> pursuits.

This comment delineates a familiar set of romantic contours. What first springs to mind is Coleridge's anxiety about the effects his metaphysical inclinations were having in later life on the well-springs of his poetry, about how his probings into the difficulties and subtleties of the German philosophers in the end conflicted with his ability to write imaginatively. (2) In Coleridge's case the conflict was deepened because it entailed renouncing the feasibility of the 'philosophic poem', the work of synthesis which stood in

relation to many a romantic poetic effort very much as the epic had
to the Augustans. (3)

In Coleridge's writings, there is considerable complexity on
these matters, for instance in 'Biographia Literaria' (1817), where
the attempt is made to reunite philosophical speculation with a
theory of poetry in order to assert the possibility of securing a
philosophically correct base for a descriptive and prescriptive
poetic. The relevant connections are effected through a series of
epistemological speculations, (4) and the crucial and resonant
distinctions between Reason and Understanding, Fancy and the
Imagination, hinge on this issue, which is the issue of how to
achieve wholeness in the face of an ideology of fragmentation, of
how to bring the future and the imaginary into relation with the
present when the accepted views of that present are governed, in
Coleridge's opinion and in Shelley's, by a dry empiricism at the
service of social conservatism. Coleridge's principal effort, in
'Biographia' and elsewhere, is towards asserting a rival truth value,
a poetic truth value which will validate the discoveries and methods
of poetic perception alongside logical truth; thus the imagination
comes to represent the activity of synthesis where logic represents
analysis, a synthesis within which facts can have a place alongside
speculation, within which the partialities of empiricism and
rationalism can be made whole.

In Coleridge again, this urge towards synthesis is also treated
in terms of subject and object; indeed, to think of 'Biographia
Literaria' again, the relations of subject and object provide not
only the theoretical impulse behind the discussion of poetic
perception, they also dictate the entire form of the book, which in
its own structure asserts that truth can be found only by juxtaposing
objective arguments and conclusions about the nature of the world
and of literature with the subjective history of an individual, the
poet himself. In 'Biographia' the systematic discussion of opinions
and conclusions is inseparable from the genetic account of how such
opinions and conclusions came to be formed. What is, of course,
apparent is that this romantic discourse of subject and object,
individual and universal, suffers from the lack of a mediating term,
can indeed be seen as an evasion of that term, the category of the
social: that the fears of intellectual fragmentation and personal
dissolution from which Coleridge paradigmatically suffered could not
be allayed without venturing into a coherent analysis of social and
economic causation.

Imagination in Coleridge is, among other things, a variety of
system, and serves thus as a substitute for the cogent forms of
integrated social life; it is a principle of interconnection, a
continuing assertion of the inseparability of different areas of
human experience. Imagination is Coleridge's mechanism for
reconnecting what our impoverished everyday perceptions put asunder.
It also claims that the act of perception, of apprehending objects
in the 'outside' world, is not at all what it appears to be, the
mere bringing into juxtaposition of two separate entities, subject
and object; rather it is a process of continual dialectical
synthesis, wherein subject and object are continually fusing and
dissolving, or wherein, in poetic terms, the identity of the poet
is continually being merged with the identity of natural objects in

a way which gives rise to a higher third term, in which not only
the objects but also the poet himself is transformed. It is this
signal transformation the failure of which Coleridge regrets so
bitterly in 'Dejection: An Ode' (1802): (5) the mere sound of the
wind, considered as the impinging of an external phenomenon, is in
itself meaningless: real, poetic perception requires a deeper
apprehension, one at the same time more exciting and more at risk,
in which the isolation and secure homogeneity of the self must be
sacrificed, at the very least in the passive receptivity frequently
imaged by Coleridge in the Aeolian harp, (6) but more satisfactorily
in an activity of continuing participation in the natural world.

Blake shared some of the presuppositions of this argument, but
characteristically transformed to take structural account of social
development. For him, the writing of history was simultaneously
'subjective' and 'objective', and it is for this reason that the
structure of the prophetic books is so complex: but 'objective' here
has a broader, more human meaning than in Coleridge. The prophetic
books assert that the history of the world, of the rise and fall of
civilizations, of the interplay and development of the great forces
and powers which determine change in society, is at the same time the
history of the development of the individual mind. Thus the giant
Albion, within whom the activity of 'Vala, or The Four Zoas' (1795-
1804) takes place, is at the same time the embodiment of England,
the stage on which history is played out, and also the individual -
not body, soul or mind but the whole concrete individual in
connection with the social forces which shape the person. And the
story of 'The Four Zoas' is the story of the fate of the individual
within a bitterly divided society, the story of the fragmentation
of Albion, of his separation into a bundle of conflicting faculties
and attributes and of the struggle for hegemony which is then played
out among these one-sided entities. It thus becomes at the same
time an extended critique of the social fragmentation which Blake
saw as accompanying an intellectual loss of the sense of totality
in human affairs, and a critique of individual fragmentation and
the consequent worship of Reason. For Blake the supremacy of Urizen
is at the same time the rule of unenlightened rationalism in the
human mind and the institutionalization of reason in the practices
of society at a given stage in history. Urizen, we might say, is a
nexus of authoritarianism: the author of repressive rules and
regulations and at the same time the father who, in various of
Blake's poems, dictates the child's entry into the cycle of pleasure
and misery and who, in time, the child becomes. (7)

Much of Blake's work is predicated on a demand for reorganization,
the reorganization of society and the human personality around
genuine needs, and the reintegration of reason, emotion, instinct
at the service of socio-psychological progress. But it is also
predicated on a strong awareness of the power of the substitute
order produced by ideology, of the way in which on the one hand
what is in fact a chaos of social and economic market forces can be
made to seem ordered, and on the other hand this chaos itself is
related to concealed interconnections between the agencies of
oppression. In 'London' ('Songs of Experience', 1794) for instance,
the issues of war, industry and marriage are worked into a single
texture: the emphasis is not on the evil of any of these phenomena

individually, but on their significance as manifestations of a
general structure of repressiveness embedded in the very form of
contemporary society. The well-known paradoxes in the poem gain their
strength not from uniqueness but from their structural similarity,
from the implicit assertion that they are all representations of a
single fissure in society, a failure of unity implicit in every
social practice and institution.

In Coleridge and in Blake, then, the concept of imagination is
closely related in different ways to the exposure of false system
and the perception of true system, and this gives us a basis on
which to approach Shelley, no less than his predecessors a poet of
the imagination despite the differences in the theory of faculties
which exist between the three poets. In all three, imagination
implies a system within which literary creativity is closely related
to other spheres of thought and feeling: partly because of the
general connectedness of life which the imagination asserts, but
more importantly because literature, as the most important art of
the imaginary and the future, needs to be complemented by a science
of the existent and the present: and this science, for Blake and
usually for Shelley if only very occasionally for Coleridge, must
be political. This essay sets out to draw an elementary topography
of Shelley's imaginative system, to point out some of the ways in
which poetry and the political relate in his work. First, I shall
look at 'Prometheus Unbound', in which he outlines the overall
meaning of the imaginative synthesis and its relation to human
lives. Second, in 'The Mask of Anarchy' I shall look at some of
the ways in which he explores the relations between words and
immediate events, and thereby suggests relations between language,
consciousness and history. Third, in the 'Ode to Liberty' I shall
look at the explicit attention which he gives to the place words
have in formulating our political beliefs and actions. And finally,
I shall try, on the basis of these investigations, to interpret a
passage from 'A Defence of Poetry' (1821), the passage wherein he
sets forth his best-known conclusions on the relation between poetry
and the social world. (8) And it is worth emphasizing at this point
that this is not a matter of outlining a static system: Shelley's
attitude towards practical politics was highly changeable, oscillating
between a conviction of the necessity of immersion in the practicali-
ties of radicalism and retreat into the elitist stance of the
alienated poet. (9)

Mary Shelley's comment clearly challenges the idea of system by
asserting that a central dualism runs through Shelley's work: on
one side is the brilliance of imagination, on the other the logical
exactness of reason. A necessary consequence of this dualism is a
certain model of the poem: to separate imagination and reason is
tantamount to asserting that these different faculties have different
objects, and thus that poetry is restricted to the perception only
of certain portions of the world. The poetic mode becomes one mode
of apprehension among others: thus, the transformation or preserva-
tion of the world which poetry effects is only partial. She is also
saying something more than this in classifying Shelley's interests
as metaphysical at all: she is implicitly placing a value judgment
on them, removing them 'beyond' the natural or social realm, and
thus condemning certain areas of speculation to a merely ideal

existence. And this, of course, is the thread on which another
aspect of the received idea of Shelley hangs: the idealism of his
opinions and concepts, his transmutation of the concrete into the
abstract. (10) And, of course, there is a pressure of this kind in
Shelley, caused by the way in which he conceived the problem of the
political: how, he asks, in several different ways, is a poet to
challenge the established realm of empirical facts, the orthodox
view of social rectitude, without seeking to attain a position above
those facts and beyond that narrow rectitude? We may answer that
this can only be done by precise and close attention to the material
world, but this was not Shelley's answer; and when we think of his
work in terms of the cloud or the skylark, floating effortlessly
above worldly transience, it is fair also to keep in mind a sharpness
of gaze, Shelley's intense desire - not at all times, but none the
less strong - somehow to bring back the wisdom of overview and use
it to re-energize life below.

'Prometheus Unbound', the lengthy verse-play of 1818-19, is a
re-telling of the Prometheus legend, the story of the Titan who,
in asserting the right of humanity to divine knowledge, offends the
gods by transgressing the boundaries of taboo and is given over by
Jupiter to infinite torture, both as punishment and as eternal
warning to the rest of mankind. Shelley's starting-point is
Aeschylus' version of the myth, in which Prometheus is eventually
reconciled with his torturer as a reward for revealing the dangers
to which Jupiter would be exposed by his intended marriage to
Thetis. In other words, as Shelley saw it, Prometheus sold out for
personal gain and salvation. In the Preface to 'Prometheus Unbound',
he makes his difference from Aeschylus clear:

> in truth, I was averse from a catastrophe so feeble as that of
> reconciling the Champion with the Oppressor of mankind. The
> moral interest of the fable, which is so powerfully sustained
> by the sufferings and endurance of Prometheus, would be annihila-
> ted if we could conceive of him as unsaying his high language
> and quailing before his successful and perfidious adversary.
> The only imaginary being resembling in any degree Prometheus, is
> Satan; and Prometheus is, in my judgement, a more poetical
> character than Satan, because, in addition to courage, and
> majesty, and firm and patient opposition to omnipotent force,
> he is susceptible of being described as exempt from the taints
> of ambition, envy, revenge, and a desire for personal aggrandise-
> ment, which, in the Hero of *Paradise Lost*, interfere with the
> interest.

The concept of the 'poetical' here is interesting: from what
Shelley says, one could fairly suppose that Satan might be considered
the more appropriate hero if the criteria were to be complexity of
character, vicarious excitement or intensity of conflict. But
Shelley's criterion is none of these: his claim here is to be less
concerned with delight than with instruction, and Prometheus is
seen as appropriate because he is a more adequate representative of
human problems. The reversal of Aeschylus clearly invites comparison
with Blake's judgment that Milton's Satan was a more admirable
character than his God, (11) and that there is a kind of purpose

inherent in 'Paradise Lost' which is opposite to what we have been
taught to think of Milton's advocacy: it was in accordance with this
idea that Blake called several of his books parts of an Infernal
Bible, (12) and some of Shelley's work should be seen as a continuation of this Infernal Bible, a rewriting of the old myths from the
point of view of the oppressed, a search to unearth the human meaning
encapsulated in the mythic code.

The virtue which underlies courage and majesty and is more admirable
than either of them is a puzzling one, for what is hinted at in the
condemnation of reconciliation and in this idea of 'firm and patient
opposition to omnipotent force' is surely a paradoxical and intransigent
quality. Shelley is concerned with the spirit which allows men to
resist kneeling before his oppressors, even while he knows their power.
And yet, what in fact is one to make of the paradox? If we are not to
put it down to mere sentimentalist exaggeration, then we must suggest
that Shelley is implicitly calling into question the meaning of
'omnipotence', asserting its relativity, driving a wedge between the
actual power and the ideological representation. The assumption is
that those powers which seem fated to press down on man and force him
into submission are not what they appear to be: that it is the major
function of ideology to naturalize, to make factors which are contingent
and changeable appear permanent and natural, and that ideology is at
its most effective when it can persuade people into acquiescing in this
operation and refusing their own right of resistance. But Shelley's
world-picture is one which permits change: omnipotence is relative.

Man is a victim thus not of an irresistible power but of his own
weak adoption of false gods, his own acceptance of the alienation
which he has previously created. (13) An important question about
'Prometheus Unbound', however, concerns the nature of this alienation,
or, in other words, the identity of Jupiter. He is described in bitter
terms in Act I, when the original curse is repeated:

> Aye, do thy worst.   Thou art omnipotent.
>   O'er all things but thyself I gave thee power,
> And my own will. Be thy swift mischiefs sent
>   To blast mankind, from yon ethereal tower
> Let thy malignant spirit move
> In darkness over those I love:
> On me and mine I imprecate
> The utmost torture of thy hate;
> And thus devote to sleepless agony,
> This undeclining head while thou must reign on high.
>   (I. 272-81)

The passage is shot through with contradiction: omnipotence is
defined as 'all things but', and in accordance with this Prometheus
asserts Jupiter's superiority in power while at the same time exposing
the temporary nature of that power, a temporariness which is evidenced
in terms of dramatic device by the secret which Prometheus possesses.
But what 'Prometheus Unbound' as a whole reveals is that this contradiction is neither a poetic device of exaggeration nor a 'metaphysical'
paradox; what it portrays is less an intransigent clash of objects or
mythic persons than the intransigent clash of two modes of perception,
of two entire systems. Jupiter's omnipotence depends on an assumption

that perceptual totality is restricted to the existent and the
present, a circular argument for there is nothing within the narrow
world of empirical facts which can challenge or threaten his rule.
But when the perception of totality is changed, when the imaginary
and the future make their entrance, Jupiter's rule is perceived as -
or rather, becomes - illusory. Jupiter's portrait is solid, but when
the pictures start to move he vanishes like the air. Or, Jupiter is
omnipotent as long as he can sustain belief in his own omnipotence
and as long as he can impress that belief on the rest of the world;
but Prometheus can threaten and demolish that omnipotence by refusing
to accede to it. Jupiter is not only a character in a myth: he
represents also a stage of the world, the Jupiter stage, wherein
behaviour and systematization are governed by belief in an omnipotent
God.

'Prometheus Unbound' is the story of Prometheus's continuous
refusal to be taken in by the false picture of the world with which
Jupiter presents him. One of Jupiter's devices to secure his
acquiescence is his sending of the Furies, but it needs to be noted
that the Furies have a highly ambivalent and synthetic form of
existence: they are not real objects, and yet they are not merely the
products of fantasy. The status of their existence depends on
Prometheus's attitude to them, and he addresses them in these terms:

> Horrible forms,
> What and who are ye? Never yet there came
> Phantasms so foul thro' monster-teeming Hell
> From the all-miscreative brain of Jove;
> Whilst I behold such execrable shapes,
> Methinks I grow like what I contemplate,
> And laugh and stare in loathsome sympathy.
>   (I.445-51)

Phantasms and shapes are Jupiter's weapons against human aspiration:
they are the fear of the future and the fear of change, and it is
through such insubstantial means that man is kept in servitude. What
Prometheus seems worried about here, though, is not fear of the
Furies, but fear that he might in some sense become like them: he is
not afraid of the revenge of the establishment, but he is afraid of
himself falling into the trap of cynical conservatism which Jupiter's
minions represent.

The battle of 'Prometheus Unbound' takes place neither in the real
world nor in the mind, but between imaginings, for Shelley believes
the imagination capable of producing real acts of synthesis, of
producing reality from its activities. Prometheus and Jupiter are
engaged in the struggle to produce a reality, and only one can exist
at a time. Thus for Shelley the collapse of Jupiter at the hands of
the mysterious Demogorgon in Act III effects a complete transformation
of the real world as the webs of ideological mystification fall away;
Ocean says:

> Henceforth the fields of Heaven-reflecting sea
> Which are my realm, will heave, unstain'd with blood,
> Beneath the uplifting winds, like plains of corn
> Swayed by the summer air; my streams will flow

> Round many-peopled continents, and round
> Fortunate isles; and from their glassy thrones
> Blue Proteus and his humid nymphs shall mark
> The shadow of fair ships, as mortals see
> The floating bark of the light-laden moon
> With that white star, its sightless pilot's crest,
> Borne down the rapid sunset's ebbing sea;
> Tracking their path no more by blood and groans,
> And desolation, and the mingled voice
> Of slavery and command; but by the light
> Of wave-reflected flowers, and floating odours,
> And music soft, and mild, free, gentle voices,
> That sweetest music, such as spirits love.
>   (III.ii.18-34)

Clearly Shelley's conception of the process of change is wildly simplistic, and it would also be possible to criticise this passage, and many others like it in 'Prometheus Unbound', as a mere catalogue. But the point is more complex than this, for Shelley is trying to provide images for a transformation which will allow individual beings to attain to their own individuality. This is one of the several meanings of the deliberately intrusive phrase, 'the mingled voice/Of slavery and command': as in Blake what appears to be order is portrayed as disorder, whereas particularity is given as the basis of the new imaginative world which is to replace that based on the logic of domination. The word 'mingled' presumably also refers to the way in which those who command are themselves also slaves: the world of Jupiter is one in which nobody can win, because there are always higher 'authorities'.

Jupiter is the system of domination by which men seek to exert control over their fellow-men and over nature, the system which denies human powers and sets up gods, kings, priests. The whole idea of superior role and hierarchy stems, according to Shelley, from this system of domination, which in turn derives from the assertion that man is not essentially a co-operative being, but needs to be coerced into a semblance of civilized behaviour, an assertion common to all conservative political theorists. Jupiter-man is at root very like Hobbes's atomistic being, devoid of organic links with his fellows and destined to submit to rules and laws which he can barely understand. (14) It is revealing that Shelley, coming as he does largely from a tradition of 'philosophical' radicalism rather than from an exposure to practical social problems, should not notice that the whole method of deriving social formations from 'pre-existing' theoretical premises is open to the same objection: to argue from 'the nature of man' is inherently conservative, whether or not the conclusions drawn are pessimistic. (15)

Thus we have an opposition between two different languages: Jupiter speaks a language of domination which is opposed by Prometheus's language, which is poetry. Thus in the final Act, Jupiter's downfall is followed by a transformation into song, and we hear the music of the liberated spirits kept so long under Jupiter's subjugation. The opposition between past domination and present liberation evidenced in the rebirth of poetry is implicit in every lyric:

Weave the dance on the floor of the breeze,
  Pierce with song heaven's silent light,
Enchant the day that too swiftly flees,
  To check its flight ere the cave of night.

Once the hungry Hours were hounds
  Which chased the day like a bleeding deer,
And it limped and stumbled with many wounds
  Through the nightly dells of the desert year.

But now, oh, weave the mystic measure
  Of music, and dance, and shapes of light,
Let the Hours, and the spirits of might and pleasure,
  Like the clouds and sunbeams, unite.
                    (IV.69-80)

There is considerable emphasis on the liberation of time in
'Prometheus Unbound', on the constraints which the world of Jupiter
has laid on our capacity for organizing our own time; (16) also of
interest here is Shelley's call for the reuniting of 'the spirits of
might and pleasure', in other words for strength and enjoyment no
longer to be considered as opposites, for the realms of work and play
to be reintegrated, and, indeed, for masculine and feminine
characteristics to be released from their stereotyping. But it is
as much as anything else the words and rhythms themselves, the words
and rhythms of poetry, which Prometheus has supposedly succeeded in
liberating: the 'plot' of 'Prometheus Unbound' is the language, the
movement from the ponderous to the light, from words weighed down
with guilt, repression and suffering to words which dance and
celebrate. And it is here that the essential contradiction of the
work lies: we can see Shelley as trying in it to reverse the
conservative movement of, say, Coleridge's thinking and to move from
the abstract to the concrete, (17) from the 'insubstantial' dominance
of Jupiter to the co-operative world liberated by Prometheus, but in
fact his language subverts the purpose: his notion of the concrete
remains unrealized because a by now conventionally romantic apparatus
of poeticization obscures it from sight.
  'The Mask of Anarchy', written at the same time as 'Prometheus',
represents a very different attempt on Shelley's part. It was written
as a direct response to the Peterloo 'Massacre', (18) and relies
heavily on contemporary reports, (19) largely because, of course,
Shelley was not in England at the time, as the opening of the poem
reminds us:

As I lay asleep in Italy
There came a voice from over the Sea,
And with great power it forth led me
To walk in the visions of Poesy.

I met Murder on the way -
He had a mask like Castlereagh -
Very smooth he looked, yet grim;
Seven blood-hounds followed him:

All were fat; and well they might
Be in admirable plight,
For one by one, and two by two,
He tossed them human hearts to chew.
Which from his wide cloak he drew.
                    (1-13)

The poem continues as a blatant allegory of the state of England;
but it is worth concentrating on this short passage for a moment.
The use of the term 'visions of Poesy' in the opening stanza is
significantly ironic: it is the kind of archaism which might well
have been appropriate to the mode of writing we find in 'Prometheus
Unbound', but here it gains its meaning from the stark contrast
between the poetry of retreat and introspection which it implies and
the England of Peterloo - or, to put it another way, between
different kinds of relation of form to content. The fact is that
these three stanzas are by no means well-constructed: the awkwardness
of 'forth led me', the grotesquely forced rhyme scheme of the third
stanza jar and jerk at our reading. Poesy, Shelley is saying, has
at this time to be this as well; the very possibility of an event
like Peterloo, which brings out political repression in such stark
colours, (20) has implications so wide that poetic form must come
into question. (21)
    'The Mask of Anarchy' makes simultaneous assertions about the
nature of society and the nature of the poet's craft. The power of
'Anarchy', which is in fact also the power of domination, is a crude
and bestial power, quite unlike the 'might' to which Shelley refers
in 'Prometheus'; because it is dehumanizing, the animal imagery is
apposite, but this imagery is also crude and forces us into
questioning our own notions of poetic order. A note of desperation
runs through the poem, which is only partly political desperation:
it is also the desperation of the poet who is trying to cut through
the tissues of ideologically charged language, and to find a bedrock
vocabulary so simple that it cannot be misunderstood. There is a
fear that the power of domination is so great that even to write
poetry is an act of bad faith, that it draws us away from the real
conflict represented at Peterloo; indeed, that the audience for whom
Shelley is now very deliberately trying to write, and who would be
readily able to understand the collage of discourses which he is
constructing, may cease to be available. (22) It might even be that
Shelley is claiming that in the state of Jupiter, poetry itself is
reduced to a jangling and discursive account, a kind of carping
journalism; but later in the poem, when the spirit of the Earth
speaks, we are made aware of the power in the straight-forward but
clumsy accents of a stump orator: (23)

What is Freedom? - ye can tell
That which Slavery is, too well -
For its very name has grown
To an echo of your own.

'Tis to work and have such pay
As just keeps life from day to day
In your limbs as in a cell
For the tyrants' use to dwell:

So that ye for them are made
Loom, and plough, and sword, and spade,
With or without your own will bent
To their defence and nourishment.

'Tis to see your children weak
With their mothers pine and peak,
When the winter winds are bleak, -
They are dying whilst I speak.

'Tis to hunger for such diet
As the rich man in his riot
Casts to the fat dogs that lie
Surfeiting beneath his eye;
                    (156-75)

This is a potent and live language, nourished from biblical anger
and expressed in stark and strongly imaged contradictions. The line
'They are dying whilst I speak' is crucial for an understanding of
Shelley, and of the radical tendency within romanticism: in it is
summarized the contradiction between an expressive poetic and a
theory of the social importance of the imagination. English
romanticism oscillated between these poles, in general and often in
specific texts: the poet claims value in accordance with his
expression of his innermost feelings, but also in accordance with
his contribution to social progress, but how are we to guarantee a
connection between these two realms, especially when the poet feels
himself to be in a situation of profound personal alienation? How
are we to know that the particular voice of the poet is 'in tune
with' - to use a significant Shelleyan and romantic metaphor - the
spirit of political rectitude? It could be said that one of Shelley's
most important political acts was simply to agonize about this
problem, in a way that Blake, with his greater degree of visionary
certitude, did not need to, and that many of the other romantics,
with their slighter degree of political commitment, did not care to.
Ideally for Shelley, the imagination was a source not only of poetic
inspiration but also of political revelation; yet he was also
painfully aware of how rarely such a synthesis actually worked.
    He takes up the same terms as in 'Prometheus Unbound', freedom
and slavery, and works them out in specific relation to his own
society; and it is indeed the terms which are important. In the
first of these stanzas, it is the 'name' of slavery which is at
stake, and its elision into the 'name' of the people of England, an
elision in consciousness and in language: Shelley's hopes for the
power of poetry are based on a prior awareness of the power of those
words which are at the service of ideology. And because of this, it
is important to Shelley to try to work different languages into a
single texture; we see in 'The Mask of Anarchy' that the old
language of radicalism is capable of connection with newer economic
facts and anxieties. The poem continues:

'Tis to let the Ghost of Gold
Take from Toil a thousandfold
More than e'er its substance could
In the tyrannies of old:

Paper coin - that forgery
Of the title deeds, which ye
Hold to something of the worth
Of the inheritance of Earth.

'Tis to be a slave in soul
And to hold no strong controul
Over your own wills, but be
All that others make of ye.

And at length when ye complain
With a murmur weak and vain
'Tis to see the Tyrant's crew
Ride over your wives and you -
Blood is on the grass like dew.
                    (176-92)

In the text, archaisms mingle with modern allusions. It might be
that Shelley was himself using this mixing of discourses as a
tactical device, but more to the point is the fact that the contemporary language of radicalism - and 'The Mask of Anarchy' is deeply
immersed in the contemporary world of political journalism and
cartoons - contained this flexibility within itself, and that Shelley
is therefore here participating in a more objective development
within writing, one which could give personal anxieties a social
base and produce a form of fusion between romantic concerns and real
political practice, if only within the text.
     The analysis of work in the previous stanzas shows a clear and
relevant grasp of the principles of alienation: the grammatical
ambiguity of the two lines, 'So that ye for them are made/Loom, and
plough, and sword, and spade', forces our attention on to the
simultaneity of production and self-production: the making of
implements for employers is simultaneously the reduction of the
worker himself to the status of implement, and this is a reduction
which can take place with or without the acquiescence of the worker's
consciousness. The emphasis, as so often within romanticism, is on
needs, although the argument is typically distorted by misprision of
historical development. The 'Ghost of Gold', paper-money, was in
fact of much less importance than other aspects of economic organization, and certainly to claim that it took from the workers 'a
thousandfold/More than e'er its substance could/In the tyrannies of
old' sounds very odd now, although the view was a common one at the
time. (24) Shelley describes bitterly the waste which is built into
production: the food that could feed children goes instead to the
dogs of the rich. But this, like the other injustices he mentions,
is referred back to mystification: it is surely no accident that
romanticism was heavily concerned with the supernatural at a time
when the concept of the 'super-natural' was an all-important one in
the analysis of economic and social life. (25) Compared with
feudalism, capitalism is often seen as a phantom oppressor, hidden
within mystery, refusing to show its face in the daylight and
wreaking violence by surreptitious means.
     'Prometheus Unbound' and 'The Mask of Anarchy' represent two
possible answers to the question of what the poet can do about the

plight of the world; they are both attempts at political disclosure,
although they clearly appeal to different audiences and employ
different tactics, in accordance with Shelley's changing views and
situation. 'Prometheus Unbound' addresses itself to the way in which
the world-view of a dominant class can distort society and enforce
its own partial vision, and deals with this problem in terms of the
myths which sustain such a vision, the myths through which the logic
of domination is enforced. 'The Mask of Anarchy' uses a different
approach, setting the possibilities of poetry against the anguish
which characterizes the position of the oppressed classes, calling
into question the poet's position as a master of words while
asserting the vitality of a literature of direct discursive statement.

The 'Ode to Liberty' was composed shortly after these two works,
early in 1820. In it Shelley traces a brief history of liberty in
civilization, focusing on the problems of moving beyond the bounds
laid down by false systems, economic, social and philosophical, and
grasping the freedom which, according to Shelley's more optimistic
doctrines, could always be within human reach. (26) The two central
stanzas are these:

O that the free would stamp the impious name
    Of Kings into the dust! or write it there,
So that this blot upon the page of fame
    Were as a serpent's path, which the light air
Erases, and the flat sands close behind!
        Ye the oracle have heard:
        Lift the victory-flashing sword,
And cut the snaky knots of this foul gordian word,
    Which weak itself as stubble, yet can bind
        Into a mass, irrefragably firm,
    The axes and the rods which awe mankind;
        The sound has poison in it, 'tis the sperm
Of what makes life foul, cankerous, and abhorred;
    Disdain not thou, at thine appointed term,
    To set thine armed heel on this reluctant worm.

O, that the wise from their bright minds would kindle
    Such lamps within the dome of this dim world,
That the pale name of Priest might shrink and dwindle
    Into the hell from which it first was hurled,
A scoff of impious pride from fiends impure;
        Till human thoughts might kneel alone,
        Each before the judgement-throne
Of its own aweless soul, or of the power unknown!
    O, that the words which make the thoughts obscure
        From which they spring, as clouds of glimmering dew
From a white lake blot heaven's blue portraiture,
        Were stript of their thin masks and various hue
And frowns and smiles and splendours not their own,
    Till in the nakedness of false and true
    They stand before their Lord, each to receive its due.
                                        (211-40)

These stanzas constitute a complexly worked statement about the power of ideology and the role of the poet in relation to it. Much of the emphasis, as in 'The Mask of Anarchy', is not so much on the institutions of domination as on names - the name of king, the name of priest. The first few lines show a characteristic ambiguity about violence: about whether to advocate stamping out the name of king altogether, presumably first by stamping out those who bear it, or to use the more subtle means at the poet's disposal through an act of writing. It seems that Shelley is suggesting that 'this blot upon the page of fame' might be removable by the poet, by means of scorn, ridicule and exposure; he is literally talking about writing ideology away, closing up the fissures in society which are opened by kingcraft and priestcraft by 'blotting' out the names of those who open and benefit from those fissures. About the strength of ideology he is characteristically double-minded: the word is 'weak itself as stubble, yet can bind/Into a mass, irrefragably firm'. The image is a sound one: there is nothing in a name apart from its function and context, yet with this function and context there comes a strength which, according to Shelley's complex image, derives not only from 'binding' but from that snake-like intertwining which is both a symbol of a further kind of rootedness and yet, by reference back to the 'serpent's path', also a point of weakness, because of the implication that the serpentine is the mythical, the unreal, and therefore amenable to the political disclosures of the poet.

The binding power of ideology, its ability to take disparate elements and pull them together into a whole, is summarized in the imagery of the 'fasces', 'the axes and the rods': again, the implication is that no single weapon of domination could enforce acquiescence, but that hegemonic systems can actually do the trick which the more obvious kinds of repression could not do. The image of rottenness in the next lines is remarkable for its thoroughness: the name of king is not only evil in itself, it is the 'sperm', the source and root of other evils, a false mode of growth which in fact does fatal injury to the 'body politic' while proclaiming its health. The implication of 'disdain' is that the 'name', by virtue of its insidious and serpentine habits, may appear too weak and crawling an enemy to fight: Shelley is convinced that this is not the case, that the ways in which we name things are essential elements in our world-view and thus in the social formation. 'Reluctant' serpents do not move in a straight line; ideological justification moves in devious paths.

The second stanza begins in a manner structurally identical to the first, substituting the 'wise' for the 'free' - the intelligentsia, in Shelley's eyes the other possible source of revolution, for the people - and the name of priest for the name of king. Again this name is seen as a blend of weakness and strength: it is 'pale', and the lighting of the lamps of wisdom will cause it to 'shrink and dwindle', but on the other hand it came to earth with the force of having been 'hurled' from hell. Within the pallor, of course, are other implications: priesthood is seen as a vampire, drawing the blood from the world both by economic parasitism and more importantly by moralistic objections to passion and love. This set of allusions merges into the line, 'A scoff of impious pride

from fiends impure': the notion of priesthood is essentially
negative, a matter of denial of powers, and human acceptance of it
is, to the fiends, a sickly joke on our gullibility. The effect of
removing the repressive layer of priesthood - or, perhaps, something
as broad as moralism - from society will be to free 'human thoughts'
from intrusive judgments, although Shelley vacillates about the
result of that: he is concerned, on the one hand, with the
individual's resumption of power over his or her own life, but he
also introduces the 'power unknown', the non-God with whom we become
familiar over the whole range of his poetry. Again it is to Shelley
'the words which make the thoughts obscure': instead of clarifying
and communicating meaning, words have been reduced to being agents
of mystification, 'clouds of glimmering dew' - attractive, as we
see from the metaphor, but delusive. The image of the lake is very
complicated: what these lying words do is 'From a white lake blot
heaven's blue portraiture', again they contribute to the pallor
which is the effect of metaphorical bloodsucking and also imprison-
ment, but what they also do is prevent the lake - the pool of
thoughts - from properly reflecting Heaven, that is, the world of
'higher reality'. Words are seen as obscuring not some ideal
freedom of the mind but the all-important relation between thoughts
and the real world, the old romantic connection between subject and
object, and liberty thus becomes the restoration of this connection,
freedom of movement between mind and world, freedom for imaginative
synthesis. As against this, ideology confronts us with words which
have 'thin masks and various hue', words which slip and slide
because they are not clearly attached to any specific object: they
are modes not of revelation but of disguise, and the final image
of the stanza has, not thoughts, but words standing before 'their
Lord, each to receive its due'. The judgment we might expect
halfway through the stanza, the judgment on free thoughts, is
obviously to be an approving one: the judgment which will be made
on the slippery, serpentine language of ideology will equally
obviously be adverse - depending, of course, on who 'their Lord'
actually is. Probably it is the 'power unknown'; yet one is left
with a suspicion that in Shelley's mind the Lord of these words
might well be no god but the devil.
     Much else could be said about these stanzas. They constitute,
among other things, a critique of the French Revolution for
remaining merely politically pragmatic, for being insufficiently
'radical' and failing to tear the names of oppression up by their
roots. A shift in the course of historical events does not become
a revolution until the very ideas which conditioned the past regime
have been obliterated. (27) Again, it may seem strange that
Shelley should use the word 'pride' of the fiends, but there are
two different kinds of pride at stake, the human pride of Prometheus
and the free people of England, and the non-human pride of those
forces which seek human restriction. And there is, of course, a
resonance running through the passage from Tom Paine, who spoke so
eloquently of the way in which religion placed barriers between
man and God, and in fact blocked the route which it claimed to
facilitate. (28)
     'A Defence of Poetry' is the text in which Shelley endeavoured
to summarize his ideas on the role and social power of poetry, and

to build a poetic theory out of them. Since he was also angrily
answering Peacock's jibes at the same time, the result is rarely as
clearly stated as one could hope, but none the less the text is one
of the most important romantic manifestoes. The most celebrated
passage comes at the end:

> the literature of England, an energetic development of which has
> ever preceded or accompanied a great and free development of
> the national will, has arisen as it were from a new birth. In
> spite of the low-thoughted envy which would undervalue contemporary
> merit, our own will be a memorable age in intellectual achievements,
> and we live among such philosophers and poets as surpass beyond
> comparison any who have appeared since the last national struggle
> for civil and religious liberty. The most unfailing herald,
> companion, and follower of the awakening of a great people to
> work a beneficial change in opinion or institution, is Poetry.
> At such periods there is an accumulation of the power of
> communicating and receiving intense and impassioned conceptions
> respecting man and nature. The persons in whom this power resides,
> may often as far as regards many portions of their nature, have
> little apparent correspondence with that spirit of good of which
> they are the ministers. But even whilst they deny and abjure,
> they are yet compelled to serve, the Power which is seated upon
> the throne of their own soul. It is impossible to read the
> compositions of the most celebrated writers of the present day
> without being startled with the electric life which burns within
> their words. They measure the circumference and sound the depths
> of human nature with a comprehensive and all-penetrating spirit,
> and they are themselves perhaps the most sincerely astonished at
> its manifestations; for it is less their spirit than the spirit
> of the age. Poets are the hierophants of an unapprehended
> inspiration; the mirrors of the gigantic shadows which futurity
> casts upon the present; the words which express what they
> understand not; the trumpets which sing to battle, and feel not
> what they inspire; the influence which is moved not, but moves.
> Poets are the unacknowledged legislators of the world.

This passage is often regarded as a noisy but rather meaningless
puff for poetry, redolent of romantic self-aggrandisement but
lacking in content; and, indeed, there is much to be criticized
in it. First, and most obviously, Shelley skirts around the principal
connection he is trying to make. 'Ever preceded or accompanied';
'herald, companion, and follower': these are the terms in which he
expresses the relation between social and literary change, and they
are not adequate. Second, in his attempt to point to the disparity
between intention and effect in poetry, he goes too far: we may
accept the image of the 'hierophants of an unapprehended inspiration',
for hierophants at least play some kind of role, however ritualized,
of a human kind in the ceremonies at which they officiate; but
'trumpets' which 'feel not what they inspire'?
    In the case of the first objection, however, while it is true
that Shelley does not commit himself as to precedence, none the less
he is solidly convinced that there must be a connection such as he
describes, and in fact his formula about an accumulation of power is

suggestive. We may now think of that power in other terms, perhaps
as the growing awareness of repression which precedes revolution,
or perhaps as a build up of cultural energy, on psychoanalytic lines,
under conditions of censorship; what is important in Shelley's
formulation of the point is that he very rightly resists a simple,
one-to-one directive correlation between society and its literature.
Instead of the facile idea that revolution is preceded - or
accompanied - by revolutionary literature, we have instead the much
more problematic concept of a superflux of ideas and energies, and
also by implication a cathexis of energies on to ideas, such that
thoughts about, conceptions of, human relations become again significant areas of questioning, loosened from the moorings of ideological
control.

And again, although perhaps poets are not trumpets, none the less
the insistence on the absence of correlation between intention and
effect is valuable. Taken to an extreme, it could result in a
ludicrous theory of automatic writing; but we can see Shelley working
towards an idea of what it is within the texture of social and
literary convention which means that, whatever the writer meant to
say, he so often ends up speaking the language of his surroundings.
'Even whilst they deny and abjure, they are yet compelled to serve'
sounds a more convincing version of the problem about Milton's
religious and political allegiance than Blake's assertion of direct
contradictions. 'Energy' is one of the key terms of this passage,
and we may initially be tempted to read it as we would in Blake;
but 'the electric life which burns within their words' alerts us to
the fact that what is going on in Shelley's mind is a more modern
metaphor. Energy, power are for him also words in a quasi-scientific
discourse, and so therefore is 'accumulation': (29) what he is
seeing is the batteries of the nation being recharged, which fits
with the emphasis on the future which emerges in the latter part of
the passage.

Again we are returned to the romantic idea of the imagination as
an alternative system, connecting subject and object, present and
future, in a way which does not bind but liberates through the
disclosure of real connections. It is in this light that we need to
interpret the final sentence of the 'Defence'. In 'Prometheus
Unbound' we saw Shelley trying to argue that liberty originates in
a change in world-view, an internal liberation whereby man comes to
realize that the world can be his if he reaches out for it. In
'The Mask of Anarchy' he points out that this change is inhibited
by a set of very precisely delineated agents of social repression,
by an economic system which distorts, among other things, the very
language we speak. And in the 'Ode to Liberty', he shows us how
words themselves become agents of repression, and can serve to bind
us to a false world-view. To Shelley, it is the imagination which
carries the major role in the struggle to break out of this circle,
because of its ability to relate real and ideal, concrete and
abstract. Poetry is not bound by ideological restriction. It
talks in terms of a different truth-value, being able to mention
human actuality and potential in the same breath. It is thus that
poets can be seen as legislators: they are the bearers of a new
system, which promises a set of truths outlawed by society.

None of this, of course, places Shelley outside his own age, or

beyond a faith in consciousness as the ultimate cause of change.
Over against his social progressivism we have to set the essentially
conservative doctrine of perfectibility, the purpose to which he
puts platonism and many other factors. Yet to write Shelley off as
a conventional idealist would be simplistic, for his central concern
was with human practice, with the connections between language and
reality, between the world of consciousness and the world as
disclosed in experience. His poetry tries to probe the obstacles
to progress which he shadowily discerned in that difficult hinterland;
and although it is bounded by aspects of the ideology of his time and
his class, that poetry, particularly in its insistence on connections
between life, work and writing, provides a significant contribution,
both to a romantic debate, and to a debate which will last much
longer.

Notes

INTRODUCTION

1 A.A. Trew in 'Language and Control', by R.G. Fowler, G.R. Kress, R. Hodge, A.A. Trew, Routledge & Kegan Paul, London, 1979, pp.95-6.
2 Aristotle, 'Politics', vol.I, p.2, Routledge & Kegan Paul, London, 1888.
3 On the dialectic here we have found the work of Herbert Marcuse especially useful; see particularly chapter 3 in 'Counter-Revolution and Revolt', Allen Lane, London, 1972, and 'The Aesthetic Dimension', Macmillan, London, 1979.
4 For the relevant work by E.P. Thompson in this area see Disenchantment or Default? A Lay Sermon, in 'Power and Consciousness', eds C.C. O'Brien and W.D. Vanech, University of London Press, 1969, pp.149-83; 'William Morris, Romantic to Revolutionary', rev. edn, Merlin Press, London, 1977; 'Poverty of Theory and other Essays', Merlin Press, London, 1978; 'London', chapter 2 in 'Interpreting Blake', ed. M. Phillips, Cambridge University Press, 1978.
5 Shelley, 'A Defence of Poetry' (1821), in 'Shelley's Prose', ed. D.L. Clark, New Mexico University Press, Alburquerque, 1954, p.293.

1   BLAKE: 'ACTIVE EVIL' AND 'PASSIVE GOOD'

1 All quotations from Blake are from 'The Poetry and Prose of William Blake', ed. D.V. Erdman, fourth edn, Doubleday, New York, 1970.
2 For polar versions of Blake's relation to the political, see H.C. White, 'The Mysticism of William Blake', Russell & Russell, New York, 1964, and G.R. Sabri Tabrizi, 'The "Heaven" and "Hell" of William Blake', Lawrence & Wishart, London, 1973. Sabri Tabrizi's book is the more offensive, but apart from that there is little to choose between their ways of failing to relate to the texts.
3 Rousseau, 'Émile', trans. B. Foxley, introd. A. Boutet de Monvel, Dent, London, 1969, p.197.

4 See J.H. Muirhead, 'Coleridge as Philosopher', Allen & Unwin,
   London, 1930, p.105.
5 Selection from Mr Coleridge's Literary Correspondence,
   'Blackwood's Magazine', vol.X, 1821, p.252.
6 See Marx, 'Early Writings', introd. L. Colletti, Penguin,
   Harmondsworth, 1975, pp.326-34.
7 See W. Kaufmann, 'Hegel: Reinterpretation, Texts and Commentary',
   Weidenfeld & Nicolson, London, 1965, p.260.
8 Commentary on Blake's concern with processes of work includes
   M. Schorer, 'William Blake: The Politics of Vision', new edn,
   Vintage, New York, 1959, pp.194-208; D.V. Erdman, 'Blake: Prophet
   Against Empire', rev. edn, Anchor Books, New York, 1969;
   J. Bronowski, 'William Blake and the Age of Revolution', Routledge
   & Kegan Paul, 1972, pp.89-131; D. Punter, Blake: Creative and
   Uncreative Labour, 'Studies in Romanticism', vol.16, no.3, 1977,
   pp.535-61; and M. Davis, 'William Blake: A New Kind of Man',
   Elek, London, 1977.
9 But it must also be noted that here the argument about passive
   and active is cast in a casuistical mould, and also utilizes an
   apparently antipathetic moralistic language of 'Vice', 'Virtue'
   and 'duty'.
10 On Blake's attitudes to the physical, see particularly T. Frosch,
   'The Awakening of Albion', Cornell University Press, 1974.
11 There are many, many analyses of 'The Tyger'; among recent ones,
   see J. Holloway, 'Blake: The Lyric Poetry', Arnold, London, 1968,
   pp.45-7; Erdman, 'Prophet Against Empire', pp.194-7; M.K. Nurmi,
   'William Blake', Hutchinson, London, 1975, pp.62-6. See also
   Nurmi, Blake's Revisions of 'The Tyger', in 'William Blake:
   "Songs of Innocence and Experience", A Casebook', ed. M. Bottrall,
   Macmillan, London, 1970, pp.198-217.
12 Although the analysis contained in 'The Tyger' seems elliptical
   and lacking in concreteness when compared with the interrogations
   of the later prophetic books, as we shall see below.
13 See, for example, J. Beer, 'Blake's Visionary Universe',
   Manchester University Press, 1969, p.176.
14 The use of imagery of feudalism for complicated and often
   ambivalent purposes is a key feature of Gothic writing: see the
   chapter on Gothic in the present volume, and also, on Gothic and
   the romantic poets, D. Punter, 'The Literature of Terror: A
   History of Gothic Fictions from 1765 to the Present Day',
   Longman, London, 1980, pp.99-129.
15 See, of course, Wordsworth's famous lines in 'The Tables Turned',
   in 'Lyrical Ballads', 1798; but also Coleridge on the 'philosophy
   of death' in, for example, 'The Statesman's Manual' in 'Collected
   Works', ed. K. Coburn and B. Winer, 16 vols, Routledge & Kegan
   Paul, 1969- , vol.VI, p.89.
16 See Erdman, 'Prophet Against Empire', pp.338-9.
17 F.W.J. Schelling, 'On University Studies', trans. E.S. Morgan,
   ed. N. Guterman, Ohio University Press, 1966, p.14.
18 Compare the ideological force of, for example, H.C. White on
   Blake, or M. Ba-Han, 'William Blake: His Mysticism', Cambette,
   Bordeaux, 1924, with Bertrand Russell on Hegel in 'History of
   Western Philosophy', Allen & Unwin, London, 1946, pp.757-73.
19 G.W.F. Hegel, 'Jenaer Realphilosophie', ed. J. Hoffmeister,
   Meiner, Hamburg, 1967, p.239.

20 F. Hölderlin, 'Hyperion', trans. W.R. Trask, Signet, New York, 1965, p.123.

21 G.W.F. Hegel, 'The Phenomenology of Mind', trans. J.B. Baillie, second edn, Allen & Unwin, London, 1931, p.81.

2 BLAKE: SEX, SOCIETY AND IDEOLOGY

1 D.V. Erdman, 'Blake: Prophet Against Empire', rev. edn, Anchor Books, New York, 1969, p.254.

2 All quotations from Blake are from 'The Poetry and Prose of William Blake', ed. D.V. Erdman, fourth edn, Doubleday, New York, 1970.

3 Commentary in 'The Poetry and Prose of William Blake', ed. Erdman, p.813.

4 Erdman summarizing criticism of VDA in 'Prophet Against Empire', p.228.

5 Erdman's discussion of VDA in 'Blake: Prophet Against Empire', pp.228-48.

6 For a discussion of dialectical method as developed within Marxism see G. Lukács, 'History and Class Consciousness', Merlin Press, London, 1971, pp.12-15, 27-9; and L. Goldmann, 'The Hidden God', Routledge & Kegan Paul, London, 1964.

7 For a lucid modern illustration of the effects of abstractionism, see C.S. Mills, 'The Sociological Imagination', Pelican, Harmondsworth, 1970, ch. 3; also relevant, A.W. Gouldner, 'Dialectics of Ideology and Technology', Macmillan, London, 1976.

8 For discussion of marriage as part of an economic market see L. Stone, 'The Crisis of the Aristocracy', Oxford University Press, 1965, ch. 11; L. Stone, 'Family, Sex and Marriage in England 1500-1800', Weidenfeld & Nicolson, London, 1976; and the chapter on Jane Austen in the present volume.

9 For a stimulating attempt to yoke insights of Marx and Freud in this area, see H. Marcuse, 'Eros and Civilization', 1955; Abacus, London, 1972. For Blake's treatment of labour, D. Punter, Blake: Creative and Uncreative Labour, 'Studies in Romanticism', vol.16, no.3, 1977, and chapter 1 of the present volume.

10 Marcuse, 'Eros and Civilization', p.77.

11 Ibid., pp.144-5.

12 Ibid., p.75.

13 Compare chapter 7 of Mary Wollstonecraft's 'Vindication of the Rights of Woman', on Modesty.

14 I have argued elsewhere that Blake already shows signs in this poem of awareness of the problems just outlined: see Aers, William Blake and the dialectics of sex, 'ELH', 44, 1977, pp.500-14.

15 For the 'history' Blake was mediating in 'America', see Erdman, 'Blake: Prophet Against Empire'.

16 Ibid., pp.213-18.

17 Plate 14 allows Enitharmon to show the reader the conscious uses of sexuality in this strategy and includes her criticism of Oothoon for demystifying sexual activity (VDA, 6).

18 On Blake's handling of sexuality in the later works, see

especially the fruitful studies by T. Frosch, 'The Awakening
of Albion', Cornell University Press, 1974, and J. Hagstrum,
Babylon Revisited, in 'Blake's Sublime Allegory', ed. S. Curran
and J.A. Wittreich, University of Wisconsin Press, 1973, pp.
101-8.

19 M. Schorer, 'William Blake: The Politics of Vision', Vintage,
New York, 1959, p.251.

20 A useful introduction to Orc is in M.D. Paley, 'Energy and
Imagination', Oxford University Press, 1970.

21 While Ololon plays an essential role in the regeneration of
Milton she never has a consciousness remotely resembling Oothoon's.

22 See Aers, William Blake and the dialectics of sex, pp.510-12.

23 However ready readers may be to take this exchange allegorically,
as relating to the potential bi-sexual individual, they should
not overlook the fact that the figuration is uncritically
grounded in traditional stereotypes of male ideology and can
only perpetuate webs of male domination - see too 'Jerusalem',
42.31-3; 61.51 (man not woman).

24 For a relevant discussion of Spenser's figurative mode see
M. O'Connell, 'Mirror and Veil', University of North Carolina
Press, 1977, chs 1-3; for Langland, D. Aers, 'Chaucer, Langland
and the Creative Imagination', Routledge & Kegan Paul, London,
1980, chs 1-3, and D. Aers, 'Piers Plowman and Christian
Allegory', Arnold, London, 1975.

25 Here Cooke, 'Romantic Will', pp.133-6, seems to miss the serious
questions concerning 'sexism' in the poetry and the power of
received ideology and dominant practices by narrowing the issue
down to his denial that Los is guilty of 'eighteenth-century
sexist dogma' in 'Jerusalem', 56.

26 Quite unequivocal and important examples of this strand in
Blake's work are 'Four Zoas', IX.122.12-14; ibid., IX.133.1-7;
'Milton', 33.1-7, and 'Milton', 30, already discussed.

27 See the commentary by W.J.T. Mitchell, 'Blake's Composite Art',
Princeton University Press, 1978, pp.186-91, and Frosch, 'The
Awakening of Albion'.

28 Some will doubtless claim that Los and Blake mean 'Person' or
'Androgynous Person' when the text puts 'Man'. But 'every word
and every letter is studied and put into its fit place'
('Jerusalem', 3), and 'Man' simply does not mean 'Person' or
'Androgynous Person' in our sexist culture. Indeed, Los's
assumptions 'confirm' Enitharmon's and my own suspicions, for
'Jerusalem', 88.12-13 is a clear perpetuation of traditional
male attitudes. Whereas Blake intervenes to correct Enitharmon
('Jerusalem' 88.16-27), he does not do so here.

29 'Poetry and Prose of Blake', 468 (see pp.467-8).

30 M.H. Abrams, 'Natural Supernaturalism', Norton, New York, 1971,
pp.147-76. Also Frosch, 'The Awakening of Albion', n.23,
pp.204-5; Damon, 'A Blake Dictionary', p.393.

31 Here see especially 'Patrologia, series Latina', ed. J.-P. Migne,
Paris, 1844 ff, 122. 825-9, and on the allegorical traditions,
Aers, 'Piers Plowman', chs 1-3.

32 See Damon, 'A Blake Dictionary', p.120, and Frosch's strenuous
attempts to rescue the body in Blake's eschatology, 'The
Awakening of Albion', pp.173, 176.

3 ROMANTIC LITERATURE AND CHILDHOOD

1 L. Stone, 'The Family, Sex and Marriage in England 1500-1800', Weidenfeld & Nicolson, London, 1977. See particularly chs 9 and 13. The most useful introduction to the subject of childhood in romantic and post-romantic literature remains P. Coveney, 'The Image of Childhood', Penguin, Harmondsworth, 1967. For a theologically grounded view of the contrast between Blake and Wordworth's treatment of childhood, see ch. 3 in R. Pattinson, 'The Child Figure in English Literature', University of Georgia Press, Athens, 1978.

2 Elements of this culture are active in the Wordsworths' attitudes toward children. For an example, see Dorothy Wordsworth's letter of 1797 on the education of Basil Montagu in 'Early Letters of William and Dorothy Wordsworth', ed. De Selincourt, Clarendon Press, Oxford, 1935, p.164.

3 E.P. Thompson, 'The Making of the English Working Class', Penguin, Harmondsworth, 1968, pp.366-84.

4 For evidence of Queeney Thrale's education see Stone, 'The Family, Sex and Marriage', pp.460-3, and for John Stuart Mill see chs 1-4 of his 'Autobiography', ed. J. Stillinger, Oxford University Press, London, 1971.

5 'Letters of Samuel Taylor Coleridge', ed. E.L. Griggs, Oxford University Press, 1956, vol.2, p.461.

6 For an informative discussion of the emergence of an expressive conception of the self in German romantic writing see ch.1 of C. Taylor, 'Hegel', Cambridge University Press, 1977, pp.3-29.

7 For an extreme expression of this opposition see Wordsworth's 'Ode on the Intimations of Immortality', particularly lines 58-108.

8 For the text of Susanna Wesley's letter and an interesting discussion, see J. and E. Newson, 'Cultural Aspects of Child-rearing in the English speaking world' in 'The Integration of a Child into a Social World', ed. M.P.M. Richards, Cambridge University Press, 1974, pp.53-83.

9 Thompson, 'The Making of the English Working Class', p.381.

10 Quotations from Blake are taken from 'The Poetry and Prose of William Blake', ed. D.V. Erdman, fourth edn, Doubleday Anchor, New York, 1970.

11 D.V. Erdman, 'Blake: Prophet Against Empire', Princeton University Press, N.J., 3rd edn, 1977, p.290.

12 For a close parallel with Blake's representation in 'The Chimney Sweeper' poems see Marx's introduction to 'Critique of Hegel's Philosophy of Right' in 'Marx, Early Writings' with introduction by L. Colletti, Penguin, Harmondsworth, 1975. See also D. Punter, ch.1, in this volume.

13 For further evidence of this point, notice the connection between a critical perspective and social isolation in 'The Chimney Sweeper' of 'Experience'. By contrast the chimney sweeper of 'Innocence' seems to speak from within a community, however illusory that community may be.

14 Contrast the closing line of 'Holy Thursday' in 'Innocence' with Blake's terse presentation of the social roots of pity in 'The Human Abstract' in Erdman, ed. 'The Poetry and Prose of William Blake', p.27.

15 Compare the engraved pictures which accompany the written text
of the two 'Nurses' Songs' in Blake's original edition of the
'Songs'. In 'Innocence' the picture shows the nurse content
to sit apart from the children. The picture accompanying the
poem of 'Experience' shows the nurse hovering over a child as
if she were trying to define his shape. For an accessible
facsimile edition of the original 'Songs' see 'Songs of Innocence
and Experience', ed. G. Keynes, Oxford University Press, London,
1970.

16 This reading poses a problem about the status of illusion in the
'Songs'. Thus the 'Nurse's Song' in 'Innocence' uses the
illusion of art to represent a valid wish for human happiness,
but in 'The Chimney Sweeper' and 'Holy Thursday' Blake explores
the part played by illusion in sustaining social domination.

17 See H. Bloom 'Blake's Apocalypse', Gollancz, London, 1963, p.39.

18 See Keynes 'Songs of Innocence and Experience', opposite plate
36.

19 'A Little Girl Lost' ends in just such a disabling contradiction;
the father cannot love his daughter and admit her sexuality.
See Erdman, 'Poetry and Prose', pp.29-30.

20 Quotations from Wordsworth poems except 'The Prelude' are taken
from 'William Wordsworth: The Poems', ed. J.O. Hayden, 2 vols,
Penguin, Harmondsworth, 1977. Quotations from 'The Prelude'
are taken from the text of the 1805 edition, ed. E. De Selincourt,
Oxford University Press, London, 1960. For a perceptive
commentary on Wordworth's treatment of childhood see D. Ferry,
'The Limits of Mortality: An Essay on Wordsworth's Major Poems',
Wesleyan University Press, Connecticut, 1959, pp.80-90.

21 Hierarchical relations are further naturalized in this passage
by Wordsworth's imagining of a dominant state power as mother
caring for her children, see, for example, 'Excursion', IX.
328-35.

22 The exclusion of the social world is a relatively unforced
outcome of the skating scene whose pastoral setting barely
distinguishes between natural and social worlds. But even when
the social world is more insistently present as in Wordsworth's
account of his residence in London in Book VII of 'The Prelude',
the same abstraction from the social environment occurs as the
necessary condition of 'vision'. See 'The Prelude', VII.588-
622.

23 For a more detailed discussion of this version of the self see
David Aers, chapter 4, below.

24 For Coleridge's comment see 'Biographia Literaria', ed. G. Watson,
Dent, London, 1965, p.260.

4 WORDSWORTH'S MODEL OF MAN IN 'THE PRELUDE'

1 See Preface to 'Lyrical Ballads' in 'Lyrical Ballads', ed.
R.L. Brett and A.R. Jones, Methuen, London, 1968, pp. 257, 259,
and 'Prelude' (1805) XII.435-6. All quotations of 'The Prelude'
come from the 1805 version in the splendid critical edition of
both texts and variant readings by E. de Selincourt and H.
Darbishire, Oxford University Press, reprint, 1968.

2 D. Ferry, 'The Limits of Mortality: An Essay on Wordsworth's

Major Poems', Wesleyan University Press, Connecticut, 1959.

3 Aristotle, 'Politics', Routledge & Kegan Paul, London, vol.I, p.2.

4 See his whole study, 'A Short History of Ethics', Routledge & Kegan Paul, London, 1967.

5 D. Aers, 'Chaucer, Langland and the Creative Imagination', Routledge & Kegan Paul, London, 1980, chs 1 and 2.

6 See C.M.L. Bouch and G.P. Jones, 'A Short Economic and Social History of the Lake Counties 1500-1830', Manchester University Press, 1961, especially pp.238-340; for more general survey see C. Hill, 'Reformation to Industrial Revolution', Penguin, Harmondsworth, 1967, and on the seventeenth century, B. Manning, 'The English People and the English Revolution', Heinemann, London, 1976, chs 6, 7, 9; for a contrasting view of the past to Wordsworth's see 'The Works of Gerrard Winstanly', ed. G.H. Sabine, Russell & Russell, New York, 1965.

7 In quoting 'The Excursion' I have used the text in 'William Wordsworth: The Poems', ed. J.O. Hayden, 2 vols, Penguin, Harmondsworth, 1977.

8 Contrast Winstanley's account of the 'covetous gentry' of the seventeenth century, or peasant experiences of the late medieval period pursued in R. Hilton, 'Bond Men Made Free', Temple Smith, London, 1973.

9 On the linguistic analysis here see Gunther Kress and Robert Hodge, 'Language as Ideology', Routledge & Kegan Paul, London, 1979, an extremely important book for those concerned with the analysis of writing of all kinds.

10 Ferry, 'The Limits of Mortality', pp.147-53.

11 On this aspect, besides David Ferry's work already cited, see the illuminating chapter on Wordsworth in Edward E. Bostetter, 'The Romantic Ventriloquists', University of Washington Press, Seattle, 1975.

12 On this period see volume one of Albert Soboul's study, 'The French Revolution', New Left Books, London, 1974.

13 On the England in question see especially E.P. Thompson, Disenchantment or Default? in 'Power and Consciousness', ed. C.C. O'Brien, University of London Press, 1969, and E.P. Thompson, 'The Making of the English Working Class', Gollancz, London, 1963.

14 Ferry, 'The Limits of Mortality', p.156.

15 For related discussions of the famous ascent of Snowdon see Bostetter, 'Romantic Ventriloquists', pp.46-51, and Ferry, 'Limits of Mortality', pp.159-61, 166-71.

16 This important poem can be fruitfully compared with Blake's critique of paradises representing false transcendence and innocence in the 'Book of Thel', 'Tiriel' (the vale of Har and Heva is especially apposite to the 'last retreat' of William and Dorothy in 'Home at Grasmere') and in the Ninth Night of 'Four Zoas'.

17 My analysis has concentrated on areas of the poem composed in 1804-5, rather than on the first two books composed in 1798-1800. Scholars such as Edward Bostetter and Alan Grob ('The Philosophical Mind', Ohio State University Press, 1973) have shown the substantial changes in many of Wordsworth's ideas

during the period, but in the areas that concern me here there is essential continuity. This can be seen by a similar reading of the version of childhood in Books I and II, which is informed by the desocializing mode analysed above. On this see Jon Cook, Romantic Literature and Childhood, ch.3 in this volume.

18 On romantic theodicies and their antecedents, see M.H. Abrams, 'Natural Supernaturalism: Tradition and Revolution in Romantic Literature', Norton, New York, 1971.

19 See especially Bostetter, 'Romantic Ventriloquists', ch.2.

20 John Barrell, 'The Idea of Landscape and the Sense of Place', Cambridge University Press, 1972.

21 Matthew Arnold, 'Culture and Anarchy', ed. J.D. Wilson, Cambridge University Press, 1966, p.203.

22 On 'The Ruined Cottage', see Bostetter, 'Romantic Ventriloquists', pp.61-6 and J. Wordsworth, 'The Music of Humanity', Nelson, London, 1969: I have used the latter's edition of the text because when writing this chapter the Cornell University Press edition was not yet available.

23 Bostetter, 'Romantic Ventriloquists', p.64.

24 William Blake, 'The Human Abstract', in 'Songs of Experience': both 'The Four Zoas' and 'Milton' return to make critical explorations of such 'pity'.

25 MacIntyre, 'Short History of Ethics', p.198.

26 See G.M. Harper, 'William Wordsworth', 3rd edn, Murray, London, 1929, ch.23, especially pp.548-51 and the 'Two addresses to the Freeholders of Westmoreland'.

5   COLERIDGE: INDIVIDUAL, COMMUNITY AND SOCIAL AGENCY

1 'The Collected Works of Coleridge' (hereafter referred to as CW) are now being produced under the general editorship of K. Coburn, published by Routledge & Kegan Paul in England: here see vol.I, pp.116, 127-30, 215-28, 240; and see his 'Collected Letters' (hereafter CL), ed. E. Griggs, Oxford University Press, 1956-9, vol. I, pp.83-4, 114. See E.P. Thompson, Disenchantment or Default, in 'Power and Consciousness', eds C.C. O'Brien and W.D. Vanech, University of London Press, 1969, pp.149-81.

2 CL, vol.I, p.214 and 'Notebooks', ed. K. Coburn, Pantheon, New York, begun in 1957, vol I. p.81.

3 For Thompson's essay see note 1; we quote Coleridge's poetry from 'Coleridge: Poetical Works', ed. E.H. Coleridge, Oxford University Press, 1961, here pp.10-11.

4 For development of the basic forms of linguistic analysis used here see Gunther Kress and Robert Hodge, 'Language as Ideology', Routledge & Kegan Paul, London, 1979.

5 On the pressures here see Thompson's essay cited in note 1, and his 'The Making of the English Working Class' (1963), Penguin, Harmondsworth, 1968. Compare K. Everest, 'Coleridge's Secret Ministry', Harvester, Hassocks, 1979.

6 On similar strategies in Wordsworth and Austen see chapters 4 and 7; also R. Williams, 'The Country and the City', Chatto, London, 1973.

7 See CL, vol.I, pp.49-50, 354 for similar examples.

8   The radical lectures reveal similar lacunae at similar decisive
    points: see CW, vol.I, pp.218-9, 226.
9   CL, vol.I, p.205; see too CL, vol.I, pp.162-3, 197.
10 CW, vol.I, p.218, Bristol, 1795.
11 For example, lines 55-8, 76-87, 110-13, 119-21, 126-31, 192-7.
12 See ch.1 in the present volume.
13 But see 'Watchman', no.8, 1796, CW, vol.II, p.xlix.
14 'Poems', pp.519-21, 100-2: our quotations are from the material
    which E.H. Coleridge quotes from the Rugby MS and dates 1797.
15 CL, vol.I, pp.394-8.
16 For the text of 'This Lime Tree Bower My Prison', see 'Poems',
    pp.178-81.
17 For the text of 'Kubla Khan', see 'Poems', p.295, for 'Christabel',
    pp.213-36, for 'The Rime of the Ancient Mariner', pp.186-209.
18 See T. McFarland, 'Coleridge and the Pantheist Tradition',
    Clarendon, Oxford, 1969, a very much more stimulating book than
    others in a similar area, e.g. J.H. Muirhead, 'Coleridge as
    Philosopher', Allen & Unwin, London, 1930; G.N.G. Orsini,
    'Coleridge and German Idealism', Southern Illinois University
    Press, Carbondale, 1969. A significant critical battle has
    raged for some time over the originality of Coleridge's thought:
    see, in particular, McFarland, pp.1-51, and N. Fruman, 'Coleridge,
    the Damaged Archangel', Allen & Unwin, London, 1971. It is to
    the point to cite his well-known comments on Schelling's
    philosophical system: 'To me it will be happiness and honour
    enough should I succeed in rendering the system itself
    intelligible to my countrymen...' (see Muirhead, p.53), for
    Coleridge considered himself to be, and requires to be considered
    as, an advocator, proselytizer, apostle, and his cultural
    importance as such outweighs the value of his speculative
    innovations.
19 See, for example, 'The Statesman's Manual', 1816, CW, vol.VI,
    p.89.
20 'Statesman's Manual', CW, vol.VI, pp.69-70; this double view
    of reason needs, of course, to be compared with Blake's account
    of the domination of Urizen, see above, pp. 13-14.
21 A.D. Snyder, 'Coleridge on Logic and Learning, with Selections
    from the unpublished Manuscripts', Yale University Press, New
    Haven, 1929, p.54.
22 'Notebooks', vol.III, 4015.
23 'Biographia Literaria' (1817), ed. J. Shawcross (2 vols),
    Clarendon, Oxford, 1907, vol.I, p.101.
24 See the comments on 'order' and 'system' in 'Anima Poetae'.
25 'Specimens of the Table Talk of Samuel Taylor Coleridge', ed.
    H.N. Coleridge, Murray, London, 1874, p.147.
26 'Statesman's Manual', CW, vol.VI, pp.49-50.
27 'The Philosophical Lectures of Samuel Taylor Coleridge', ed.
    K. Coburn, Pilot Press, London, 1949, pp.67-8.
28 See Snyder, 'Coleridge on Logic', pp.54-66, for these and
    similar instances.
29 See, in particular, 'Biographia Literaria', vol.I, pp.88-93.
30 'The Friend' (1818), vol.I, essay xiii, CW, vol.IV, part I, p.94n.
31 Which, of course, calls to mind the contemporary Gothic fiction
    which Coleridge, for the most part, admired. The connection is

often made clear in his own vocabulary: the search for a non-dualistic philosophy and the search for transcendence of fear in the Gothic novel are parallel reactions to social fragmentation: see pp.110-11 below.

32   See 'Biographia Literaria', vol.I, pp.163-9.

33   'Notebooks', vol.III, 4057.

34   'Inquiring Spirit: A New Presentation of Coleridge from his published and unpublished Prose Writings', ed. K. Coburn, Routledge & Kegan Paul, London, 1951, p.31.

35   The opposite side of the metaphor is the openness which we have already seen in his observation on childhood at p. 94 above.

36   'Notebooks', vol.III, 3950.

37   See 'Biographia Literaria', vol.II, p.107; and 'The Letters of John Keats', ed. H.E. Rollins, 2 vols, Cambridge University Press, 1958, vol.I, p.193. There is no direct evidence that Keats read 'Biographia'.

38   'Notebooks', vol.II, 2086.   The connections between the imagery and the speculation in this note are fascinating.

39   'On Poesy or Art', in 'Biographia Literaria', II.263.

40   See Coburn (ed.), 'Inquiring Spirit', p.40; and, relevantly, Snyder, 'Coleridge on Logic', p.73.

41   'Statesman's Manual', CW, vol.VI, p.65; the passage is followed by a reference to Milton.

42   CL, vol.IV, p.893.

6   SOCIAL RELATIONS OF GOTHIC FICTION

1   For a more substantial contribution, see D. Punter, 'The Literature of Terror: A History of Gothic Fictions from 1765 to the Present Day', Longman, London, 1980, which this chapter partly follows.

2   Although this realization is only hesitantly finding its way into print, where D.P. Varma, 'The Gothic Flame', Barker, London, 1957, was until recently the only available full-length study. Varma's work suppresses the category of the social completely. C.A. Howells, 'Love, Mystery and Misery: Feeling in Gothic Fiction', Athlone Press, London, 1978, is a slight improvement; R. Kiely, 'The Romantic Novel in England', Harvard University Press, 1972, more interesting again.

3   Writers of the time were clearly aware of the distinctness of the mode, but on the whole they reacted with either anger or amused contempt. See, on the one hand, Wordsworth, 'Lyrical Ballads', ed. R.L. Brett and A.R. Jones, Methuen, London, 1968, p.249 (Preface); and on the other, Jane Austen, 'Northanger Abbey', ed. A.H. Ehrenpreis, Penguin, Harmondsworth, 1972.

4   This is an important point, and needs emphasizing. The fact that a specific class conflict receives attention in a particular literary genre and at a particular time does not imply that that conflict is an active one within the society, nor does it even imply that the terms, structures and categories within which the texts operate can be helpfully taken as co-ordinates of the social grid. There are negative aspects to the connections: figures of pre-bourgeois power seem to have acted as nodes on

which accumulated various aspects of the self-boredom of the bourgeoisie. Thus the figures themselves are composites, their relation to history mediated through a specific, and itself contradictory, class consciousness; none the less important for that, but to be read along the axis of the imaginary, as, perhaps, unstable syntheses of social fear and desire. A reading list on the reality of these class relations would include G.E. Mingay, 'English Landed Society in the Eighteenth Century', Routledge & Kegan Paul, London, 1963; F.M.L. Thompson, 'English Landed Society in the Nineteenth Century', Routledge & Kegan Paul, London, 1963; D. Hay et al., 'Albion's Fatal Tree: Crime and Society in Eighteenth-Century England', Allen Lane, London, 1975; L. Stone, 'The Family, Sex and Marriage in England, 1500-1800', Weidenfeld & Nicolson, London, 1977; E.P. Thompson, The Peculiarities of the English, in 'The Poverty of Theory and Other Essays', Merlin, London, 1978.

5   Horace Walpole, 'The Castle of Otranto: A Gothic Story', ed. W.S. Lewis, Oxford University Press, 1964, pp.7-11 (Preface to the 2nd edn).

6   The 'locus classicus' for the description of realism in the eighteenth-century novel is, of course, I. Watt, 'The Rise of the Novel: Studies in Defoe, Richardson and Fielding', Chatto & Windus, London, 1957; see especially pp.9-34.

7   See Varma, 'The Gothic Flame', p.3; and J.M.S. Tompkins, 'The Popular Novel in England, 1770-1800', Constable, London, 1932, pp.215-17.

8   See his review reprinted in 'Coleridge's Miscellaneous Criticism', ed. T.M. Raysor, Constable, London, 1936, pp.355-70.

9   Ann Radcliffe, 'The Mysteries of Udolpho', ed. B. Dobrée, Oxford University Press, 1966, p.221.

10   Matthew Lewis, 'The Monk', New English Library, London, 1973, p.111.

11   Ann Radcliffe, 'The Italian, or The Confessional of the Black Penitents', ed. F. Garber, Oxford University Press, 1968, p.284.

12   See 'The Letters of John Keats', ed. H.E. Rollins (2 vols), Cambridge University Press, 1958, vol.II, p.62, for the usually cited 'locus'; but Keats's familial attitudes were interesting in themselves. Less than a year before Radcliffe had been a 'Damosel' ('Letters', vol.I, p.245), but any deductions can be only symbolic.

13   See again, of course, Wordsworth, 'Lyrical Ballads', p.249; and also, in general, R. Williams, 'The Country and the City', Chatto & Windus, London, 1973.

14   See in particular the jauntily self-pitying passage in 'Monk', p.157.

15   This is, of course, a misquotation from 'As You Like It', IV.i.

16   As the articulation of a clash between residual and developing components in ideology, this should be compared with comments on Blake in chapter 2 above.

17   See, for example, C. Hill, Clarissa Harlowe and her Times, in 'Puritanism and Revolution', Panther edn, 1968, pp.351-76, and the references that Hill cites.

18   See, crucially, C.R. Maturin, 'Melmoth the Wanderer', ed. D. Grant, Oxford University Press, 1968, p.532, and the doubts

about narrative structure implied in Isidore's deployment of
the terms 'wandering' and 'dream'.

19 As evidence of the various purposes for which the poets used
Gothic, see Punter, 'Literature of Terror', pp.100-1.

7 COMMUNITY AND MORALITY: TOWARDS READING JANE AUSTEN

1 'Gentleman's Magazine' for September 1816 and Scott in 'Quarterly
Review', 14 October 1815, issued May 1816, spelling and punctua-
tion modernized; quoted from 'Jane Austen: The Critical Heritage',
ed. B.C. Southam, Routledge & Kegan Paul, London, 1965.

2 Quoted from E.P. Thompson, 'The Making of the English Working
Class', Penguin, Harmondsworth, 1968, pp.240-1, 257.

3 Jane Austen's Emma, in 'Jane Austen: Emma', ed. D. Lodge,
Macmillan, London, 1968, p.220.

4 See E.P. Thompson, 'Making of the English Working Class'; D. Hay
et al., 'Albion's Fatal Tree: Crime and Society in Eighteenth
Century England', Penguin, Harmondsworth, 1977, especially chs 1,
5, 6; E.J. Hobsbawm and G. Rudé, 'Captain Swing', 2nd edn,
Penguin, Harmondsworth, 1973; A.J. Peacock, 'Bread or Blood',
Gollancz, London, 1965; D. Jones, 'Before Rebecca', Allen Lane,
London, 1973. For a sense of the developments in and from the
Middle Ages see R. Hilton, 'English Peasantry in the Later Middle
Ages', Oxford University Press, 1975; G. Duby, 'Rural Economy
and Country Life in the Medieval West', Arnold, London, 1968;
C. Hill, 'Reformation to Industrial Revolution', Penguin,
Harmondsworth, 1967; R. Brenner, Agrarian class structure and
economic development in pre-industrial Europe, 'Past and Present',
70, 1976, pp.30-75.

5 Marilyn Butler, 'Jane Austen and the War of Ideas', Oxford
University Press, 1975, pp.294, 299, 285; for another attempt,
W. Roberts, 'Jane Austen and the French Revolution', Macmillan,
London, 1979.

6 Butler, 'Jane Austen', passim; A.M. Duckworth, 'The Improvement
of the Estate', Johns Hopkins University Press, 1971, pp.46-7;
on Burke and Austen, Butler, 'Jane Austen', pp.37-40, 228-9, 287.

7 Ed. C.C. O'Brien, Penguin, Harmondsworth, 1968, p.372.

8 Hobsbawn and Rudé, 'Captain Swing', p.27; see too Roberts,
'Jane Austen', p.63. And note Burke himself describing labour
as 'a community, and, as such, as article of trade ... subject
to all the laws and principles of trade', 'Thoughts and Details
on Scarcity' in 'The Debate on the French Revolution', ed.
A. Cobban, Black, London, 1960, p.409.

9 When it suits him, however, Burke uses the doctrine of original
sin, which could have made him suspicious of what seemed
'natural' (e.g. 'Letters on a Regicide Peace', 1796, where the
Revolution's 'spirit lies deep in the corruption of our common
nature').

10 See the judge's 'Address to the convicts' at Cardiff Great
Session, 8 April 1801, printed in D. Jones, 'Before Rebecca',
pp.215-20.

11 Butler, 'Jane Austen', p.250; see too Bradbury, 'Jane Austen's
Emma' p.218.

12 Quotations of 'Emma' from the edition by R. Blythe, Penguin, Harmondsworth, 1966: page references are given in the text in brackets, here p.54.
13 Trilling's essay printed in D. Lodge, 'Jane Austen: Emma'.
14 Emma is seriously mistaken here: Austen has no wish that the middle classes should simply separate marital property (wife) from the market and its relations - a topic I return to at the close of this chapter. Only rakes like Crawford and Tom Bertram are not so engaged!
15 J. Robinson, 'Economic Philosophy', Pelican, 1970, p.25.
16 On the strains in this model as far back as the fourteenth century, see D. Aers, 'Chaucer, Langland and the Creative Imagination', Routledge & Kegan Paul, London, 1980, ch.1.
17 Duckworth, 'Improvement', pp.155-6; Butler, 'Jane Austen', pp.257-61, 265-6, 273.
18 Butler, 'Jane Austen', pp.259-60.
19 'Mansfield Park', ed. T. Tanner, Penguin, Harmondsworth, 1975, page references in text.
20 Besides works cited in note 3, see C. Lis and H. Soly, 'Poverty and Capitalism in Pre-Industrial Europe', Harvester, Hassocks, 1979, p.131.
21 Duckworth, 'Improvement', p.73.
22 See especially here, Lis and Soly, 'Poverty and Capitalism', p.103, works cited in note 3, and on enclosures in the period, Thompson, 'Making of the English Working Class', ch.4.
23 For example, D.V. Erdman, 'Blake: Prophet Against Empire', Doubleday, New York, 1969; see index under 'slave', 'slavery' and J.G. Stedman.
24 L. Stone, 'The Family, Sex and Marriage in England, 1500-1800', Weidenfeld & Nicolson, London, 1977, p.261.
25 'The Complete English Tradesman' (1725) in 'Select Writings of Defoe', ed. J.T. Boulton, Cambridge University Press, 1975, pp.232-3: see too Duckworth's excellent observations on 'Pride and Prejudice', 'Improvement', p.132.
26 On this see R. Williams, 'Country and City', Chatto & Windus, London, 1973.
27 Lis and Soly, 'Capitalism and Poverty', pp.102-3 and chs 4 and 5.
28 See earlier chapters on Blake by Punter and Aers.
29 Quoted in Lis and Soly, 'Capitalism and Poverty', pp.194-5.
30 See Lis and Soly, 'Capitalism and Poverty', chs 4 and 5, especially pp.188-202.
31 Contrast John Clare's admiring attitude to gipsies as those who manage to evade the domination of agrarian capitalists and their 'tyrant justice': 'The Shepherd's Calendar', ed. E. Robinson and G. Summerfield, Oxford University Press, 1964, 'October'.
32 In 'Albion's Fatal Tree', ch. 1; and, of course, see Thompson, 'Making of the English Working Class' and his 'Whigs and Hunters', Allen Lane, London, 1975.
33 Stone, 'Family, Sex and Marriage', pp.384-5: see too M. Walter in 'The Rights and Wrongs of Women', ed. J. Mitchell and A. Oakley, Penguin, Harmondsworth, 1977, pp.307-29.
34 'It is hardly surprising', Stone comments, 'that ... governesses

were among the largest occupational groups to be found in lunatic asylums', 'Family, Sex and Marriage', p.385.

35 Butler, 'Jane Austen', pp.267-9.

36 Stone, 'Family, Sex and Marriage', see pp.666-8, 673-4, 677-8.

37 Stone, 'Family, Sex and Marriage', p.678: see ch.13.

38 See Aers, 'Chaucer, Langland', chs 1 and 4; for the quotation from Stone, 'Family, Sex and Marriage', p.678.

39 Besides Stone's work, see Roberta Hamilton, 'The Liberation of Women', Allen & Unwin, London, 1978, and on the critical and creative treatment of such issues in an earlier period, Aers, 'Chaucer, Langland', ch.6.

40 See too Fanny's comment, pp.211-12.

41 Especially pp.73, 315-21, 363-4 and Lady Bertram on p.331. He scruples at Maria's match (pp.214-16) but this, as Austen stresses, is an extreme case; he still assents.

42 In 'Critical Essays on Austen', ed. B.C. Southam, Routledge & Kegan Paul, London, 1970, p.198; for an example of the brother-sister relation between Edmund and Fanny, see 'Mansfield Park', p.57.

8 HAZLITT: CRITICISM AND IDEOLOGY

1 See R. Park, 'Hazlitt and the Spirit of the Age', Clarendon Press, Oxford, 1971. For a concise if abstract discussion of Hazlitt's political ideas see W.P. Albrecht, 'Hazlitt and the Creative Imagination', University of Kansas Press, Lawrence, 1965, pp.29-33. In this essay references to Hazlitt's writing are from 'The Complete Works of William Hazlitt' (hereafter CW), ed. P.P. Howe, 21 vols, Centenary Edition, Dent, London, 1930-4. Where possible I have also referred to two readily available anthologies, 'Selected Essays of William Hazlitt', ed. G. Keynes, Nonesuch Press, London, 1970, and 'Selected Writings of William Hazlitt', ed. C. Salveson, New American Library, New York, 1972 - hereafter referred to as Keynes and Salveson.

2 See Raymond Williams, 'Culture and Society', Penguin, Harmonds-worth, 1963, pp.23-39.

3 CW, vol.13, p.38; Keynes, pp.366-7.

4 CW, vol.13, p.41; Keynes, p.372.

5 CW, vol.13, p.40; Keynes, p.370.

6 For Comte, see, for example, 'Système de Politique Positive', first published 1851, 'Au Siège de la Société Positiviste', Paris, 1929, vol.I, pp.141, 145-55. For George Eliot see 'Felix Holt', first published 1866, Penguin, Harmondsworth, 1972, pp.399-402.

7 CW, vol.13, p.42; Keynes, pp.372-3.

8 'Reflections on the Revolution in France' in 'The Works of Burke', vol.IV, Oxford University Press, London, 1906-7, p.10. All references to the writings of Burke are from this edition, hereafter referred to as Burke.

9 CW, vol.13, p.ix; Salveson, p.409.

10 For the opposition between tyranny and liberty see E.P. Thompson, 'The Making of the English Working Class', Penguin, Harmondsworth, 1968, particularly, chs 4, 5, 15, 16.

11 CW, vol.13, p.41; Keynes, p.371. For Burke's views on the
    importance of writers to political life, see Burke, vol.IV,
    pp.121-3.
12 For 'On the Prose Style of Poets', see CW, vol.12; see also
    Keynes, pp.482-500; Salveson, 229-43.
13 CW, vol.7, p.301.
14 CW, vol.7, p.226.
15 CW, vol.7, p.228.
16 CW, vol.7, p.229. For Coleridge's comments see 'Biographia
    Literaria', ed. G. Watson, Dent, London, 1965, pp.105-6.
17 For the relevant passage in Gramsci's writings see 'Selections
    from the Prison Notebooks', eds Q. Hoare and G. Nowell Smith,
    Lawrence & Wishart, London, 1971, pp.432-3.
18 CW, vol.7, pp.259-81.
19 See Burke, vol.V, pp.89-102; vol.VI, pp.162-3.
20 Burke, vol.IV, pp.24-30.
21 Burke, vol.VI, p.88.
22 CW, vol.7, p.260.
23 Ibid., p.260.
24 Ibid., p.261.
25 Burke, vol.IV, pp.33-4.
26 CW, vol.7, p.262.
27 Burke, vol.IV, p.86.
28 For examples see Raymond Williams, 'Culture and Society', pp.
    65-84, 120-36, 224-38, 246-57.
29 CW, vol.7, p.269.
30 For Hazlitt's awareness of the effects of eloquence, see CW,
    vol.12, pp.11-13; Keynes, pp.492-3; Salveson, pp.236-7.
31 Burke, vol.V, pp.100-1.
32 CW, vol.7, pp.262-3.
33 Burke, vol.V, pp.100-1.
34 CW, vol.7, p.263.
35 CW, vol.7, p.268.
36 Ibid., p.145.
37 For 'Project for a New Theory of Civil and Criminal Legislation',
    see CW, vol.19, pp.302-20.
38 CW, vol.7, p.12.
39 Park, 'Hazlitt and the Spirit of the Age', p.213.
40 CW, vol.12, pp.347, 355. See also Park, 'Hazlitt and the Spirit
    of the Age', pp.213-14.
41 CW, vol.11, p.79.
42 Ibid., p.37; Keynes, pp.737-8; Salveson, p.314.
43 CW, vol.11, p.37; Keynes, p.738; Salveson, p.314,
44 For a useful commentary on the social function of literary forms
    in eighteenth-century culture, see L. Lowenthal, 'Literature,
    Popular Culture and Society', Pacific Books, Palo Alto, 1968,
    pp.52-108.
45 David Aers, Community and Morality: Towards Reading Jane Austen,
    pp. 127-8 above.
46 CW, vol.11, pp.64-5; Salveson, pp.328-9.
47 See E.P. Thompson, 'Making of the English Working Class', p.660.
48 For evidence on Hackney College see R.M. Wardle, 'Hazlitt',
    University of Nebraska Press, Lincoln, 1971, pp.44-7, and P.P.
    Howe, 'The Life of Willial Hazlitt', Secker, London, 1922, pp. 22n,
    52.

49 For Hazlitt's early response to Coleridge see CW, vol.12;
    Keynes, pp.502-3; Salveson, 244-245.
50 Frederic Jameson, The Vanishing Mediator: Narrative Structure in
    Max Weber, in 'Working Papers in Cultural Studies', vol.5,
    Centre for Contemporary Cultural Studies, Birmingham, 1974, p.115.
51 CW, vol.13, p.212; Salveson, p.413.
52 CW, vol.4, p.214; Salveson, pp.49-50.
53 Coleridge, 'Biographia Literaria', pp.167, 173-4.
54 CW, vol.7, p.142.
55 Ibid., pp.135, 144.

9 SHELLEY: POETRY AND POLITICS

1 Mary Shelley, Notes to 'The Revolt of Islam' (1818), in 'The
   Complete Works of Percy Bysshe Shelley', ed. R. Ingpen and W.E.
   Peck (10 vols), Benn, London, 1926-30, vol.I, p.409. All
   subsequent references to Shelley's works are to this edition.
2 This is a commonplace of Coleridge's criticism: see, for example,
   R. Parker, 'Coleridge's Meditative Art', Cornell University
   Press, Ithaca, 1975, pp.62-89; T. McFarland, 'Coleridge and the
   Pantheist Tradition', Clarendon, Oxford, 1969, pp.107-90.
3 The 'philosophic poem' is the subject of M.H. Abrams, 'Natural
   Supernaturalism: Tradition and Revolution in Romantic Literature',
   Oxford University Press, London, 1971; see, for example, pp.19-
   32, 201-37, 299-307.
4 See 'Biographia Literaria', ed. J. Shawcross (2 vols), Clarendon,
   Oxford, 1907, vol.I, pp.65-107, leading up to the distinctions
   on vol.I, p.202.
5 In 'Coleridge, Poetical Works', ed. E.H. Coleridge, Oxford
   University Press, London, 1967, pp.362-8.
6 See 'The Eolian Harp' (1795) in 'Poetical Works', pp.100-2; but
   also the associated imagery of trembling receptivity in, for
   example, 'Songs of the Pixies' (1793) and, more disturbingly,
   'Lines at Shurton Bars' (1795), 'Poetical Works', pp.40-4,
   96-100.
7 For different aspects of this structure, see Blake, 'in a
   mirtle shade' (from the 'Notebook', 1793); 'Infant Sorrow'
   ('Songs of Experience', 1794); 'The Mental Traveller' (from the
   Pickering Manuscript, c.1803); also cf. the textual reconstruction
   of 'Infant Sorrow' in 'The Poetry and Prose of William Blake',
   ed. D.V. Erdman, fourth edn, Doubleday, New York, 1970, pp.719-
   21. All Blake references are to the Erdman edition.
8 In the Ingpen and Peck edition, 'Prometheus Unbound' is at
   vol.II, pp.179-267; 'The Mask of Anarchy', vol.III, pp.235-50;
   'Ode to Liberty', vol.II, pp.306-15; 'A Defence of Poetry',
   vol.VII, pp.107-40.
9 Shelley's experience of practical politics in Ireland is of
   obvious importance, but is symptomatic of wider uncertainties;
   see one of the two sound biographies. The better is K.N. Cameron's
   two-volume work, 'The Young Shelley: Genesis of a Radical',
   Gollancz, London, 1951, and 'Shelley: The Golden Years', Harvard
   University Press, Cambridge, Mass., 1974; alternatively there is
   R. Holmes, 'Shelley: The Pursuit', Weidenfeld & Nicolson, London,
   1974.

10   See, for example, E.R. Wasserman, 'Shelley: A Critical Reading',
     Johns Hopkins University Press, Baltimore, 1971, pp.255-502;
     the parts of the book which appear on these pages are entitled
     'The Poetry of Idealism: Utopia' and 'The Poetry of Idealism:
     Immortality'.
11   Cf. Blake, 'The Marriage of Heaven and Hell', Plate 5.
12   See in particular 'Marriage of Heaven and Hell', Plates 22-4,
     'A Memorable Fancy'.
13   Again cf. Blake, 'Marriage of Heaven and Hell', in particular
     the account of alienation given in Plate 11.
14   For an understanding of the model of a 'non-organic' individual-
     istic society against which writers like Blake, Coleridge and
     Shelley all struggled, it is essential to read Hobbes,
     'Leviathan', ed. C.B. Macpherson, Penguin, Harmondsworth, 1968.
     Blake's argument against the Hobbesian version of man runs
     through the prophetic books, but is most neatly encapsulated in
     'Marriage of Heaven and Hell', Plates 17-20, 'A Memorable Fancy';
     Coleridge's is apparent in, for instance, 'Religious Musings'
     (1795), lines 126-58, 'Poetical Works', pp.113-15, but see also
     pp. 86-90.
15   Clearly, to talk about Shelley as within a tradition of
     philosophical radicalism is a simplification, but it does point
     to important affinities: see, as well as Cameron, Holmes,
     pp.97-8, 120-2, 138-40 et seq.; D. King-Hele, 'Shelley: His
     Thought and Work', Macmillan, London, 2nd edn, 1971, pp.27-31,
     139-45. What lies most importantly behind Shelley's political
     attitudes is the work of William Godwin; see particularly his
     'Enquiry concerning Political Justice', ed. K.C. Carter, Oxford
     University Press, London, 1971.
16   One of the most interesting comparisons here is with the
     unfortunately very dense Note on Eternity, Time and the Concept,
     in A. Kojève, 'Introduction to the Reading of Hegel', ed. A.
     Bloom, trans. J.H. Nichols Jr, Basic Books, New York, 1969,
     pp.100-49.
17   See above, pp.98-9.
18   It would be impossible here to go into detail on Peterloo, on
     its political significance and its relation to the Seditious
     Meetings Act of 1817: see, among many other works, J. Stevenson,
     'Popular Disturbances in England 1700-1870', Longman, London,
     1979, and references in E.P. Thompson, 'The Making of the English
     Working Class', Gollancz, London, 1963. For my discussion of
     'The Mask of Anarchy', I am greatly indebted to conversations
     with Dr R.B. Sales, of East Anglia.
19   Particularly those in the 'Examiner'. See Holmes, pp.529-32
     for a factually useful but rather effusive account of the
     transmission of the relevant information; also 'Three Accounts
     of Peterloo', ed. F.A. Bruton, Manchester University Press,
     Manchester, 1921, to which Holmes helpfully refers.
20   The starkness is important; Peterloo was virtually, it appears,
     a festival occasion before the intrusion of the authorities. It
     is interesting that, to point up the contrast between peaceful
     demonstration and military violence, Shelley gives much of the
     authority in the poem to a female protagonist, in an account
     based on fact: see Holmes, p.532. Yet he does not take up the

widely reported presence of women's groups in the poem; the two
details together constitute a diminution of group political
activity to the dimensions of individual heroics.

21 'The Mask of Anarchy' belongs in literary terms with Blake's
'Gwin, King of Norway', Coleridge's 'Ancient Mariner' and Keats's
'La Belle Dame sans Merci' as revitalizations of the ballad;
but more important is the distinction between Blake and Shelley
on the one hand, who adopt not only ballad versification but
also the associated vocabulary, and Coleridge and Keats on the
other, who were more interested in the ghostly resonance of a
'dying' form.

22 One of the most important aspects of this 'collage' is Shelley's
inverted adoption of an archaic, feudal discourse: cf. above,
pp.104-6.

23 A stump orator who, as far as can be made out, is a long way
from 'Orator' Hunt, the principal speaker at Peterloo, who
belonged to the 'independent gentleman' school of radical, like
Cobbett and, in a rather less public way, Shelley himself.
See Hunt's own account of Peterloo in 'Memoirs of Henry Hunt'
(3 vols), T. Dolby, London, 1820-2, vol.III, pp.604-40, which
is a very powerful reconstruction of the events, and also conveys
considerable insight into Hunt's own attitudes.

24 Cf. also, for instance, Cobbett, 'Rural Rides' (1830), ed. G.
Woodcock, Penguin, Harmondsworth, 1967, in which paper money is
continually referred to as a major contributing factor in
economic inequity and collapse.

25 This is a conjunction which also needs to be related to Gothic
fiction: see above, p.106 ff.

26 See, for example, the early 'Queen Mab' (1813), in Ingpen and
Peck, vol.I, pp.67-165; and also Wasserman, pp.3 et seq.

27 Cf. on this Shelley's important comments on the power of pre-
revolutionary habits in his Preface to 'The Revolt of Islam',
in Ingpen and Peck, pp.241-2.

28 See Tom Paine, 'The Rights of Man' (1791-2), introd. A. Seldon,
Dent, London, 1969, p.44.

29 This scientific metaphor for vitality, rebirth and change should
be compared with the one operant throughout Mary Shelley,
'Frankenstein, or The Modern Prometheus' (1818), ed. M.K.
Joseph, Oxford University Press, London, 1969.

Index of Authors and Titles

Abrams, M.H., 41-2
Aers, David, 27, 64, 82, 118, 150
Aikin, Lucy, 134
'Alice Fell' (Wordsworth), 58-9
'America' (Blake), 13, 32, 35, 39
'Ancient Mariner, The' (Coleridge), 93, 95, 102
'Anima Poetae' (Coleridge), 99
'Aphorisms' (Lavater), 9
'Appeal from the New to the Old Whigs' (Burke), 141, 144-5
Aquinas, St Thomas, 64-5
Arnold, Matthew, 79
Austen, Jane, 118-36, 150

Ball, John, 81, 118, 130
Barrell, John, 77
'Biographia Literaria' (Coleridge), 99, 153, 156
Blake, William, 118, 130, 134; 'active evil' and 'passive good', 7-26; and childhood, 46-54, 59, 63; and Coleridge, 85, 87, 89, 101; sex, society and ideology, 27-43; and Shelley, 155, 157-8, 160; and Wordsworth, 12, 66, 80
Bloom, H., 27-8
Boehme, Jakob, 42, 96
'Book of Ahania, The' (Blake), 36
'Book of Urizen' (Blake), 32, 41
Bostetter, Edward, 79
Bradbury, Prof., 119

Bruno, G., 99
Burke, Edmund, 120-2, 124, 137, 139-47
Butler, Marilyn, 120, 122, 133

'Castle of Otranto, The' (Walpole), 104-7, 110
'Chimney Sweeper' (Blake), 10, 47-50, 55
'Christabel' (Coleridge), 93-5
Clare, John, 77
Coleridge, Samuel Taylor, 82-102; and Blake, 85, 87, 89, 101; and childhood, 45; correspondence of, 7-8, 91, 102; and Gothic, 117; and Hazlitt, 137-9, 141, 147, 149-50, 152-3; and philosophy, 155-7; and Shelley, 155-6, 158, 163; and Wordsworth, 62, 64, 73
'Comus' (Milton), 29
Comte, Auguste, 138
Cook, Jonathan, 44, 82, 137
'Coriolanus', essay on (Hazlitt), 153-4
'Culture and Society' (Williams), 137, 143

'Defence of Poetry, A' (Shelley), 158, 169-71
'Dejection: An Ode' (Coleridge), 157
'Depth and Superficiality, On' (Hazlitt), 149

'Destruction of the Bastille'
    (Coleridge), 83
Duncan, Alistair, 120, 125
'Duty, Ode to' (Wordsworth), 80

'Earth's Answer' (Blake), 51
'Economic and Philosophical
    Manuscripts of 1844' (Marx), 8
Eliot, George, 138
'Eloquence of the British Senate,
    The' (Hazlitt), 140
'Emma' (Austen), 118, 122-33, 135
'Émile' (Rousseau), 7
'Eolian Harp, The' (Coleridge),
    90-1
Erdman, D.V., 27-8, 47
'Europe' (Blake), 13, 27, 31-4
'Excursion, The' (Wordsworth),
    54-8, 63, 67-9, 75

'Family, Sex and Marriage in
    England 1500-1800, The'
    (Stone), 44, 133
Ferry, David, 64, 69, 74
'First Letter on a Regicide
    Peace' (Burke), 141-2
'Four Zoas' (Blake), 29-31,
    34-41 passim, 87, 157
'France: An Ode' (Coleridge), 93
Freud, S., 30, 36

'Gentleman's Magazine, The',
    118, 120
'German Ideology' (Marx), 65
Gramsci, A., 141

Hay, Douglas, 131
Hazlitt, William, 137-54
'Hazlitt and the Spirit of the
    Age' (Park), 148
Hegel, G.W.F., 8, 25, 102
Hill, Christopher, 115
Hobsbawm, E.J., 120
Hölderlin, F., 25
'Holy Thursday' (Blake),
    49-50
'Home at Grasmere' (Wordsworth),
    75
'Hyperion' (Hölderlin), 25

'Illustrations of "The Times"
    Newspaper' (Hazlitt), 154
'Infant Joy' (Blake), 61
'Infant Sorrow' (Blake), 61
'Inquiring Spirit' (Coleridge),
    99-100
'Intimations of Immortality, Ode'
    (Wordsworth), 59, 62
'Introduction' (Blake), 51
'Island in the Moon' (Blake), 10
'Italian, The' (Radcliffe), 104,
    109-11, 114-17

'Jane Austen and the War of Ideas'
    (Butler), 120
'Jerusalem' (Blake), 9, 22-7,
    35-6, 38-42, 87

Kant, I., 80, 96
Keynes, Geoffrey, 52, 137
'Kubla Khan' (Coleridge), 93-4,
    99

Langland, William, 65-6
Lavater, J.C., 9
Lewis, Matthew, 107, 109-11,
    113-14
'Liberty, Ode to' (Shelley),
    158, 167-9, 171
'Life of Napoleon, The' (Hazlitt),
    138-40, 147
Lis, Catherine, 130
'Little Boy Lost, A' (Blake), 50
'Little Girl Lost, The' (Blake),
    51-4, 61
'Little Girl Found, The' (Blake),
    51, 53, 61
'Little Vagabond, The' (Blake),
    50
'London' (Blake), 32, 157-8

MacIntyre, Alasdair, 80
'Making of the English Working
    Class, The' (Thompson), 44,
    46
'Mansfield Park' (Austen), 122,
    126-8, 134-5
Marcuse, H., 30
'Marriage of Heaven and Hell'
    (Blake), 9

Marx, Karl, 8, 31-2, 65
'Mask of Anarchy, The' (Shelley),
    158, 163-7, 171
'Melmoth the Wanderer' (Maturin),
    117
'Mental Traveller, The' (Blake),
    8, 16-22, 30
Mill, James, 45
Mill, John Stuart, 45
'Milton' (Blake), 34-5, 37-8, 40
Milton, John, 81, 159-60
'Monk, The' (Lewis), 104, 108-9,
    111, 113-14, 117
'Mysteries of Udolpho, The'
    (Radcliffe), 104, 107-9,
    111-16

'Nurses' Songs' (Blake), 50-1

Ode, see 'Dejection'; 'Duty';
    'France'; 'Intimations of
    Immortality'; 'Liberty'
'Opus Maximum' (Coleridge), 101
Owen, Robert, 137, 146

Paine, Thomas, 146, 169
'Paradise Lost' (Milton), 40,
    159-60
Park, Roy, 148-9
'Phenomenology of Spirit'
    (Hegel), 25
'Philosophical Lectures'
    (Coleridge), 98
'Piers Plowman' (Langland), 65
'Political Essays' (Hazlitt),
    140, 147-8
'Popular Novel in England
    1770-1800' (Tompkins), 115
'Prelude, The' (Wordsworth), 56,
    59-62, 64-81
'Project for a New Theory of
    Civil and Criminal Legislation'
    (Hazlitt), 147
'Prometheus Unbound' (Shelley),
    158-67, 171
'Prose Style of Poets, On the'
    (Hazlitt), 140
Punter, David, 7, 82, 103, 155

'Quarterly Review', 118

Radcliffe, Ann, 107-16
'Recluse, The' (Wordsworth), 66
'Reflections on having left a
    place of retirement'
    (Coleridge), 84-6, 93
'Reflections on the Revolution
    in France' (Burke), 120-1,
    141-3
'Religious Musings' (Coleridge),
    86-90, 93, 95
'Rights of Man' (Paine), 146
'Rise of the Novel, The' (Watt),
    110
Robinson, Joan, 124
Rousseau, J.J., 7, 44-5
Rudé, G., 120
'Ruined Cottage' (Wordsworth),
    77, 79

Schelling, F.W.J., 25, 96
'School Boy, The' (Blake), 50
Scott, Sir Walter, 150-1
Scotus, John, 42
Shelley, Mary, 155, 158
Shelley, Percy Bysshe, 117-18,
    155-72
Smith, Adam, 75, 124
Snyder, A.D., 97-8, 101
Soly, Hugo, 130
'Song of Los, The' (Blake), 0,
    13-16, 23
'Songs of Innocence and
    Experience' (Blake), 8,
    10-11, 35, 46-51, 55, 59,
    157
Southey, Robert, 137, 139, 141,
    147, 149
'Spirit of the Age, The'
    (Hazlitt), 140, 148-50
Stone, Lawrence, 127, 132-3

'This Lime Tree Bower, my
    Prison' (Coleridge), 92-4
Thompson, E.P., 44, 46, 82, 86,
    151
Thrale, Queeney, 45
'Times, The', 146, 154
'Tintern Abbey' (Wordsworth),
    64, 77
'To the Reverend W.J. Hart'
    (Coleridge), 84
'To a Young Ass' (Coleridge), 84

Tompkins, J.M.S., 115-16
Trilling, L., 123
'Tyger' (Blake), 8, 11-13

'University Studies, On'
    (Schelling), 25

'Vision of the Last Judgement'
    (Blake), 27, 41-2
'Visions of the Daughters of
    Albion' (Blake), 27-34, 38-9

Walpole, Horace, 104-7, 117
'What is the People?' (Hazlitt),
    137, 141, 143-4, 146-7
Williams, Raymond, 137, 143
Wilson, Angus, 136
Winstanley, G., 81, 130
Wollstonecraft, Mary, 118
Wordsworth, William: and Blake,
    12, 66, 80; and childhood,
    54-63; and Coleridge, 62, 64,
    73; and politics, 137-9, 141,
    147, his 'Prelude', 64-81;